International Political Economy Series

General Editor: Timothy M. Shaw, Professor of Human Security & Peacebuilding, School of Peace & Conflict Management, Royal Roads University, Victoria, BC, Canada

Titles include:

Leslie Elliott Armijo (*editor*)
FINANCIAL GLOBALIZATION AND DEMOCRACY IN EMERGING MARKETS

Robert Boardman
THE POLITICAL ECONOMY OF NATURE
Environmental Debates and the Social Sciences

Jörn Brömmelhörster and Wolf-Christian Paes (*editors*)
THE MILITARY AS AN ECONOMIC ACTOR
Soldiers in Business

Gordon Crawford
FOREIGN AID AND POLITICAL REFORM
A Comparative Analysis of Democracy Assistance and Political Conditionality

Matt Davies
INTERNATIONAL POLITICAL ECONOMY AND MASS COMMUNICATION IN CHILE
National Intellectuals and Transnational Hegemony

Martin Doornbos
INSTITUTIONALIZING DEVELOPMENT POLICIES AND RESOURCE STRATEGIES IN EASTERN AFRICA AND INDIA
Developing Winners and Losers

Fred P. Gale
THE TROPICAL TIMBER TRADE REGIME

Meric S. Gertler and David A. Wolfe
INNOVATION AND SOCIAL LEARNING
Institutional Adaptation in an Era of Technological Change

Anne Marie Goetz and Rob Jenkins
REINVENTING ACCOUNTABILITY
Making Democracy Work for the Poor

Andrea Goldstein
MULTINATIONAL COMPANIES FROM EMERGING ECONOMIES
Composition, Conceptualization and Direction in the Global Economy

Mary Ann Haley
FREEDOM AND FINANCE
Democratization and Institutional Investors in Developing Countries

Keith M. Henderson and O. P. Dwivedi (*editors*)
BUREAUCRACY AND THE ALTERNATIVES IN WORLD PERSPECTIVES

Jomo K.S. and Shyamala Nagaraj (*editors*)
GLOBALIZATION VERSUS DEVELOPMENT

Angela W. Little
LABOURING TO LEARN
Towards a Political Economy of Plantations, People and Education
in Sri Lanka

John Loxley (*editor*)
INTERDEPENDENCE, DISEQUILIBRIUM AND GROWTH
Reflections on the Political Economy of North–South Relations at the
Turn of the Century

Don D. Marshall
CARIBBEAN POLITICAL ECONOMY AT THE CROSSROADS
NAFTA and Regional Developmentalism

Susan M. McMillan
FOREIGN DIRECT INVESTMENT IN THREE REGIONS OF THE SOUTH AT
THE END OF THE TWENTIETH CENTURY

S.Javed Maswood
THE SOUTH IN INTERNATIONAL ECONOMIC REGIMES
Whose Globalization?

John Minns
THE POLITICS OF DEVELOPMENTALISM
The Midas States of Mexico, South Korea and Taiwan

Lars Rudebeck, Olle Törnquist and Virgilio Rojas (*editors*)
DEMOCRATIZATION IN THE THIRD WORLD
Concrete Cases in Comparative and Theoretical Perspective

Benu Schneider (*editor*)
THE ROAD TO INTERNATIONAL FINANCIAL STABILITY
Are Key Financial Standards the Answer?

Howard Stein (*editor*)
ASIAN INDUSTRIALIZATION AND AFRICA
Studies in Policy Alternatives to Structural Adjustment

International Political Economy Series
Series Standing Order ISBN 0–333–71708–2 hardcover
Series Standing Order ISBN 0–333–71110–6 paperback
(*outside North America only*)

You can receive future titles in this series as they are published by placing a standing order. Please contact your bookseller or, in case of difficulty, write to us at the address below with your name and address, the title of the series and one of the ISBNs quoted above.

Customer Services Department, Macmillan Distribution Ltd, Houndmills, Basingstoke, Hampshire RG216XS, England

Multinational Companies from Emerging Economies

Composition, Conceptualization and Direction in the Global Economy

Andrea Goldstein

Foreword by Louis T. Wells

© Andrea Goldstein 2007
Foreword © Louis T. Wells 2007

All rights reserved. No reproduction, copy or transmission of this publication may be made without written permission.

No paragraph of this publication may be reproduced, copied or transmitted save with written permission or in accordance with the provisions of the Copyright, Designs and Patents Act 1988, or under the terms of any licence permitting limited copying issued by the Copyright Licensing Agency, 90 Tottenham Court Road, London W1T 4LP.

Any person who does any unauthorized act in relation to this publication may be liable to criminal prosecution and civil claims for damages.

The author has asserted his right to be identified as the author of this work in accordance with the Copyright, Designs and Patents Act 1988.

First published in 2007 by
PALGRAVE MACMILLAN
Houndmills, Basingstoke, Hampshire RG21 6XS and
175 Fifth Avenue, New York, N.Y. 10010
Companies and representatives throughout the world.

PALGRAVE MACMILLAN is the global academic imprint of the Palgrave Macmillan division of St. Martin's Press, LLC and of Palgrave Macmillan Ltd. Macmillan® is a registered trademark in the United States, United Kingdom and other countries. Palgrave is a registered trademark in the European Union and other countries.

ISBN-13: 978–0–230–00704–8
ISBN-10: 0–230–00704–X

This book is printed on paper suitable for recycling and made from fully managed and sustained forest sources. Logging, pulping and manufacturing processes are expected to conform to the environmental regulations of the country of origin.

A catalogue record for this book is available from the British Library.

Library of Congress Cataloging-in-Publication Data

Goldstein, Andrea E.
    Multinational companies from emerging economies : composition, conceptualization and direction in the global economy / Andrea Goldstein ; foreword by Louis T. Wells.
      p. cm.—(International political economy series)
    Includes bibliographical references and index.
    ISBN-13: 978–0–230–00704–8 (cloth)
    ISBN-10: 0–230–00704–X (cloth)
    1. International business enterprises – Developing countries. I. Title.

HD2932.G62 2007
338.8′881724—dc22   2006053272

Printed and bound in Great Britain by
CPI Antony Rowe, Chippenham and Eastbourne

Contents

List of Tables	vii
List of Boxes	ix
Foreword by Louis T. Wells	x
Preface	xiii
Acknowledgments	xx
List of Abbreviations	xxii

1	Introduction	1
2	Trends in Southern OFDI	7
	2.1 What is corporate nationality?	7
	2.2 The quality of the data	10
	2.3 Aggregate statistics	11
	2.4 The geography of investment	15
	2.5 Enterprise data	24
3	Toward an Industry Categorization	31
	3.1 General features	31
	3.2 EMNCs in oil and gas	33
	3.3 EMNCs in non-financial services	40
4	The New Asian Multinationals	52
	4.1 Asian Tiger multinationals	52
	4.2 Nurturing and sustaining competencies in Chinese MNCs	61
5	Multilatinas	67
	5.1 The early phase	67
	5.2 The consequences of market reforms	68
6	Existing Theories and Their Relevance to EMNCs	74
	6.1 The monopolistic advantage and the product lifecycle	74
	6.2 Behavioral models	77
	6.3 The eclectic paradigm – ownership, location, internalization	79

	6.4	Dynamic capabilities and the resource-based view	84
	6.5	Conglomeration and internationalization	87
7	The Role of Governments	94
	7.1	The role of support policies	94
	7.2	The role of competition policies	99
	7.3	The role of international policies	102
	7.4	The political economy of EMNCs	104
8	Some Key Questions	117
	8.1	The role of diaspora entrepreneurship in homeland FDI	117
	8.2	The challenge of multinational management	122
	8.3	Financial market issues	127
	8.4	The impact on the host economies	130
9	Consequences for OECD Governments, Firms, and Workers	136
	9.1	Motivations and entry modes	136
	9.2	Performance	139
	9.3	The risk of protectionism	142
	9.4	Proactive strategies	144
	9.5	A complex issue	146
10	Conclusions – The Way Ahead	148

Appendix 1 Selected EMNCs' acquisitions in the OECD market	153
Appendix 2 Representative disputes between EMNCs and host governments in developing countries	165
Notes	169
References	181
Company Names Index	199
Subject Index	205

List of Tables

2.1	FDI outflows from emerging and transition economies	12
2.2	Outward FDI stocks from emerging and transition economies	13
2.3	Geographical destinations of FDI from selected emerging and transition economies	18
2.4	Geographical origin of FDI in selected economies	20
2.5	Surveys of investment abroad in emerging economies	22
2.6	Employment at emerging multinationals' affiliates in selected OECD countries	23
2.7	Summary statistics for the world's largest MNCs	25
2.8	The top 50 MNCs based in developing countries	26
2.9	The top MNCs based in developing countries	29
3.1	The top 50 MNCs based in developing countries	32
3.2	Overseas expansion by main non-OECD national oil companies	35
3.3	Fast-food chains from the developing world	48
3.4	Selected foreign investments by Indian BPO companies	50
4.1	Major Korean greenfield investments in Europe and North America	54
4.2	Singapore's industrial township projects	57
6.1	The world's 100 largest contractors	77
6.2	The eclectic framework of different industrial typologies	80
6.3	The investment development path (IDP) model	83
7.1	The regulation of outward FDI in selected countries	97
7.2	EMNCs' participation in the MIGA portfolio	104
8.1	Foreign directors on the boards of some of the world's largest EMNCs	127
8.2	Major deals since 2004 in energy and telecommunications industries	128

8.3	Russian and CIS listings on London's main market	131
9.1	OECD countries' initiatives to attract Chinese MNCs	137
9.2	Selected Chinese MNCs' R&D centers in OECD countries	139

List of Boxes

2.1	Regional strategies in Central and Eastern European energy markets	16
2.2	Typologies of FDI activity data	21
3.1	The Orascom Group: an Arab multinational	42
4.1	The role of Temasek in Singapore's regionalization strategy	55
4.2	Asian investors in the Southern Africa textile industry	60
4.3	Making a Chinese global brand: the Haier case	64
5.1	Two EMNCs follow their customers	71
6.1	Cemex: linking, leveraging, and learning	85
6.2	Tata: from Indian to global conglomerate	90
6.3	A Thai conglomerate in China: the Charoen Pokphand Group	91
6.4	D'Long Strategic Investment: a multinational conglomerate	92
7.1	Recent policy changes in South Africa	96
7.2	The Malaysian South–South Corporation Berhad (MASSCORP)	98
7.3	Economic diplomacy and corporate internationalization: the case of Venezuela	107
7.4	Cemex in Indonesia	111
7.5	Petrobrás in Bolivia	114
8.1	Ethnic ties and FDI: the case of Techint	121
8.2	Human resource management at SABMiller	124
8.3	Ramatex Namibia	134
9.1	China International Marine Containers (Group) in the United States	140
9.2	EMNCs to the rescue: the case of MG Rover	145

Foreword

It may come as a surprise to some to discover that emerging economies have produced their own large multinationals. Neither conventional economic theories nor more modern theories of multinational enterprise would have predicted such an outcome. Theories say that capital should flow into poor countries, not out of them, or that enterprises should become multinational primarily as the result of innovations that are likely in the rich and high-labor-cost countries, not in the emerging markets. Moreover, many business managers from the traditional multinationals of the rich countries have overlooked the new multinationals; only recently have the new firms posed a threat – or sometimes provided opportunities – to businesses from the industrialized countries.

Just a few years ago most of the developing world followed import-substitution policies, restricting the import of goods produced efficiently elsewhere and protecting many services and infrastructure sectors from foreign investors. The goal was to support locally owned businesses. Many development experts became convinced that these types of policies would produce coddled, uncompetitive firms that could survive only inside protected markets. In the "worst" cases, governments even created and owned protected firms. State ownership has been widely seen as the kiss of death to competitiveness. Nevertheless, some of these protected firms have turned into the "new" multinationals. Moreover, some of the strongest of the new multinationals have come from what were only recently among the most protected home markets: South Africa, China, and India, for example.

Past research

A wave of research on Third World multinationals appeared about twenty years ago putting forth explanations based on the specific conditions of the era. For example, skills developed from the special needs of protected markets gave a few companies advantages that enabled them to compete in other protected markets. Authors differed about exactly which skills were important and how lasting they might be, but the explanations for the multinationalization of these firms meant that their foreign investments could be force-fitted into theories of multinational enterprise.[1] And the investors proved to be only minor threats to firms from the rich countries.

At the same time, a number of firms from developing countries were going to other low-wage countries to escape the quotas that restricted exports from their home countries. Their advantage over local firms in their new production sites often lay in their carefully built reputation with buyers for quality and reliability. Principal sources of these internationalized firms were Korea, Taiwan, and Hong Kong.

Some of the explanations offered in the 1980s now seem quite out of date. The participation of the Third World in the move toward globalization has eroded most of the advantages associated with the ability to manufacture efficiently at small volumes and to substitute less-than-ideal inputs for materials not easily imported. The end of the textile quota system has removed an important drive for East Asian firms to set up factories in other low-wage countries, although export firms do still go down the ladder of development to seek lower labor costs. Most of these multinationals, however, were and remain small and are not the focus of this study.

In earlier times, as now, some firms from emerging economies went abroad in an effort to build a vertically integrated business. In some cases, they sought raw materials; more often, they built downstream facilities in the richer countries to assemble or service their exports. Today, more seem motivated to build vertical systems. One wonders, however, whether a few of the new multinationals have chosen integration because their competitors from the richer countries did so at an earlier time, even though today's more open markets have made the strategy obsolete.

Earlier researchers noted another phenomenon that was rather rare at the time: similar to their competitors from richer countries, some firms from emerging economies saw investment in richer markets as a way of learning new technologies and skills. Recently, more firms appear to be following this path.

Implications of new research

Even though a few of the old explanations of multinationals from emerging markets are still useful, they fail to encompass a number of the

[1] See Sanjaya Lall (ed.), *The New Multinationals: The Spread of Third World Enterprises* (Chichester, UK: Wiley, 1983) and Louis T. Wells, *Third World Multinationals: The Rise of Foreign Investment from Developing Countries* (Cambridge, MA: MIT Press, 1983). Although these two books emphasize different strengths that created early multinationals from the emerging markets, they are similar in their conceptual approaches.

most important new multinationals, and especially the large ones on which this book focuses. As a result, the research presented here adds greatly to the earlier studies of multinationals from emerging markets and to theories of why firms invest abroad. The author explores the characteristics of multinationals from various regions. Although there are common elements in the stories of the new multinationals, the firms do differ according to the region they call home.

Even more important, the following chapters explore the implications of the new phenomena for policy. This book goes much farther than previous work in examining the impact of these firms on their home and their host countries. What roles do – and should – government policies in the emerging markets play in encouraging or discouraging the new multinationals? Do the firms represent a loss of much-needed capital and management to their home countries? What, if any, gains compensate for the outflows? Are some of these firms pioneers, willing to invest in countries where other multinationals have feared to go? Firms from South Africa and China suggest that this may well be the case. If so, is this always a good thing for the emerging markets where they locate their subsidiaries? In the end, does it matter which country a multinational calls home? Can Indonesia, for example, expect a better deal from a Chinese firm than from a European or U.S. investor when it needs an electric power plant? Should the United States care whether a British investor or an emerging market investor operates some of its ports or acquires one of its breweries?

Managers of traditional multinationals must decide how they will react to the rise of these new international businesses: simply ignore them, as did many firms when Japanese competitors first appeared, or view them as serious competitors to whose moves they must respond? Their decisions will be wiser if they have a better understanding of the new multinationals.

For sure, some of the new multinationals will fail, but the research in this book suggests that many will survive as serious competitors in a global market. The surprising fact that protected markets did produce such strong firms might even lead development specialists to reconsider their belief that protection inevitably produces only uncompetitive firms.

Louis T. Wells
Herbert F. Johnson Professor of International Management
Harvard Business School

Preface

Productivity growth is a milestone for sustainable development, and a vibrant private sector is the harbinger of such growth. On the basis of this regularity in economic history, the development community is assigning increasing importance to private sector development, with a strong emphasis on small and medium-sized enterprises and local entrepreneurship. It would be wrong, however, to lose sight of the importance of "big business" in economic development. Large industrial enterprises have historically played a vital role in developing new technologies, marketing new products, and introducing new organizational forms. In this way, they have contributed to economic growth and development in industrial countries. Even in the current phase of globalization, characterized by widespread adoption of information and communication technologies, shorter product cycles, fragmentation and increasing dematerialization of production, creation of global value chains, and geographical extension of corporate networks, scale and scope factors remain important. There is therefore no reason to expect big business to play a less crucial role in the new millennium and in developing countries than it did in the economy history of currently high-income countries during past industrial revolutions.

By focusing on the international operations of large corporations in the form of outward foreign direct investment (OFDI), this study aims to provide a better understanding of their contribution to economic growth in emerging, transition, and developing countries. In the analysis of developing economies, the role of exporting as a tool for learning has long been recognized in the literature. The analysis of OFDI flows, on the other hand, is much less developed. The reasons for this are multiple. Possibly the most important is simply the fact that until only a few years ago the amounts were negligible and the multinational corporations (MNCs) from developing countries – that is, the emerging MNCs (EMNCs) that are the object of study in this book – were hardly world leaders in their market niches, let alone in their industries. For decades, the term "multinational" has been synonymous with the expansion of American firms; in fact, even firms from other OECD countries became major investors only recently. Hence, the fact that managers and scholars could discount the competitive threat from Asia, Latin America, South Africa, and the former communist countries – and that OECD policymakers did not devote resources to attracting MNCs from these sources – is far from surprising.

Another possible reason is that analysts and scholars pay more attention to net FDI as a metric, and on this account most developing countries are still net recipients of cross-border investment flows. This focus, however, risks losing sight of the fact that even the United States and other industrial countries were, in their early industrialization days, both home and host to large FDI. At the same time, some countries may be net exporters of capital for the wrong reasons, that is, because they are not attractive enough to foreign investors, and not because they have managed to groom their own MNCs.

These days, to neglect EMNCs would be perilous for policymakers, competitors, and scholars of the global economy alike. Korean MNCs started to emerge more than a decade ago and, despite the slowdown in the aftermath of the Asian crisis, some such companies boast sales volumes, transnationalization indices, and brand recognition levels on a par with established Western companies. In the case of MNCs from the other so-called Asian Tigers (Hong Kong, Singapore, Taiwan), by enlarging capacity in China many have improved the terms of their participation in global production networks. Likewise, some Latin American, Indian, and South African companies have amply expanded their global production base since the mid-1990s either through organic growth or through sequential mergers and acquisitions. More recently, it has been large Chinese firms that have attracted popular attention, most notably when Lenovo acquired the PC business of IBM in December 2004 in exchange for a sizeable equity stake. When, a few months later, CNOOC (the China National Offshore Oil Corporation) made an unsolicited takeover bid for Unocal, a middle-sized oil company, the fear that Chinese companies might be on the verge of conquering the American economy caused an outcry that was out of proportion to the importance of the bid. Across Africa and Central Asia, the activities of Chinese and Indian oil companies, and also of national companies from oil-producing countries, are driving a new Great Game and strongly influencing the foreign policies of Western powers.

A key assumption that underpins this research is that, in today's global economy, EMNCs are much more than simple niche players. In some sectors, such as construction and steel making, EMNCs occupy high positions in the global rankings and operate on the basis of some form of competitive advantage. In services such as air transport and telecommunications, where growth rates outside of the so-called Triad (Europe, North America, and Japan) are set to rise exponentially over the next few decades, MNCs from countries as diverse as Singapore and Mexico rank among the world's largest and most internationalized. Analyzing the strategies of developing countries' investors is thus important for several reasons: to understand the trends, characteristics, structure, dynamics, and opportunities of global and regional foreign investment; to develop strategies of selective incentives (rather than generalized, redundant, and costly systems) that may support this phenomenon in source countries; to assist host economies in intercepting these flows and identifying their bargaining position vis-à-vis specific foreign investment projects; to draw up and implement strategies that maximize both the diffusion of capacities, linkages, and other dynamic gains to the host economy and the balance of payment gains from foreign investment, without compromising diversification of productive and trade capacities; to identify the sources of business excellence and spread them, whenever possible, to the rest of the economy; and to assess the consequences that the emergence of new business actors have on North–South and South–South economic and political relations.

A first step in this endeavor involves the analysis of existing quantitative information. FDI statistics generally suffer from important limitations, including the fact that data on cross-border financial flows are not necessarily the best indicators of global production activity. The quality of developing countries' data is generally poor and that for outward FDI probably even poorer – the problem of "round-tripping," for instance, is particularly severe, and the use of tax havens as a conduit for cross-border investment is also very common. With these caveats in mind, and not without taking note of the efforts that some countries such as Brazil and Singapore are making to collect more meaningful statistics, some trends are clear.

Asian investors contribute the lion's share of Southern OFDI. Outward flows have accompanied the emergence of the so-called Asian Tigers and are now also on the rise from China. For the two largest Tigers, Korea and Taiwan, there is evidence of a "flying geese" dynamics, with the more labor-intensive stages of the value chain moving progressively to the rest of Asia and, increasingly, China, while core corporate functions remain in the source countries. For Hong Kong, the level of integration with mainland China is even higher, although its textiles and clothing MNCs have also long invested in other developing countries to take advantage of Multi Fiber Agreement quotas and preferential market access. In the 1970s, Hong Kong firms moved resources to Mauritius as quota restraints became binding. Whereas factories in the city-state once churned out garments themselves, production has migrated, but many of the executives, traders, and logistics experts who handle a good portion of the world's garment trade are still based there. Singapore is yet another case, with foreign MNCs and state-owned enterprises playing a very prominent role in the economy and, as a result, also in outward FDI activities.

Latin American MNCs, or *multilatinas*, on the other hand, have lost the leadership among EMNCs that was once theirs. For most of the 20th century, Latin America played host to the handful of then-existing multinationals from developing countries, although none ever reached a globally competitive dimension. Those few *multilatinas* that survived two decades of structural adjustment and market reform policies started investing overseas in the late 1990s. In the competition with traditional MNCs, *multilatinas* have tried to leverage their superior knowledge of policy innovations such as trade and financial liberalization, privatization, public–private partnerships, and regulatory reform and their ability to replicate them across regional markets.

Finally, new source countries are emerging in other places, with a strong regional profile. In many sub-Saharan countries, where FDI inflows are notoriously low, South Africa is often the largest investor, even when its firms tend to invest in OECD markets rather than in the rest of the continent. Similarly, incipient MNCs in Eastern Europe have so far mainly ventured into other transition economies, although they are now starting to be more ambitious in the aftermath of EU accession. The regional profile is also very evident in Russia, especially toward the rest of the Commonwealth of Independent States, and in the Middle East. For all these regions, the emergence of companies capable of acting as "international owners" signals a reversal of fortunes following a recent economic history marked first by colonialism, built on foreign capital, and then by socialism, characterized by closure to that capital.

On the basis of this acceleration in OFDI flows from developing countries, numerous questions arise. Different social sciences, including economics, management, and sociology, have studied the internationalization patterns of corporate entities in developed economies. Each of them has contributed rich insights that can increase our understanding of the EMNC phenomenon: in particular, the so-called eclectic paradigm, with its emphasis on the categories of ownership, localization, and internalization, remains useful as an instrument to categorize the motives of foreign investors. Such theories, however, must be adapted to EMNCs' idiosyncratic features – accelerated internationalization, ability to make up for weak proprietary advantages with other assets such as the talent to adapt and to experiment, reliance on governance forms that depart in various ways from the so-called Anglo-Saxon model and yet prove equally capable of surfing the waves of globalization, and, last but not least, the role that public policies, politics, and migration (the presence of a diaspora) play in the decision to invest overseas, as well as in the modalities and location of their expansion.

Another issue that remains insufficiently analyzed is the emergence of developing countries' investors in non-financial services. In sectors such as utilities (telecommunications, electricity, gas, and water), hospitality management (hotels and restaurants), transport, and retail trade, the productivity gap between industrial and developing countries is huge and it is counter-intuitive to expect firms from the latter to invest abroad. And yet this is what is happening, mostly in other developing countries but also and increasingly in industrial ones – the purchase of Europe's largest perfumery chain and Italy's third-largest telecom operator by Hong Kong and Egyptian investors, respectively, being two recent and important examples.

In the contemporary global economy, firms can achieve competitive advantage by building managerial know-how, project-execution capabilities, and brands in activities such as banking, public utilities, telecommunication services, and construction where these features are more important than technology. Given the importance of the process by which the interaction between the regulator and the regulated firms evolve, EMNCs that have operated under a new regime in their home country may also have a superior knowledge of the intricacies of post-privatization regulatory games – a point that, as already mentioned, is particularly important for *multilatinas*, and also for companies in Central Europe and elsewhere. Moreover, in services, building a sympathetic relationship with the customer is crucial, and EMNCs can generally benefit from cultural and psychic proximity. In fact, even when actors are private, ethnicity and the network of interpersonal relationships that the former creates play a role. It suffices here to highlight how diasporic groups across Southeast Asia have played a key role as investors in mainland China.

Government policies to promote both inward and outward FDI must be seen within the broader framework of the role of the state in promoting a country's process of economic development and structural transformation. On a broad level, the progressive liberalization of the capital account is clearly a major component of the policy package that makes it possible for EMNCs to flourish and expand, especially for those countries that have accumulated huge foreign exchange reserves. Increasingly, more specific measures are being taken, such as adhering to regional trade and investment agreements, signing bilateral investment treaties, extending credit lines and insurance guarantees to outward foreign investors, and creating *ad hoc* agencies.

A more contentious issue concerns the possibility that governments may use a mild approach to competition policy to protect national champions and support their overseas drive. Not only is this strategy not infallible in spurring corporate growth – it may indeed give managers a sense of complacency and weaken the basis of competitiveness – but even if successful it may simply result in a transfer of economic welfare from consumers to producers. On the other hand, an assertive pro-competition stance may reinforce corporate productivity and push companies outside national borders, as documented by some examples in this study.

As economic and business historians have long noticed, in any global economic system corporate strategies are embedded in dense networks. As a result, they must be analyzed in the context of the political economy of both host and home countries – when not of the global economy. All governments provide direct political assistance to big business (although hardly ever to smaller enterprises) in their foreign ventures. This is particularly important in natural resources and extractive industries. Probably nowhere is this clearer than in the oil and gas business. After a two-decade hiatus, energy consumption and economic growth appear to be linked again as a result of the faster development of emerging countries, the emergence of carbon as a commodity in its own right, and the search for energy security. These factors, combined with the heightened insecurity brought about by the September 11, 2001, terror attacks on the United States, as well as the Enron crisis, potentially lead to far more politicized energy relations, create new sources of tensions among countries, and open new opportunities for entrepreneurship and cooperation. EMNCs are already important in this business – either as the world's largest companies in terms of reserves (e.g., Saudi Aramco, NIOC, Gazprom, and Sonatrach) or as some of the most acquisitive new players (e.g., CNPC, Sinopec, and ONGC) – and their protagonism has undoubted, although far from clear, consequences. Likewise in other manufacturing and service sectors, some EMNCs, especially from China, remain state-owned and their strategies and tactics cannot be analyzed in isolation from the broader political economy.

The final section of this book discusses the consequences of South-to-North FDI flows for OECD governments and firms. EMNCs want – and indeed need – to establish a direct presence in OECD countries to develop new resources and capabilities. Their rise introduces a wide range of new issues in the policy debate in OECD countries. These issues include the importance of nationality in determining corporate behavior, the adaptability of non-OECD investors to the policy environment and the informal norms that characterize business in OECD countries, the opportunity of tailoring investment promotion to specific circumstances, and the consequences for national security. On all these counts, in order to take a long-term view, it is crucial to understand critical trends and uncertainties that may affect the future environment. Recent episodes, of which the debate concerning the possible CNOOC–Unocal deal was only the first, have highlighted the risk of a return of protectionism. Blocking the doors of the global economy to Chinese and other up-and-coming investors – after spending years to open doors to their markets – is clearly an error. However, the global economy is undergoing profound changes and in industrial nations the efforts to gain a better understanding of the underlying trends, of the emerging issues, and of the necessary adaptations to the policy environment must encompass all stakeholders. If debating these issues remains the privilege of few deal makers in business and government, it will be harder to build a convincing case for open markets.

The opinions expressed and arguments employed are the author's sole responsibility and do not necessarily reflect those of the OECD, the OECD Development Centre, and their Members.

Acknowledgments

If the pleasure of writing a book does not stand only in the constant intellectual challenge, but also in the opportunity to engage with people, visit places, accumulate air miles, and make friends, with multinational corporations from emerging economies I probably chose the best possible topic. With this, however, also comes the responsibility of doing justice to the many people who have helped me in many moments, ways, and places. Needless to add, none of them may even remotely be held responsible for the content of this book.

This study was initiated in 2004 while I was working at the Foreign Investment Advisory Service of the World Bank Group. It was a short period, but it allowed me to test some of the arguments in some of the world's least development-friendly environments with colleagues and practitioners. My thanks go in particular to Xavier Forneris and Rich Stern for introducing me to the mysteries of Lebanese cuisine in Freetown, Kinshasa, and Ouaga and to Shyam Khemani for convincing me of the importance of competition policy in reducing poverty in the developing world. Upon my return to the OECD Development Centre, I was fortunate enough to reinforce a long-running friendship with Federico Bonaglia and Lucia Wegner, while also working together with them, especially in Lusophone Africa.

John Dunning (as Palgrave referee), Danny Van den Bulcke, Lou Wells, and Mira Wilkins all provided thorough commentaries on earlier drafts. As co-authors of separate, but contemporary, papers on multinationals and international business, I am in debt to Dilek Aykut, Federico Bonaglia, Neo Chabane, Michael Chen, John Mathews, Serge Perrin, Nicolas Pinaud, Lucia Piscitello, Helmut Reisen, Simon Roberts, Omar Toulan, and Ted Tschang. I also presented this work in front of seminar audiences at Bologna (Buenos Aires branch), Koç (Istanbul), and Tsinghua (Beijing) universities, Banque de France, Sciences-Po, and OECD Development Centre (Paris), the Danish and South African Institutes for International Affairs (Copenhagen and Johannesburg), the Swiss Development Cooperation (Bern), the United Nations Economic Commission for Latin America and the Caribbean (Santiago), the World Bank Group task force on Southern multinationals (Washington, DC), and, on three separate occasions, the United Nations Conference on Trade and Development (Geneva). I thank Joe Battat, Daniel Chudnovsky, Tom

Davenport, Torbjørn Fredriksson, Neuma Grobelaar, Anne Miroux, Michael Mortimore, Ziya Onis, Stefano Ponte, Marcia Tavares, Kee Hwee Wee, and Max von Zedtwitz for their support and suggestions during these seminars. I also benefited from interactions with participants in two projects on "Can Latin American Companies Compete?" (directed by Robert Grosse at Thunderbird) and "The Strategies of Chinese and Indian Multinationals in Europe," initially supported by Fondazione Courmayeur. For more than a few years now, Cino Molajoni and Henrique Rzezinski at Organización Techint and Embraer, respectively, have accompanied my efforts at gaining a deeper knowledge of these two Latin American firms. Mike Spicer has facilitated useful meetings with South African multinationals. Pavida Pananond was a source of precisions on outward FDI in Thailand. Many other friends and colleagues, far too numerous to list separately, provided data, information, and help in different forms.

At Palgrave, Tim Shaw was an enthusiastic editor when I first approached him with the idea of including a book on this subject in the International Political Economy series; Alison Howson and Jennifer Nelson were equally supportive publishers. J. Vidhya was a fantastic project manager in Chennai and my father Jorge had the dubious pleasure of proof-reading the manuscript and helping with the indices. This is also an opportunity to thank Alessia Graziano, my Italian editor at Il Mulino.

In my days as a graduate student, a book that influenced me greatly was *Dependent Development*. As time has passed, I may have forgotten some of Peter Evans's arguments, but certainly not his acknowledgments section. I was then too young to understand fully the importance of talking about superheroes with one's sons, but in the meantime I have tried to catch up and can now say that no book can even remotely be as important as *fare la bagarre* with Edoardo and Filippo. To them, Nonna Ada, and Luisa, who made all this possible, goes all my love.

List of Abbreviations

3WMNC	Third World multinational corporation
AGOA	African Growth and Opportunity Act
ASEAN	Association of Southeast Asian Nations
BIT	bilateral investment treaty
BOT	build-operate-and-transfer
BPO	business process outsourcing
BTO	build-transfer-and-operate
CAFTA	Central American Free Trade Agreement
CEO	chief executive officer
Cfius	Committee on Foreign Investments in the United States
COMECON	Council for Mutual Economic Cooperation
DTT	double taxation treaty
EMA	*empresa multinacional andina*
EMNC	emerging market multinational corporation
FDI	foreign direct investment
GATS	General Agreement on Trade in Services
GDP	gross domestic product
GSM	global system for mobile communications
HIPC	highly indebted poor country
ICIIE	Islamic Corporation for the Insurance of Investment and Export
ICSID	International Centre for Settlement of Investment Dispute
ICT	information and communication technologies
IDP	investment development path
IFDI	inward foreign direct investment
ILO	International Labour Organisation
IMF	International Monetary Fund
IPA	Investment Promotion Agency
IPO	initial public offer
LDC	less developed country
LNG	liquefied natural gas
M&A	merger and acquisition
MIGA	Multilateral Investment Guarantee Agency
MNC	multinational corporation
MOFCOM	Ministry of Commerce (China)

NOIP	net outward investment position
OBM	original brand manufacturer
OECD	Organisation for Economic Co-operation and Development
OEM	original equipment manufacturer
OFDI	outward foreign direct investment
OLI	ownership, location, internalization
PTIA	preferential trade and investment agreement
R&D	research and development
ROE	return-on-earnings
SAARC	South Asian Association for Regional Cooperation
SAFE	State Administration of Foreign Exchange (China)
SME	small- and medium-sized enterprise
SOE	state-owned enterprise
SPE	special purpose entity
SSIA	South–South investment agreement
TNI	transnationality index
UNCTAD	United Nations Conference on Trade and Development
UNCTC	United Nations Centre on Transnational Corporations
UN/DESA	United Nations Department of Economic and Social Affairs
WTO	World Trade Organization

1
Introduction

Summary

In this early part of the 21st century, deals such as the acquisition of the IBM personal computer business by Lenovo of China, Cemex's emergence as one of the world's largest producers of cement, and Chinese investments in the Canadian energy sector have made evident the increasing relevance of outward foreign direct investment (OFDI) flows from developing countries. The phenomenon is not completely new – indeed, the term "Third World multinationals" gained currency in the 1970s and 1980s – but its foundations have fundamentally changed. In today's global economy, emerging multinationals are no longer niche players; they operate on the basis of some form of competitive advantage. Identifying them, however, remains a key research and policy issue.

Cross-border capital flows are a distinguishing feature of the contemporary global economy, possibly to an even larger extent than international trade. Therefore, the takeover of Ikegai, the opening of a new restaurant in Singapore, and a recruitment drive by restaurants in the United States – all events that took place in July–August 2004, when this study was started – should hardly raise an eyebrow. Yet, what was unusual was that the investor that rescued the first company, Japan's oldest lathe manufacturer, is China's Shanghai Electric; the eateries that made their debut in the very competitive Singapore market, Cabbages and Condoms, distinguish themselves by being Thai, serving condoms instead of after-meal mints, and funneling all profits into AIDS education and environmental protection;[1] and the restaurants that sponsor US entry visas for skilled waiters, arguing that *churrasco* skills are unavailable in the US job market, hail from Brazil.[2] Such deals are not confined to bankrupt companies and admittedly low-tech service sectors such as fast-food restaurants. In that same period, Noranda, a Canadian copper and nickel mining company, entered into exclusive negotiations with China Minmetals, China's biggest base metals company, after shareholders turned down a rival bid by Brazil's CVRD.[3]

These examples, and many others of acquisitions of companies based in industrial countries by competitors from the developing world (see Appendix 1), show that even when they lack the scale, the intellectual property portfolio, and the market power to push their own brands, emerging market multinational corporations (EMNCs) intend to use acquisitions to build global recognition and expand their innovation and manufacturing bases. What are relatively new, moreover, are the forms that foreign direct investment (FDI) from non-developed countries is taking, the motivations, and the effects. In sum, the ability to fund considerable financial arrangements in sophisticated markets, or to build distinctive and highly competitive corporate characteristics and resources, is no longer confined to "Northern" firms.

The rise of so-called Third World multinational companies (3WMNCs) was documented by a number of authors two decades and more ago.[4] Wells (1983) explores why firms based in developing countries have chosen to invest in branches, joint ventures, and wholly owned subsidiaries overseas rather than simply export goods or enter into licensing arrangements abroad. Drawing on the product-cycle model, his analysis emphasizes the ability of 3WMNCs to adapt existing process and product technologies (including second-hand equipment), "descale" them (i.e., modify them so they work at smaller scales) and produce at low costs with small production runs and inexpensive labor. Lall (1983), on the other hand, gives pride of place to proprietary advantage in industrial technology: 3WMNCs "may develop advantages in specialized products and processes only if the localization of technical change ... affords scope for the development of proprietary technological assets" (p. 261).[5] Technology may be the main driver of international expansion if this expansion is to countries with a lower level of development (Diaz-Alejandro 1977) and if firms gain the capacity to internationalize through a cumulative learning-by-doing process (Tolentino 1993). The studies in Oman (1986) also underline the fact that 3WMNCs supply resources and services that are better adapted to the needs of developing countries. A non-technological dimension is added to explain their success in penetrating new markets. These firms are willing to use non-traditional forms of investment (joint equity ventures, licensing, management agreements, turnkey operations) that both host governments and home-country authorities prefer – the former because of the expectation that more know-how will be transferred, the latter because the associated cash outflows abroad will be smaller.

Although such monographs and collections of country studies to some extent emphasized different factors, these early studies reported that international Third World firms operated in a wide range of industries and were by no means confined to either labor-intensive or mining sectors. Country chapters showed Indian and Argentinean firms to be particularly strong on production engineering and basic design capability (Lall 1983), while Brazilian civil engineering contractors mastered some specific technologies and learned how to execute large-scale works under very tough environmental conditions (Guimaraes 1986). And yet, albeit with nuances, the general belief was that companies from non-industrial economies could hardly ever rise to become formidable global competitors (see especially Heenan and Keegan 1979). In particular, evidence for innovation-generating development activities was found to be very sparse (Wells 1983: 156). In his study of 3WMNCs in Mauritius and the Philippines, Busjeet (1980) makes it clear that "external market and cost considerations were more important in the foreign investment decision than the desire to exploit the skills and resources of the firm" (p. 61).

Following the widespread, albeit incomplete and at times flawed, process of economic reform and liberalization that the "South" has gone through since the late 1980s, EMNCs have learned at least some of the tricks of the global economy. Domestic trade liberalization has increased competition on hitherto protected markets, reduced margins at home, and pushed surviving firms into export expansion. Sometimes, firms in developing countries have had to learn new business tricks well before they have become common in OECD (Organisation for Economic Co-operation and Development) markets – possibly the best example being the pro-market regulatory regimes in network industries that were introduced in Latin America during the late 1980s/early 1990s, when in most industrial countries utilities were still largely state-owned monopolists. As a result, such firms found themselves at an advantage when competing with OECD firms on third markets. In other instances, EMNCs have created value by identifying and successfully exploiting opportunities that were opened up by operating in turbulent environments (Sull and Escobari 2004).

Rather than conventional notions of corporate strategy, such as the imperative to predict accurately efficient combinations of position, resources, and competencies, EMNCs have mastered the art of experimenting with flexible solutions to respond to unexpected twists in the business environment. In this sense they have been able to turn what was *prima facie* a liability – unpredictable, when not missing, markets – into an asset (for instance, the proclivity to build up slack resources as a valuable cushion against unforeseen crises). Also, big business in developing countries has become an active player in the global alliance game that defines modern capitalism (Dunning 1995), first by setting up joint ventures in home markets, then expanding together into regional ones, and eventually, in some cases, buying out its OECD-based partners. Some businesses have also ridden the waves of paradigm changes: in electronic equipment, in particular, it was the transition from analog to digital that gave Samsung and other Korean companies the opening they needed to compete with long-established rivals.

These developments call for new research into the international expansion of such companies, bridging the gap between the existing literature on business in emerging economies – which often portrays corporations as rent seekers that flourish as a result of privileged access to political, financial, and transactional resources – and the increasing attention that scholars are devoting to dynamic capabilities as the basis for corporate success (Dosi *et al.* 2000). Factors such as protecting proprietary processes and competitive advantages, "learning by competing" in high-income markets, following important customers, and the increasingly global nature of management (in terms of citizenship, education, recruitment, and professional background) all combine to explain the decision to invest abroad. In this sense, theories and research methodologies developed in international business research can provide new insights into the dynamics of EMNCs.[6] In particular, they may help clarify the conditions under which EMNCs move from "exploiting" existing technologies to "explore" potentially superior ones and generate patterns of self-sustaining growth. And yet there is probably some truth in the expectation that MNCs will differ depending on the income level of their home economies – in particular that EMNCs, instead of relying primarily on non-imitable technological advantages when expanding abroad, seek sources of advantage in their social capital and distribution capabilities.

To advance this research agenda, scholars need to analyze the specific activities and capabilities of the firms involved, and the dynamic reconfiguration that links corporate strategies, FDI, and the broader social and environmental context. In particular, research must come to terms with the concept of heterogeneity across firms as the best way to extend existing models and make them more realistic but still theoretically sound. To a large, albeit still undetermined, degree, the resource and capability endowments enjoyed by MNCs differ in accordance with variations in institutional structures and business systems (Yeung 2002). Standard economic models do not usually account for both the systematic heterogeneity observed in corporate competencies and the nuances of the mechanisms governing the dynamics of interactions among agents (firms, governments, institutions). However, there can be little doubt that soft factors (e.g., vision, ambition, commitment), microeconomic diversity, and institutional settings affect in non-trivial ways aggregate dynamics. Rather than considering only economic factors, an account of companies' internationalization trajectories needs to incorporate the formation and development of strategies, routines, objectives, and behaviors in specific social, cultural, and historical contexts. To this end, this book includes a fair number of embedded and longitudinal "business vignettes" to back up broader analytical observations with concrete examples. I hope it does not sound too presumptuous to remember that some of the founding scholars of international business studies, such as Raymond Vernon, John Dunning, and Edith Penrose, "placed a high priority on evolutionary and historical perspectives and methodology" (Jones and Khanna 2006).

Obviously, the reliance on case studies and anecdotal narratives is not without its risks, especially insofar as it does not lend itself to the quantitative testing that is now the standard social science methodology. This study, at any rate, is not so much about identifying regularities and making predictions as it is about shedding some light on the following research questions:

- What forms are FDI flows from the South taking in terms of target countries and industries, manner of entry and financing, macro- and microeconomic impact, and stage in the history of the MNC? What are the motivations for the corporate decision to internationalize via overseas investment in marketing, distribution, production, and innovation activities rather than pursue the alternative of exporting from the home country?
- What are the similarities and differences between EMNCs and their more established counterparts from the industrialized countries, both large and small? Can existing theories of international business serve for analyzing EMNCs? And, vice versa, what contribution does the study of EMNCs make to theories of international production? In particular, are firms from developing countries "dragon MNCs" that internationalize through investment at an earlier stage in their life than their counterparts from industrial nations?
- Will China and India, and developing Asia more broadly, become an important source of FDI to developing countries? What would be the

beneficiary sectors – only natural-resource-intensive sectors? Would the poor benefit from these developments, or would they remain outside any benefits, especially if most FDI goes to resource-intensive industries? Does OFDI from emerging economies play a positive role in facilitating home economies' competitive insertion into the world economy? Is the development impact of EMNCs any different?

- What are the implications of these developments for North–South and South–South relations in general, and for relations between specific home and host countries? How should OECD governments react to this process? Is there reason to fear a disruption of the progressive economic and political liberalization that is seen as a core element of development assistance? Might EMNCs come to the rescue of sunset industries and ailing firms in OECD countries?

The following chapter reviews available data, highlighting the rise of the Asian Tigers and large emerging economies such as Brazil, China, India, Mexico, Russia, and South Africa as sources of global FDI flows. Attention is also drawn to some key methodological issues – on the one hand, the role of the diasporas and the broader difficulty in clearly classifying increasingly complex ownership structures; on the other hand, the so-called round-tripping phenomenon whereby domestic investors take advantage of incentives accorded to foreign companies by routing their investments through third countries. Chapters 3 analyzes industry dynamics, with particular emphasis on oil and service industries, while Chapters 4 and 5 focus on the entry and performance record of Asian and Latin American MNCs, respectively. Chapter 6 reviews the main threads in the economic and business literature on multinationals and their theoretical relevance for non-OECD countries. In particular, it is argued that a huge effort is needed to explore in greater depth and with more rigorous parameters the sources of corporate success, the extent of firm-level capabilities in innovation and knowledge management relative to competitors, and the heterogeneity of company trajectories, relying on both macro and co-evolutionary approaches. The multiple roles of governments – at the level of both policies and international political economy – are discussed in Chapter 7. Three main topics are identified in Chapter 8 as still gravely wanting in terms of deeper and better research – the role of diasporas in homeland FDI, the challenge of multinational management, and the impact of EMNCs on host economies. The consequences for OECD governments and firms are explored in Chapter 9.

2
Trends in Southern OFDI

Summary

FDI statistics generally suffer from important limitations, including the fact that data on cross-border financial flows are not necessarily the best indicators of global production activity. The quality of developing countries' data is probably even poorer – the problem of round-tripping, for instance, is particularly severe and the use of tax havens is also very common. With these caveats in mind, some trends are clear. Asian investors contribute the lion's share of Southern OFDI, while Latin American multinationals have lost the leadership that was theirs for most of the 20th century. Other countries are also emerging, with South Africa being especially present in the rest of sub-Saharan Africa.

In the area of international investment flows, data collection, comparison, and interpretation are fraught with difficulties. Methodologies change relatively often, time series are short, and monitoring is of uneven quality and reliability. In general terms, it is questionable whether balance-of-payments measures of FDI flows and stocks represent well enough production owned and operated across international borders (Lipsey 2000).[1]

2.1 What is corporate nationality?

Definitions of what constitute an EMNC may be problematic. Ownership is certainly an important element, but the internationalization of the world's business activities is possibly more about the cross-border extension of managerial control and the transfer of know-how than it is about the transfer of financial funds. Nonetheless, data availability compels most analyses of international investment to use financial flows indicators as a vehicle and a major component of globalization.

The issue of immediate versus ultimate ownership of direct investment enterprises is also crucial. The focus of this book is on companies incorporated in developing and transition economies whose ultimate beneficial owner is an investor from one or more such countries. Numerous problems arise, however, in trying to identify the ultimate source or destination of FDI. Leaving aside the possible semantic confusion between emerging and new multinationals – no matter whether from OECD countries or from emerging economies – there are other definitions that may dovetail with that of EMNCs and yet refer to other phenomena.

First, what of companies established in developed countries by non-resident entrepreneurs? A very large MNC for which the assignment of nationality is not obvious is Mittal Steel. The company is registered in Amsterdam and is 88 percent controlled by an Indian citizen who lives in London. Lakshmi Mittal and his two children sit on the board of directors alongside another Indian, a Mauritian of Indian descent, and four North Americans. The team overseeing the many major acquisitions, including those in Romania, the Czech Republic, Poland, and South Africa, that have made the company the world's largest steel producer mostly comprises Indian engineers, led by Mittal Steel's chief operating officer. Although Lakshmi Mittal has personal property in India, he has not lived there for more than three decades and his company does not operate any steel mills in India. However, when Mittal Steel launched a takeover bid for Arcelor in January 2006, the managers of the European company began referring to the suitor as an Indian company and the government in Delhi also timidly supported the deal. Less well known, Brightstar is a Miami-based company owned by a Bolivian entrepreneur that in less than a decade has grown into a US$2.2 billion business and the world's largest distributor of mobile phones, centered on emerging markets.[2]

Second, what of companies that move their primary listing to an advanced country's financial market in order to benefit from lower currency risk and higher liquidity, and yet maintain a strong association with their countries of origin? The story of South African MNCs is particularly complex. SABMiller, for instance, is British-registered, with dual listing in London and Johannesburg; its management is overwhelmingly of South African nationality, although it is unclear where the managers reside;[3] its main shareholder (Altria) is American and the second-largest (the Santo Domingo family) is Colombian. In a similar vein, investors from developing countries may sometimes buy a company that is registered in an industrial country to improve their financial standing. Antofagasta is a British company also traded in New York that is controlled by the Luksic family of Chile. The predecessor of the modern Antofagasta was incorporated in London in 1888 and raised money on the London Stock Exchange to build and operate a railway from Antofagasta, a port on the Pacific Coast of Northern Chile, to La Paz, in Bolivia. The Luksics bought the company in 1980 and then merged Antofagasta's banking and industrial interests with those of its diversified Chilean company Quiñenco. Although Antofagasta still has most of its assets in Chile and Peru, it is now attempting to acquire Tethyan Copper, the Australian owner of the Reko Diq copper-gold project in Pakistan.

Third, what of companies incorporated in developing countries that are in turn subsidiaries of OECD MNCs? Brazil's Embraco, for instance, is the world's largest producer of compressors, with plants in China, Italy, and Slovakia. Although Whirlpool acquired a majority position in 1997, and integrated the company into its global operations, Embraco's management is still almost exclusively Brazilian. A few Swedish-owned MNCs expanded into Eastern Europe via subsidiaries in Central Europe to exploit accumulated knowledge and experience of local markets and reduce market entry risk, while another one – Lundin Petroleum – used a subsidiary in the United Arab Emirates to make its first investment in Sudan (Patey 2006). Volkswagen of Germany is using Skoda Auto, its Czech subsidiary, to enter the former Soviet Union. Not only is Volkswagen using the Skoda brand, but it is also using Skoda as the corporate entity investing in new assembly plants in Ukraine and Kazakhstan.

And fourth, what of companies from developing countries that are owned by financial investors based in OECD countries? Leciva is a generic drugs maker that Warburg Pincus, a US private equity firm, bought from the Czech state in 1998. In 2003 Leciva acquired its Slovak counterpart Slovakofarma to create Zentiva, ahead of an initial public offer (IPO) in London and Prague that helped to cut debt. Since 2004 Zentiva has expanded into Poland and Russia.

In all such cases, assigning corporate citizenship is something of a moot point. At any rate, international statistics will classify as British investments by Antofagasta, Mittal, or SABMiller, even when – as discussed – these companies are probably at least as much Chilean, Indian, or South African. There are possibly interesting similarities with the story of Simon Patiño, a Bolivian entrepreneur who in the 1920s and

1930s worked through companies registered in advanced countries to obtain control of one of two Malaya smelters and build the world's largest tin empire (Jones 2005: 63).[4]

2.2 The quality of the data

In the early 1980s, when the pioneering attempts at analyzing OFDI from non-OECD countries were made, available statistics tended to be patchy and unreliable. Wells (1983) resorted to numerous sources to compile validated data and viable estimates, while Lall (1983) concludes that "despite all our efforts, it did not prove possible to get accurate comparable data on total foreign investments by all the sample countries" (p. 250). The publication of the United Nations Conference on Trade and Development (UNCTAD) annual *World Investment Report* – which relies on investment promotion agencies (IPAs) for data collection (based on approvals or projections rather than actual investment inflows) – has resulted in considerable improvements on the situation prevailing two decades ago. Yet, many flaws persist in terms of reliability, comparability, usefulness, comprehensiveness, and timeliness (UNCTAD 2006).

Discrepancies between reported inward and outward flows are still large (see the International Monetary Fund's *IMF Balance of Payments Yearbook*). In particular, FDI outflows from developing countries are notoriously underreported. The official statistics on overseas investment differ significantly from those provided by the countries in which the investments take place. In the Taiwanese case, for instance, investors that choose to pursue overseas investment do not necessarily register this with the Investment Commission at the Ministry of Economic Affairs.[7] The proportion of unregistered investment tends to be higher in Southeast Asia and China than in the United States, and complex administrative procedures have a reinforcing influence on this type of behavior (Yang and Tu 2004). Franco and De Lombaerde (2000) lament that Colombian official data on OFDI are difficult to reconcile with those of recipient countries and that Colombian MNCs are very reluctant to share information and data. Likewise, "the reluctance of many Thai firms to provide information on their international activities remains a major obstacle in studying their behaviors" (Pavida 2004: 107).

Moreover, any large comparative dataset compiled from national sources has weaknesses and caution is appropriate. In many countries, central bank data are not very "pure," as they likely contain portfolio investment and some service flows (remittances). Still, they are better than they used to be and are improving owing to the efforts of international institutions such as the IMF and OECD to upgrade quality, coverage, and consistency at the country level (despite the poor accounting practices in many countries).[5] In addition, in 2003 the IMF Committee on Balance of Payments Statistics convened its Task Force to examine the Feasibility of a Coordinated Direct Investment Survey. The Direct Investment Technical Expert Group was established by the IMF and OECD in 2004 to make recommendations on the methodology for measuring FDI for the harmonized revisions of the IMF Balance of Payments Manual and the OECD Benchmark Definition of Foreign Direct Investment. The IMF Committee on Balance of Payments Statistics and the OECD Workshop on International Investment Statistics reviewed these recommendations. Finally, there are gaps between FDI flows (compiled by a national source) and merger and acquisition (M&A) data (usually compiled by a non-national source).

2.3 Aggregate statistics

It is very important to consider all these caveats, and the fact that year-on-year variance is so large, when examining available aggregate statistics. Table 2.1 provides a snapshot of FDI outflows from developing countries for the past decade. The rise in the absolute value is certainly impressive – from slightly more than US$53 billion in 1992–98 to more than US$85 billion in 1999–2004, with a peak of US$147 billion in 2000. Outflows in 2004 were slightly higher than for 2002 and 2003 combined. Global FDI flows over this period, however, rose much faster, and as a result the developing countries' weight diminished from 14.7 percent in 1992–98 to 9.9 percent in 1999–2004 (the 2004 share being the highest since 1997). This trend does not diminish the importance of EMNCs as much as it underlines the fact that the 1990s saw stronger investment integration, spurred by M&As, among OECD economies (Cantwell and Santangelo 2002).

Stock data over a longer time span paint a slightly different picture (Table 2.2).[6] Developing countries saw their global share plummet in the aftermath of the debt crisis, from 13.33 percent in 1982 to a low of 7.74 percent in 1991. Their participation rose substantially later in the decade, reaching a zenith in 1997 at 15.26 percent, before falling again to 11.63 percent in 2003. However, the quality of the stock data is such that it is very difficult to make any conclusive argument.

Among developing economies, those in Asia remain by far the largest *active* investors. The so-called Tigers – Korea, Singapore, Hong Kong, and Taiwan – accounted for almost 59 percent of the total in 1992–98 and

Table 2.1 FDI outflows from emerging and transition economies (US$ m., countries ranked by cumulative 1992–2004 figures)[a]

	1992–98	1999	2000	2001	2002	2003	2004
World	381,439	1,104,937	1,239,149	743,465	652,181	616,923	730,257
Developed economies	*329,273*	*1,016,555*	*1,095,077*	*664,045*	*603,380*	*585,149*	*644,206*
Developing economies	*53,525*	*91,007*	*147,247*	*82,114*	*53,312*	*42,358*	*95,758*
Hong Kong	20,047	19,369	59,352	11,345	17,463	5,492	39,753
Singapore	5,020	7,778	5,085	22,711	4,095	3,705	10,667
Taiwan	3,303	4,420	6,701	5,480	4,886	5,682	7,145
Korea	3,196	4,198	4,999	2,420	2,617	3,426	4,792
Russia	1,132	2,208	3,177	2,533	3,533	9,727	9,601
China	2,816	1,774	916	6,885	2,518	−152	1,805
Malaysia	1,900	1,422	2,026	267	1,905	1,369	2,061
Brazil	845	1,690	2,282	−2,258	2,482	249	9,471
Chile	939	2,558	3,987	1,610	343	1,884	943
Mexico	549	1,475	984	4,404	930	1,784	2,240
Argentina	1,709	1,730	901	161	−627	774	319
South Africa	1,592	1,580	271	−3,180	−399	577	1,606
Indonesia	946	72	150	125	182	15	107
Venezuela	514	872	521	204	1,026	1,318	−348
India	89	80	509	1,397	1,107	913	2,222
Thailand	487	349	−22	346	106	486	362
Colombia	358	116	325	16	857	938	142
Hungary	122	250	621	368	278	1,647	538
Turkey	138	645	870	497	175	499	859
Nigeria	310	173	169	94	172	167	261

[a] Excluding tax havens (see text).
Source: UNCTAD data at www.worldinvestmentreport.com.

52 percent in 1999–2004. If we add China, the five largest economies, all in Asia, accounted for more than two-thirds of the total in 2004. Conversely, Hong Kong firms allocated 53.2 percent of their total 2001–03 investment to foreign markets; Singapore channeled 23.3 percent; and Taiwan 6.4 percent. For the two latter countries, a large chunk of FDI outflows went to mainland China. Again, the quality of the data on OFDI flows as a percentage of gross fixed capital formation is debatable: this indicator also reaches suspiciously high levels for countries such as Albania, Gambia, and Laos, which host precious few MNCs.

Extreme care is notoriously important with Chinese data, as FDI enjoys favorable treatment compared with domestic investment, resulting in an incentive to label projects as foreign. According to Giroud and Mirza (2006), "the stock of Chinese OFDI in 2003 was $11.4 billion according to the Ministry of Commerce (MOFCOM), whereas the SAFE (State Administration of Foreign Exchange) figure is around $39 billion (and OFDI through informal channels would boost the latter figure even

Table 2.2 Outward FDI stocks from emerging and transition economies (US$ m., countries ranked by 2004 figure)[a]

	1989	1995	2000	2001	2002	2003	2004
World	1,479,889	2,917,546	6,148,284	6,564,217	7,288,417	8,731,240	9,732,233
Developed economies	*1,346,555*	*2,579,117*	*5,252,602*	*5,667,699*	*6,360,693*	*7,715,676*	*8,594,838*
Developing economies	*133,335*	*338,429*	*895,682*	*896,518*	*927,724*	*1,015,563*	*1,137,394*
Hong Kong	9,653	78,833	388,380	352,602	309,430	339,649	405,589
Singapore	5,775	35,050	56,766	72,184	85,759	90,242	100,910
Taiwan	7,645	25,144	66,655	70,758	76,850	84,092	91,237
Russia	n.a.	345	20,141	32,437	54,608	72,273	81,874
Brazil	40,420	44,474	51,946	49,689	54,423	54,892	64,363
Korea	1,488	10,231	26,833	29,020	31,102	34,527	39,319
China	1,659	15,802	27,768	34,654	37,172	37,020	38,825
South Africa	13,143	23,305	32,333	17,579	21,980	27,184	28,790
Argentina	6,022	10,696	21,141	21,283	20,618	21,500	21,819
Mexico	840	2,572	7,540	11,944	12,067	13,645	15,885
Chile	147	2,774	11,154	11,720	12,239	13,852	14,447
Malaysia	2,136	11,042	21,276	8,354	10,119	11,735	13,796
Venezuela	866	3,427	7,676	7,894	8,732	9,548	9,204
Turkey	173	1,425	3,668	4,581	5,847	6,138	6,997
India	118	495	1,859	2,615	4,005	5,054	6,592
Nigeria	792	2,931	4,132	4,226	4,398	4,565	4,826
Hungary	0	278	1,280	1,556	2,167	3,537	4,472
Colombia	392	1,027	2,989	2,952	3,553	4,390	4,284
Thailand	258	2,276	2,203	2,626	2,594	3,031	3,393
Czech Rep.	0	346	738	1,136	1,473	2,284	3,061

[a] Excluding tax havens and offshore centers (see text).
Source: UNCTAD data at www.worldinvestmentreport.com.

further). Although the MOFCOM figure is probably a significant understatement of the scale of Chinese OFDI, there are concerns that 'round-tripping' inflates the SAFE data" (p. 2). In fact, a significant proportion of investments pouring from Taiwan, Hong Kong, and Singapore is round-tripping from China's mainland. Based on the most recent statistical information, Xiao (2004) argues that around 40 percent of China's FDI inflows are likely to be spurious, a much higher estimate than previous authors had suggested. Despite the distorting effect of round-tripping on Chinese FDI statistics, its abuse of existing government measures to attract foreign investment, and the negative consequences for tax revenues, Cross *et al.* (2004) argue that it has brought certain benefits – a sort of second-best practice that has promoted access to international capital markets and has catalyzed the internationalization of Chinese enterprises.

On the other hand, Latin American investors – such as Argentinean companies, which established cross-border production as early as the beginning of the 20th century and were still dominating the geography of Southern FDI in the 1970s – now account for a much smaller share (11.71 percent in 1992–98, falling to 10.62 in 1999–2004). Chile, which has the smallest population among the six largest Latin American investors, has been consistently ranked among the top three. The experience of *multilatinas* is analyzed in greater detail in Chapter 5.

Russia is another major source of Southern FDI, with a heavy concentration in the natural resources and transportation sectors of the countries of the former Soviet Union (UNCTAD 2005b). Russian metallurgical companies have also become important MNCs. Flat-steel producer Severstal is aiming to diversify into higher-margin products and to become one of the world's six biggest steel producers, while Russian Aluminum (RusAl) is the world's second-largest producer of primary aluminum, with refineries and smelters in Guinea and Australia. The Cypriot offshore sector has developed into a landing place for Russian capital, to the extent that Cyprus is currently the biggest direct investor in Russia (Hunya 2006: table 4). In addition, the investment flow from (or via) Cyprus to other Eastern European countries is relatively large, and a significant share of these "Cypriot" investments is considered to be of Russian origin (Vahtra and Liuhto 2004). There is nothing completely new here: in the early years of the 20th century, Russian interests set up and registered in London a company to make direct investments in Tsarist Russia (Gurushina 1998). By virtue of its Britishness, the Russian Tobacco Company could avoid certain regulations in the commercial code that discouraged the creation of monopolies in the Russian Empire.

In India, which remains a relatively smaller outward investor, round-tripping takes place too, although the phenomenon is less developed in terms of size. Mauritius has been the dominant source of FDI into India since 1995, accounting for 36 percent of total inflows from August 1991 to September 2005 (Reserve Bank of India 2005 *Annual Report*). Most such investments are effected through Mauritius Offshore Companies, which are special-purpose vehicles best suited to foreign investors who wish to utilize Mauritius as an investment platform, thereby benefiting from its network of double taxation treaties.

It is only recently that companies headquartered in other transition economies in Central and Eastern Europe have become outward investors, although some early attempts were made in the 1970s (Svetličič and Rojec 2003). The bulk of cross-border investment takes place within the region, as companies and managers are familiar with post-communist business culture, can often communicate without an interpreter, may have contacts from the past, are more tolerant of bureaucracy, and show a greater awareness of national sensitivities. The foreign presence of "transition MNCs" is also gaining momentum in Western Europe as a result of the May 2004 European Union (EU) enlargement, although from a very low basis. In the case of Poland, for instance, investment in Germany is estimated at around €500 million – mostly sole-proprietor businesses but also including big-ticket operations such as PKN Orlen's 494 petrol stations and Unimil, which became Europe's largest producer of condoms following the acquisition of the Condomi brand.[8] The value of Polish investment in the Czech Republic is also estimated at around €500 million, of which most reflects PKN Orlen's takeover of Unipetrol. Following the US$2.3 billion purchase of Mazeikiu Nafta in May 2006, PKN Orlen has become Central Europe's largest energy group.

Finally, the evolution of South African data reflects the decision of many of the country's traditional groups and mining houses to transfer their primary listing from Johannesburg to London, as well as the reverse takeover of De Beers by Anglo-American. The end of the Apartheid regime has certainly contributed to the acceleration of South African investment in other countries in the region, but the majority of the firms surveyed by the SA Foundation (2004) already had a presence in other African countries well before 1994.

2.4 The geography of investment

Even in the age of globalization, FDI flows still show a high degree of geographical proximity. Many of the world's largest firms are not global but regionally based in terms of breadth and depth of market coverage. Data on the activities of the 500 largest MNCs – which are overwhelmingly OECD-based – reveal that very few are successful globally. For 320 of the 380 firms for which geographic sales data are available, an average of 80.3 percent of total sales are in their home region of the Triad (Japan, the EU, and the United States); (Rugman and Verbeke 2004).

The expectations in the case of developing economies are not clear. On the one hand, EMNCs may have an even stronger "local bias" than their more sophisticated competitors, which have had the time to develop the managerial and logistics skills to control a complex web of multi-country subsidiaries. Instead of entering into direct competition with Northern majors, EMNCs may try to replicate in neighboring countries their own transformation on the home market (see Box 2.1 for two examples from energy markets in Central and Eastern Europe). On the other hand, to

Box 2.1 Regional strategies in Central and Eastern European energy markets

The Czech electricity utility CEZ and the Hungarian oil company MOL are two of New Europe's largest MNCs. Although the markets they operate in are slightly different, they are both characterized by a heavy government role in regulation and intense competition from Western majors. Both companies have focused on post-socialist markets, where they perceive themselves to have a competitive advantage.

MOL went public in 1993, and Austria's OMV has a 9.1 percent stake, although voting rights are limited to 5 percent per shareholder. With the EU enlargement, Western majors have invested in Hungary, cutting MOL's share of domestic retail sales (now 43 percent), depressing margins, and therefore making it imperative to diversify the resource base. MOL is also saddled with huge debts caused by its price-capped gas business. Since the late 1990s, MOL has created a regional powerhouse with more than 1,200 petrol stations across nine countries. MOL initially used licensing to spread its retail operations abroad. In 2000 it snapped up 36 percent of Slovnaft, Slovakia's sole refinery, before acquiring majority control in November 2002, the first time an Eastern European company took over a competitor of any size elsewhere in the region. In 2003 it bought 25 percent of INA, its Croatian state-owned counterpart, outbidding OMV with an offer of US$505 million. MOL has already reaped synergies in refining and marketing from its merger with Slovnaft, and a presence in Croatia gives it direct access to Russian crude oil supplies from the Adriatic Sea.

Initially, MOL aimed at securing supply channels via acquiring stakes in foreign fields and through production-sharing agreements. Management now believes that the region's oil companies have a bleak future as national minnows, but stand a chance of competing with the industry's giants if they come together, jettison high-cost businesses such as exploration, and concentrate on refining and marketing. As MOL's financial resources are rather modest, it has embraced cooperation as a modal choice in securing raw material supply. MOL divested in Egypt and Tunisia, where its exploration experiences were less encouraging, and chose to concentrate exploration and production in Siberia, through a joint venture with Yukos of Russia.

In November 2003, MOL signed a memorandum of understanding with PKN Orlen, Poland's biggest oil firm. Although the alliance makes strategic sense, with parliamentary elections approaching and nationalistic sentiment running high, in mid-2004 the Polish government drew up laws giving the state the right to veto important decisions in "strategic" firms, including PKN. It is understood that MOL, OMV, and PKN may form some kind of strategic alliance if an outside predator were to enter the region.

The experience of CEZ, in which the Czech government holds a 72 percent stake, is similar, although in this case the firm enjoys a higher degree of market power at home (72 percent of generation in 2006). Using its cheap baseload from two nuclear power stations, CEZ has become the second-largest power exporter in Europe, and the government has also helped by selling it two-thirds of the country's distribution network and the biggest brown coal mine in what were considered sweetheart deals. Cash flows will continue to grow as domestic prices converge to those of Germany, which are currently 20 percent higher.

In the 18 months to February 2006, CEZ's market capitalization almost quadrupled, making the company the most valuable in New Europe outside Russia. CEZ bought Romanian and Bulgarian distributors (bringing in almost 7 million new customers), a Polish generating company, and Bulgaria's second-largest thermal power plant in March 2006. If anything, management has been criticized for being too timid in its bids – its caution made it lose Slovenske Elektrarne, which could have provided the biggest synergies, to Italy's Enel.

Sources: "MOL's milestone," *The Economist*, April 6, 2000; "Hungary's new empire builder," *The Economist*, July 17, 2003; "Attention to cultural detail pays off at Mol," *Financial Times*, August 20, 2003; "Eastern Europe's consolidators pause (briefly) for breath," *International Petroleum Finance*, September 2004; "A state utility turns up the juice," *Business Week*, April 4, 2005; "CEZ powers ahead with Central Europe expansion," *Financial Times*, February 23, 2006; Heinrich (2004).

the extent that EMNCs use foreign acquisitions to gain market access and knowledge, they are likely to do this in distant countries that they cannot otherwise conquer. To add to the complexity of this exercise, EMNCs may be particularly apt to shift assets and income to special-purpose entities (SPEs) registered in foreign economies with favorable tax treatments. Many studies of the process of globalization are based on FDI statistics that include transactions involving SPEs that do not conduct any "real" economic activities in those economies (UNCTAD 2006). Financial flows through FDI enterprises that are SPEs have increased substantially in recent years, and many such tax havens are in zones that are OECD-contiguous – for instance Bermuda and Gibraltar. These "in transit" flows constitute – on a world level – double counting, which may lead to an overvaluation of the weight of South-to-North FDI flows.

Data differ widely in nature, coverage, and trustworthiness and are at most suggestive of broader trends.[9] Indirect estimates, using data from several sources, suggest that more than one-third of Southern FDI inflows in the 1990s originated in other developing economies (Aykut and Ratha 2004). Table 2.3 makes it clear that, depending on the country, each of these various hypotheses is somehow confirmed.

- Korean and Russian firms have invested heavily in their respective neighborhoods, either to take advantage of high growth rates and export potential (Koreans in China and ASEAN [Association of Southeast Asian Nations] countries) or to access natural resources and exploit a common recent history and culture (Russians in former Soviet republics). Korean firms have also invested heavily in Central Asia.
- Chinese firms have so far mostly sought natural resources (oil, mining, and forestry) in Africa, Canada, and Latin America, as well as Australia.

They are also active in information and communication technologies (ICT), computer, and software industries, although data are poor.[10]

- South African blue chips have mostly invested in European markets, although this is partly an accounting artifice resulting from the decision to seek primary listing in London. The paradox is that, while largely shying away from the rest of Africa, in most African countries they do account for at least a large part of inward FDI (see below).
- Finally, tax havens and offshore centers – mainly in the Caribbean and the Pacific, but also around Europe (the Channel Islands, Cyprus, Gibraltar, Liechtenstein, and Madeira) and Africa (Mauritius) – account for very sizeable shares of OFDI, in particular in the cases of Brazil, India, Russia, and Singapore.[11] They are also being increasingly used by Chinese investors.[12]

Table 2.3 Geographical destinations of FDI from selected emerging and transition economies

	Same region	EU15 and EFTA	Japan and Oceania	Canada and USA	Rest of the world
Brazil[a]	4.02	17.14	0.10	2.38	76.35
China[b,c]	46.80	6.64	3.71	17.84	25.01
Hungary[d]	75.11	17.70	1.32	3.27	2.61
India[c,e]	19.43	12.43	2.75	16.43	48.96
Korea[f]	40.30	20.70	1.90	32.00	5.00
Russia[g]	37.02	24.74	n.a.	23.11	15.12
Singapore[a]	46.99	9.68	7.55	5.25	30.53
S. Africa[a]	10.90	76.43	3.14	7.11	2.42
Thailand[h]	58.75	6.74	1.78	15.17	17.56
Turkey[i]	32.01	57.70	0	2.79	7.51

[a] End-2004 stock.
[b] Cumulative flows 1991–2003; same region includes all of Asia.
[c] Approved projects.
[d] Cumulative flows 1999–2003 Q1; same region includes former COMECON countries and CIS countries.
[e] Cumulative flows April 1996–August 2005.
[f] 1999 stock
[g] Cumulative flows 1995–99; same region includes former COMECON countries and CIS countries.
[h] Cumulative flows 1978–2002.
[i] Cumulative flows through mid-2004; same region includes Balkans, Central Asia, Russia, and Northern Cyprus.

Sources: Banco Central do Brasil, *Capitais Brasileiros no Exterior*, 2004; Hazine İstatistikleri, Treasury Statistics, 2004; Ministry of Commerce and Industry, Department of Industrial Policy and Promotion, *India FDI Fact Sheet*, January 2006; Singapore Statistics, *Survey of Singapore's Investment Abroad*, 2006; South African Reserve Bank, *Quarterly Bulletin*, no. 240, 2004; Giroud and Mirza (2006): Lee (2004); Pavida (2004); Spányik (2003); Vahtra and Liuhto (2004).

Furthermore, at the aggregate level, various indicators point to the importance of emerging economies as sources of FDI inflows to other, usually less developed, non-OECD countries. In fact this is not a new phenomenon – already in 1968–77, for instance, 11 percent of the foreign equity in investments approved in the Philippines was held by less developed country (LDC) firms (Busjeet 1980: 22). The quality of the data is such that any comparison must be made with a great deal of caution (Table 2.4). The importance of South Africa as a major FDI source for the rest of sub-Saharan Africa, however, is clear, as is, albeit to a smaller degree, that of Russia and Turkey in Central Asia.[13] In the case of Argentina, while the weight of Brazil is relatively minor compared with traditional North Atlantic investors if the benchmark for analysis is the 1990–2000 period (Goldstein 2004b), shifting the focus to cumulative flows following the 2001 debt default changes the picture. Over the past few years, Brazilian investors have snatched various Argentinean assets, including Loma Negra (bought by Camargo Corrêa), Perez Companc (by Petrobrás), Quilmes (by AmBev), Acindar (by Belgo Mineira), and Swift Armour (by Friboi).[14] In the first 11 months of 2005, Brazil accounted for 48 percent of M&A activity in its Southern neighbor.[15] Brazilian MNCs found that the opportunities of buying in a fire sale (Krugman 2000) more than offset the risks of operating in a poor business environment. Moreover, for them, financial market pressures not to invest in a country in default were not as constraining as for their OECD rivals.

Data on cross-border M&A deals completed in developing and transition countries in 2004 reveal that in value terms EMNCs accounted for 47 percent of regional activity in Africa, 13 percent in Latin America, 24 percent in Asia and Oceania, and 25 percent in Southeast Europe and the Commonwealth of Independent States (UNCTAD 2005a: annex table A.II.1). In the case of telecommunications, intra-regional South–South FDI in 1990–2003 was as high as 49 percent in sub-Saharan Africa and 48 percent in North Africa and the Middle East (Guislain and Qiang 2006). In fact, since 2001 the retreat of some of the traditional international operators from infrastructure projects in the developing world has left a significant gap that local and regional operators and investors have begun to fill to some extent (PPIAF 2005). Although developing country investors accounted, in terms of value, for only 27 percent in energy and 18 percent in water, compared with 59 percent in transport and 51 percent in telecom, in rural electrification innovative companies such as NetGroup (South Africa), Electricity Distribution Management (Namibia), and IPS Power (a subsidiary of the Aga Khan Foundation) have sought to leverage experience gained in low-cost projects

Table 2.4 Geographical origin of FDI in selected economies

	AR	AZ	BG	BH	BW	CR	KZ	LK	MO	MT	NP	VN	UZ
Brazil	16												
Chile	4												
China			2				4		38		11		
Croatia				16									
Hong Kong			6					10				7	
India			2						2	7	36		
Indonesia							2						
Korea			4				12	12	8		4	10	3
Malaysia			8						3	6		3	
Mauritius									1				
Mexico	4					8							
Russia		5							3				26
Singapore			5					17	1	9		19	
Slovenia				14									
South Africa	1				49					14			
Taiwan	1			1								15	
Thailand	1											3	
Turkey		13					4						

Notes: Source countries in rows; destination countries in columns. Figures correspond to cumulative FDI inflows for the following countries: AR – Argentina, 2002–05; AZ – Azerbaijan, 1994–2001; BG – Bangladesh; BH – Bosnia Herzegovina, 1994–2003; BW – Botswana, end-1999 stock; CR – Costa Rica, 1992–2003; KZ – Kazakhstan, 1993–2000; LK – Sri Lanka, 1979–2000; MO – Mongolia, 1990–2003; MT – Mauritius, 1990–98; NP – Nepal, until 2001; PE – Peru, 1990–96; VN – Vietnam, 1988–2003 (commitments); UZ – Uzbekistan, 1997.

Sources: Centro de Estudios para la Producción, Base de Inversiones; Foreign Investment Promotion Agency of Bosnia and Herzegovina; UNCTAD, Investment Policy Review, various issues; UN Economic and Social Commission for Asia and the Pacific, International Economic Conference and Regional Roundtable on FDI for Central Asia, Dushanbe, April 2–4, 2003; Banco Central de Costa Rica; Leproux and Brooks (2004); Nachin (2004).

Box 2.2 Typologies of FDI activity data

A first category of government statistics includes the Canadian Census of Manufacturers, which provides rich firm-specific data on industry sector, entry mode (acquisition, greenfield investments, joint ventures, strategic alliances, licensing, etc.), size, performance, and nationality. The Canadian statistics are unique, providing data both on foreign and domestic incumbents and on entrants, over time.

Second, there are university databases on representative samples of MNCs, such as the Harvard Database on American and Foreign MNCs. Despite being the source of much early empirical work on MNCs, including entry form and mode studies, the Harvard database ends in 1975. The Research Institute of Industrial Economics in Stockholm collects data on Swedish MNCs approximately every four years, providing a consistent database since 1965. All Swedish multinationals in manufacturing are included, and the affiliates of the participating firms cover approximately 85 percent of the total number of employees at foreign affiliates of Swedish MNCs. The response rate was 30 percent in 2003. In the earlier surveys, the response rate was 80–90 percent.

Third, researchers have frequently constructed *ad hoc* databases from published material. For example, Hennart and collaborators constructed a database on Japanese investment in the United States using data from Toyo Keizai, the Japan Economic Institute, the Lexis-Nexis news retrieval service, the Nikkei database, Japan Company Handbook, and the US Census of Manufacturers. They derived variables on advertising and research and development (R&D) expenditures, entry form and mode, year of entry, number of subsidiaries and years in the United States, SIC industry categories, first-tier supplier, sales, and concentration levels.

Risk of duplication, lack of standardization, failure to amalgamate results into a consistent database, and limitations on user access plague surveys. Maintaining longitudinal databases is a massive undertaking for private researchers, and might be more profitably undertaken in collaboration with statistical bureaux. Interview data are very expensive to gather and are limited by interview resources, access to firms, and constraints on the scope of the research agenda. Reliance on open-ended questions also poses data analysis challenges for econometric model estimation. Finally, international data collection suffer from the lack of collaboration mechanisms and it is almost impossible for a single or small group of researchers to collect datasets of sufficient size for cross-country comparisons.

Sources: Hakkala and Zimmermann (2005); Nicholas and Maitland (2002).

at home into broader investment and management opportunities. On a larger scale, Barmek Holdings of Turkey has entered into a long-term electricity distribution concession in Baku (Azerbaijan).

A different way of looking at the same trends is provided by data on the overall activities of direct investment enterprises, for example in respect of employment. In OECD countries, regular activity surveys, such as the benchmark survey of US FDI conducted by the Bureau of Economic Analysis, provide more meaningful bases to gauge the true impact of multinational activities (Box 2.2). Similar surveys to produce much more detailed, reliable, and useful data are now conducted in a few emerging economies (Table 2.5). In the case of Brazil, the survey covered 11,245 firms in 2004 and could be completed online. In the case of developing countries, however, resource constraints limit the scope for business survey development, and FDI ones ought probably to be combined with existing surveys to avoid placing too great a burden on respondents and institutions (UNCTAD 2006).

In addition, the approximate size of the EMNC universe in the OECD area can be gauged through host-country statistics on employment by country of control (Table 2.6).[16] Not all countries produce the same data – Statistics Canada, for instance, has data on assets, operating revenue, and operating profits by country of control for corporations operating in Canada, but not on employment – and in some countries the number of companies involved is very small and statistical offices are nervous about releasing it given the ease with which particular companies could be identified. In Ireland, for instance, the Annual Employment Survey provides a fairly detailed breakdown, but the 2004 data are available only at the level of

Table 2.5 Surveys of investment abroad in emerging economies

Country	Institution	Periodicity (since)	Firm coverage
Argentina	Central bank	Semi-annual (2005, Circular "A" 4237)	Foreign assets above 10% of proportional assets value (VPP)
Brazil	Central bank	Annual (2002)	Foreign assets above US$100,000
Korea	EXIM bank	Annual	Country and industry
Singapore	Statistics board	Annual (1991)	All locally incorporated companies and local branches of foreign companies that had investment abroad; includes financial institutions since 1994

Table 2.6 Employment at emerging multinationals' affiliates in selected OECD countries

	USA[a]	Japan[b]	Germany[c]	France[d]	Italy[e]	Sweden[f]	Netherlands[g]	Austria[h]	Total
World	5,420,300	581,054	2,129,900	1,904,300	938,545	544,579	507,000	315,025	12,340,703
Hong Kong	11,300	631	1,300	700	2,529	827	1,200	103	18,590
Singapore	15,200	500	1,200	300	1,213	6,323	1,500	1,006	27,242
Taiwan	18,600	1,331	600	100	1,271	47	0	0	21,949
Korea	11,900	483	3,800	900	420	112	100	0	17,715
China	3,400	0	200	400	506	231	0	0	4,737
Russia	700	0	700	500	19	13	0	143	2,075
Malaysia	5,400	0	200	700	311	0	300	0	6,911
Chile	500	0	100	—	31	0	0	0	631
Argentina	200	0	1,100	—	5,041	0	0	0	6,341
Mexico	47,100	215	400	200	3	0	0	0	47,918
South Africa	9,700	0	3,100	100	1,289	266	0	0	14,455
Brazil	5,300	0	1,100	S	12	0	0	0	6,412
Venezuela	7,600	0	—	100	748	0	0	0	8,448
Iran	0	0	300	—	0	0	0	0	300
Colombia	900	0	0	—	0	0	0	0	900
India	1,700	0	100	S	864	101	0	0	2,765
UAE	1,600	0	100	100	0	0	0	0	1,800
Hungary	750	0	5,000	S	17	0	0	183	5,950
Turkey	700	0	3,100	500	265	0	0	0	4,565
Azerbaijan	0	0	—	—	0	0	0	0	0
Czech Republic	0	0	300	0	9	0	0	152	461
Top 21 total	*142,550*	*3,160*	*22,700*	*4,600*	*14,548*	*7,920*	*3,100*	*1,587*	*200,165*

[a] Foreign Direct Investment in the United States: Operations of U.S. Affiliates of Foreign Companies, Preliminary Results for the 2002 Benchmark Survey.
[b] Year-end 2002 figures from *Gaishikei Kigyo* CD-ROM 2003 [Foreign Firm CD-ROM 2003], Tokyo: Toyo Keizai.
[c] Year-end 2003 figures.
[d] Year-end 2002 figures: number of employees, agriculture and finance excluded; "S" = secret (fewer than three affiliates). *Source*: Insee (Lifi survey) – Diane.
[e] Mariotti and Mutinelli (2005).
[f] ITPS (2005).
[g] Statistics Netherlands analysis of Inward FATS information (Business register, 2005, and data collection, 2003, on Enterprise Group financial statistics).
[h] Figures for 2001, joint Oesterreichische Nationalbank and Statistics Austria pilot study on Inward FATS.

three aggregated geographical groups – Greater China, Other Asia, and Rest of the World – for a grand total of 361 employees (38, 280, and 43, respectively).[17] Nonetheless, these sources are probably as accurate as any. In the eight high-income OECD countries for which data are available, the top 21 emerging economy investors account for 200,165 jobs, equal to 1.62 percent of total employment in foreign-owned affiliates. To provide an additional comparator, in 1990 NV Philips alone employed more than 50,000 people in the United States (Wilkins 2005), more than MNCs from Mexico, which is home to the EMNCs with the largest number of employees in the United States. Still, there may be individual instances where EMNCs are important employers. South Carolina, which took an early lead in targeting Chinese MNCs, has generated more than 2,500 manufacturing jobs as a result, a not insignificant number in terms of the total manufacturing employment in foreign-owned subsidiaries in the state (roughly 62,000).[18] In the United Kingdom, 36 new Indian projects were recorded in 2004–05, mostly in the ICT and drugs sectors, creating 1,418 jobs.

2.5 Enterprise data

Mention must also be made of enterprise data sources, which, no matter how incomplete in coverage, are probably more reliable than either balance-of-payments or IPA statistics. Based on the UNCTAD annual database of the world's largest MNCs, Table 2.7 provides comparative statistics on the top 50 EMNCs the world's 100 largest MNCs. For both categories of firms, the transnationality index (TNI) – a non-weighted average of the incidence of foreign assets, sales, and employment in the total for each indicator – shows an increase since 1998. For the top EMNCs, however, the increase is far more dramatic – from 36.6 percent to 49.2 percent in 2002. In sum, although their TNI remains considerably lower than that of their OECD peers, EMNCs are converging at a fast pace.

Of the top ten EMNCs in 1993, only four survive in the 2003 listing (Table 2.8) – a relatively low proportion, albeit equal to that for the world at large (UNCTAD, various years).[19] Hong Kong–based Hutchinson Whampoa is by far the largest MNC based in an emerging market. It is a diversified group that grew out of a shipping company – in 1977, in what was then one of the most visible investments by an Asian company, Hutchinson Whampoa began operations on both approaches to the Panama Canal, in Balboa and Cristobal – and now manages a diverse array of holdings (from some of the world's biggest retailers to property development and infrastructure to 3G telecommunications operators).

Table 2.7 Summary statistics for the world's largest MNCs

	1998	2000	2001	2002	2003	% Change, 1998–2003
(a) World's top 100						
Assets (US$)						
Foreign	1,922	3,113	2,958	3,317	3,993	107.8
Total	4,610	6,184	6,052	6,891	8,023	74.0
Sales (US$)						
Foreign	2,063	2,356	2,247	2,446	3,003	45.6
Total	4,099	4,748	4,450	4,749	5,551	35.4
Employment						
Foreign	6,547,719	6,791,647	7,038,000	7,036,000	7,242,000	10.6
Total	12,741,173	14,197,264	13,783,000	14,332,000	14,626,000	14.8
Average TNI (Transnationality Index) (%)	53.9	55.7	58.0	57.0	55.8	3.5
(b) Emerging economies top 50						
Assets (US$)						
Foreign	109	155	186	195	249	128.4
Total	449	541	528	464	711	58.4
Sales (US$)						
Foreign	109	186	145	140	202	85.3
Total	289	393	362	308	513	77.5
Employment						
Foreign	400,475	403,000	541,361	713,624	1,077,200	169.0
Total	1,546,883	1,321,449	1,275,493	1,503,279	3,096,600	100.2
Average TNI (%)	36.6	35.3	44.8	49.2	47.8	30.6

Table 2.8 The top 50 MNCs based in developing countries (by 2003 foreign assets, annual ranking, 1993–2003)

	1993	1995	1996	1997	1998	1999	2000	2001	2002	2003
Hutchinson Whampoa (Hong Kong)	2	7	24	6	7	1	1	1	1	1
Singtel (Singapore)		15		18			22	2	2	2
Petronas (Malaysia)			19		5	4	5	6	3	3
Samsung Electronics (Korea)	4	12	15		23	10	8	11	5	4
Cemex (Mexico)	1	3	3	5	4	3	2	3	4	5
América Móvil (Mexico)								21	25	6
China Ocean Shipping Group										7
Petrobrás (Brazil)	6	14	13	12	10				18	8
Lukoil (Russia)						7			8	9
LG Electronics (Korea)	15	5	18	10	14		3	4	6	10
Jardine Matheson (Hong Kong)	5	6	7	3	3		25	10	7	11
Sappi (South Africa)			5	7	6		11	14	11	12
Sasol (South Africa)									13	13
CNPC (China)										14
Capitaland (Hong Kong)									16	15
City Developments (China)								17	17	16
Shangri-La Asia (Hong Kong)								13	12	17
Citic Pacific (China)	19	20	20	17	19			9	10	18
CLP Holdings (Hong Kong)									27	19
China State Construction Engineering										20
MTN Group (South Africa)									19	21
Asia Food Products (Singapore)										22
Flextronics (Singapore)							10	16	15	23
CVRD (Brazil)		17	21		17				22	24
YTL (Malaysia)										25

Company						Rank
Hon Hai (Taiwan)						26
China Resources (Hong Kong)						27
ONGC (India)						28
Neptune Orient (Singapore)				9	9	29
United Microelectronics (Taiwan)				8	33	30
SIA (Singapore)		23			26	31
Gerdau (Brazil)					23	32
Barlworld (South Africa)					32	33
Quanta (Taiwan)	4					34
First Pacific (Hong Kong)			17	25	21	35
Hyundai Motor (Korea)	4	4			35	36
Norilsk (Russia)						37
Taiwan Semiconductor (Taiwan)				24		38
BenQ (Taiwan)						39
CNOOC (China)						40
Fraser & Neave (Singapore)					34	41
Swire Pacific (Hong Kong)					41	42
Keppel (Singapore)					30	43
Yue Yuen (Taiwan)						44
Acer (Taiwan)						45
Delta (Taiwan)						46
Bimbo (Mexico)		8			37	47
China Minmetals						48
MUJI Group (Malaysia)						49
Novoship (Russia)						50
Guandong Inv't (China)		16	21	13	12	42
Anglogold (South Africa)					14	
Perez Companc (Argentina)				22	20	
Samsung (Korea)				18	24	
Kulim (Malaysia)					28	
					29	

Continued

Table 2.8 Continued

	1993	1995	1996	1997	1998	1999	2000	2001	2002	2003
Naspers (South Africa)									31	
Nan Ya Plastics (Taiwan)									36	
Orient Overseas (Hong Kong)									38	
CP Pokphand (Thailand)									39	
Gruma (Mexico)									40	
Savia (Mexico)									43	
Grupo Imsa (Mexico)									44	
Asia Pacific Breweries (Singapore)									45	
Nampak (Singapore)									46	
Kumpulan Guthrie (Malaysia)									47	
Li & Fung (China)									48	
Cintra (Mexico)									49	
ASE Group (Taiwan)									50	
Petróleos de Venezuela (PDVSA)	13	2	2					5		
New World Development (Hong Kong)	7	19	16					7		
Hyundai (Korea)		16	17					15		
China National Chemicals Import–Export		13	8					19		
SABMiller (South Africa)								20		
Guangzhou Investment (China)								23		

Source: UNCTAD data.

In 2005 it concluded an important acquisition in Europe, purchasing Marionnaud, France's biggest chain of perfumeries. Other "established" EMNCs such as Cemex, Jardine Matheson, PDVSA (for which 2002 data are unfortunately unavailable), and the subsidiaries of Singapore's Temasek are analyzed in greater depth in some of the boxes in this study. Unfortunately, data limitations make it impossible to explore EMNCs' demography – that is, their survival and size mobility – along the lines suggested by Hannah (1998). His observation that "the 'emerging markets' on the 1912 list ... have in fact regressed: the largest Russian oil company of today (Lukoil) cannot yet match its Tsarist predecessor (Nobel Brothers)" (pp. 62–63) deserves to be explored further.

Companies from Asia clearly dominate the country ranking (Table 2.9). The four Tigers were represented by 17 companies (out of 25) in 1993 and, although their share is now lower, by 25 companies on average (out of 50) in 2001–03. The number of Latin American MNCs in the top 50 has fluctuated since 1994, ranging from a maximum of 15 in 1997 to a minimum of 11 during 2001–03. The downward trend mimics the one identified by Sklair and Robbins (2002) in their study of *Fortune*

Table 2.9 The top MNCs based in developing countries (by country)

	1993	1995	1996	1997	1998	1999	2000	2001	2002	2003
Argentina	0	1	1	2	2	2	1	1	1	
Brazil	2	4	5	5	6	3	4	2	3	3
Chile	0	1	3	4	3	2	1	1	0	
China	0	7	4	5	5	0	3	1	0	5
Colombia	0	0	1	0	0	0	0	0		
Croatia	0	0	0	0	0	0	0	0	1	
Hong Kong	6	10	11	9	9	10	11	11	10	9
India	0	0	1	1	1	1	0	0	0	1
Korea	6	7	6	6	6	9	5	5	4	3
Malaysia	2	2	3	3	2	3	4	4	3	3
Mexico	3	6	4	3	2	4	4	6	7	3
Philippines	1	1	1	1	1	1	1	1	0	
Russia	0	0	0	0	1	1	2	2	2	3
Saudi Arabia	0	0	0	1	0	0	1	0	0	
Singapore	1	4	3	4	6	7	6	6	9	9
South Africa	0	2	4	3	3	4	4	5	7	4
Taiwan	4	4	2	2	2	2	2	4	2	7
Thailand	0	0	0	0	0	0	0	0	1	
Venezuela	0	1	1	1	1	1	1	1	0	

Source: Author's elaboration on UNCTAD data.

500 rankings. They find that the three Latin American newly industrialized countries – Argentina, Brazil, and Mexico – had 33 percent of Third World representatives in 1965 and only 16 percent in 2001 (Table 2.4). A somewhat puzzling phenomenon is the fact that the numbers of Brazilian and Mexican companies have moved in different directions: Mexican MNCs were more numerous during the first half of the 1990s, the Brazilians rose during the second half of the decade and then decreased again during the early 2000s, while the Mexicans rose in turn. These statistics have to be treated with great caution, however; in particular, the sudden disappearance of Chinese companies in 1999 and 2002 is most likely due to the lack of data.

FDI activity from emerging economies is very concentrated in a small number of companies. In the case of Hungary, in early 2001 barely 2 percent of investors were responsible for around 52 percent of the total accumulated FDI stock (Heinrich 2004). In India, software small- and medium-size enterprises (SMEs) contribute 47 percent of the OFDI stock, whereas SMEs' contribution is small in the case of manufacturing (Pradhan and Sahoo 2005). In Brazil, where no such reliable data exist, the Fundação Dom Cabral is currently undertaking a survey.

Finally, it is worth looking at the weight of individual EMNCs in selected host economies. Here again, the problem is one of data availability and quality, so it is necessary to resort to anecdotal information. In Angola, a diversified group from Brazil is the largest non-oil foreign firm, employing 6,400 people (Goldstein 2004a).[20] Odebrecht built the Capanda hydropower station, obtained the water and sanitation concessions in Luanda and Benguela, and jointly exploits the Catoca diamond mine. The fact that Odebrecht (which is also active in many other developing countries) received more than half of Proex resources – a main export support instrument – in 1991–97 is a testament to the support that Brazilian authorities have given to business ventures in Angola. Angola alone accounted for 22.5 percent of total Brazil's financed exports. In Bangladesh, the Tata Group's proposed US$2 billion investment plan – five times total FDI inflows in 2003 and two-thirds of the cumulative flows since 1972 – is expected to be put into operation by the end of 2008.[21] The Tata Group plans to build a 1,000 megawatt power plant, a 2.4 million ton steel mill and a 1 million ton per year fertilizer factory. Posco's US$12 billion integrated steel complex in Orissa is the single biggest FDI in India and also the largest overseas investment made by a Korean company.

3
Toward an Industry Categorization

Summary

Emerging multinationals are active in a wide range of sectors, with an especially high profile in energy and construction. In particular, national oil companies have access to unprecedented levels of hard currency liquidity and an interest in investing abroad, either to reach a higher degree of vertical integration or to widen the geographical spread of their proven reserves. In the case of services, extensive South–South investment has accompanied the emergence of notable telecom companies, such as América Móvil and Orascom and, in air transport (where cross-border flows are very low), of some of the most international carriers, such as Emirates and Singapore Airlines.

3.1 General features

The same problems of data quality and coverage obviously plague the categorization of EMNCs by sector (Table 3.1). For example, in the case of China the most notable outward investments have been in the energy and resource sectors, by companies such as CITIC (China International Trust and Investment Corporation), Shougang (Capital Steel), and SinoChem (China National Chemical Import and Export Co-operation), the country's largest trading company. But these companies appear in the UNCTAD rankings only for some years. For this reason, it is probably more accurate and wiser to sketch major trends from the data available, without aiming to provide a precise and exhaustive portrait.

Diversified groups account for a large proportion of EMNCs, and the links between conglomerates and OFDI in emerging economies are explored at greater length below. A second cluster of EMNCs comprises

Table 3.1 The top 50 MNCs based in developing countries (by sector)

	1993	1994	1995	1996	1997	1998	1999	2000	2001	2002	2003
Business services	0	0	0	0	0	0	0	2	1	1	1
Chemicals	1	1	3	2	3	2	2	1	0	4	1
Construction	2	4	4	3	4	5	2	1	0	1	1
Construction materials	1	2	1	1	1	1	1	1	1	1	1
Diversified	7	10	12	10	12	9	12	11	12	6	5
Electronics & electronic equipment	5	6	6	5	6	5	7	7	9	6	11
Food & beverages	2	6	7	8	7	7	5	5	5	6	3
Glass	0	1	1	2	1	0	0	0	0	0	0
Hotels	1	2	2	2	1	1	2	0	3	2	3
Media	1	1	1	0	0	0	0	0	1	1	0
Metals	1	4	0	1	0	3	3	3	3	2	1
Mining	0	0	1	1	1	1	2	1	0	2	3
Motor vehicles	1	0	0	0	0	0	1	1	1	1	1
Paper	0	2	1	2	2	1	1	1	1	1	1
Petroleum	2	2	4	5	6	7	5	7	6	4	7
Pharmaceuticals	0	0	0	0	0	0	0	0	0	1	0
Real estate	0	0	0	0	0	0	0	0	0	1	1
Retailing	0	0	2	2	1	0	0	1	0	0	0
Telecoms	0	1	1	1	0	0	2	1	3	3	3
Textiles & leather	0	0	0	0	0	0	0	0	0	0	1
Tobacco	1	1	0	1	1	1	0	0	0	0	0
Transport & storage	0	3	2	4	3	2	3	5	3	5	4
Utilities	0	0	0	0	1	3	2	2	1	1	2
Wholesale trade	0	4	2	0	0	2	0	0	0	1	0

Source: Author's elaboration on UNCTAD data.

those in mining and petroleum (Section 3.2), and a third includes construction, public utilities, and transport services (Section 3.3).[1] In both cases EMNCs have used a combination of corporate and political resources (the latter often resulting from their state-owned nature) to expand overseas and compete with more established competitors, as discussed below.

Finally, a fourth cluster groups manufacturing firms, producing both capital-intensive industrial commodities (cement, glass, motor vehicles, paper) and food and beverages. Although this cluster represents a relatively small proportion of EMNCs, whereas it has traditionally been the largest cluster among OECD-based MNCs, it includes well-known companies such as Cemex or SABMiller. Other manufacturing EMNCs, solely from Asia, operate in electronics and include both producers of consumer goods, such as Samsung, and contract manufacturers, such as Quanta, the world's largest producer of personal computers as an original design manufacturer (ODM). No matter how successful they are, for few of these companies does the number of patents owned or the value of their brands seem *prima facie* a sufficient explanation of their global success. The challenge in this case is to identify the dynamic capabilities they have accumulated and the sources of their competitive advantage on global markets (see Section 6.4).

3.2 EMNCs in oil and gas

Since oil prices started to rise in 2002, much attention has been devoted to the increased importance of the main non-OECD economies. On the demand side, China's oil consumption already accounts for more than 18 percent of global oil-demand growth and will increase by 3.4 percent per year to 2030, driven by transport requirements (IEA 2004). With marginal growth in domestic production over the past several years, China's oil-import dependence, which was 23 percent in 1998, reached 37 percent in 2003.

On the supply side – as mentioned above – national oil companies have access to unprecedented levels of hard currency liquidity and an interest in investing abroad, either to reach a higher degree of vertical integration or to widen the geographical spread of their proven reserves. Consequently, the balance of power between producing countries and international oil companies is rapidly changing. As the former demand a bigger share of profits from oil extraction and trading, countries such as Angola, Azerbaijan, Bolivia, Kazakhstan, Russia, and Venezuela have decided to claw back some of their energy fields, increase export taxes, and/or link their share of the profits to the oil price and the profitability of a project. This development – which, interestingly enough, has seen oil producers in the OECD area behave in the same fashion[2] – is opening the way to contract renegotiations and hence to the entry of new players.

A brief analysis of non-OECD national oil companies' strategies (Table 3.2) reveals some key issues.[3] While all remain state-controlled – which was once the case in almost all OECD countries but is now an exception – they differ in their nature and hence in their strategies.[4] Some are large producers and exporters on their own and expand abroad to acquire competencies and to integrate downstream into refining, distribution, and retailing. This is true most notably of PDVSA and KPC. Venezuela and Kuwait, which mostly produce cheaper heavy- or medium-grade oil not suitable for all refineries, have sought more capacity to refine this oil into high-grade petroleum and oil products (see Box 7.3 for more on PDVSA). Brazil and Malaysia also produce enough oil to meet current demand levels, although their reserves are not large enough to guarantee long-term supplies. Petrobrás and Petronas did not venture abroad to import, however, as much as they did to gain global market presence and, especially in the former case, to deploy their strong technical competencies in deep-water exploration. As Acha and Finch (2005) note, "The success of Petrobras' expertise and technology in the geoscience and engineering of deepwater, particularly in the 1980s and 1990s, has been underscored by drilling milestones and technology awards" (p. 86).

For other national oil companies, growing energy needs combined with limited domestic energy resources necessitate the search for appropriate solutions capable of securing long-term supplies through investment in exploration and production. In China, government policy to reduce the probability and the cost of a supply disruption has emphasized strategic means rather than market mechanisms (e.g., creating stockpiles or drawing up emergency response plans). China's increasingly acute dependence on oil imports, especially from the Gulf, and an ingrained ideology of self-reliance are driving the country's frenetic global search to lock up future energy supplies and lessen the competition for oil assets. China's oil companies made their first experimental forays into overseas investment in the mid-1990s, started seeking opportunities in Central Asia and Russia later in the decade (Andrews-Speed *et al.* 2004), and are now very active also in Africa and the Americas. In Canada, in particular, Chinese and other national oil companies are interested in both oil sand (which can be refined into crude oil after it has been extracted using a relatively high-cost process that has been

Table 3.2 Overseas expansion by main non-OECD national oil companies

Company	Comments
China National Petroleum Corp. (CNPC)	Has invested in Sudan, Venezuela, Kazakhstan (85% of the Aktobemunaigaz joint venture to develop the Aktobe and Zhanazhol fields; 10 m. tons-a-year pipeline from Atasu to Xinjiang province), Mauritania (with Australia's Barako), and Myanmar. Participates in the Sino-Russian oil pipeline project. Together with Sonangol, has shown interest in partnering with Argentina's state-owned Enarsa. In April 2005 bought a 17% stake in Canada's MEGEnergy (recoverable bitumen) for US$150 m. In September 2005, led a group of Chinese firms that bought oil and pipeline assets in Ecuador from Canada's EnCana for US$1.4 bn. in cash
China National Offshore Oil Corp.(CNOOC)	In 2002, formed a joint venture with Australia's North West Shelf gas field project's partners, including Chevron, Exxon Mobil, and Shell, to take a 5% stake (equivalent to LNG shipments of approximately 3.3 m. metric tons a year over two decades starting in 2006); the venture supplies as much as 10% of Japan's LNG imports. Signed an agreement in 2003 that called on the partners to earmark a significant volume of Gorgon LNG for use in the Chinese market; was reported to be seeking a 12.5% stake in the project; talks have failed so far to produce an agreement on price. Placed successful bid in Libyan auctions in October 2005 and reached an agreement in 2006 to explore six blocks in Kenya. With Sinopec, cut a deal to purchase BG's interest in the Kashagan field project, but this foundered when other partners exercised their pre-emption rights
Indian Oil Corporation (IOC)	Will invest US$1 bn. to develop jointly with Petropars one of Iran's largest natural gas fields. Had an offer to take over France's Maurel & Prom turned down as too low. Joined forces with Oil India to pursue overseas exploration and production opportunities and in early 2005 bagged an oil block in Libya, the first ever overseas block won by an Indian firm through the competitive bidding route

Continued

Table 3.2 Continued

Company	Comments
Kuwait Petroleum International (KPI)	Acquired Santa Fe, a US-based drilling contractor. Between 1983 and 1987, acquired most of Gulf Oil's refining and marketing operations in Western Europe, in addition to BP's Danish and Luxembourg operations. In 1986, the Q8 brand was launched. Other major expansions occurred in Italy (purchase of Mobil's network and a refining joint venture with AGIP in Milazzo) and Sweden. In 2004, decided to leave the UK market and acquired part of the BP network as well as an Automat network (TANGO) in the Netherlands. In Belgium, is the second-biggest market player following acquisition of BP and Aral networks. Markets approximately 30,000 barrels of products per day in Western Europe through more than 4,000 retail stations. Assumed responsibility for development of international operations from Kuwait Petroleum Corp. in September 2004. In 2005 struck separate deals with Royal Dutch/Shell and BP to explore refining and marketing ventures in China and India
Lukoil	Has purchased stakes in oil fields, especially in the Caspian Sea region and in Iraq, and controlling shares in refineries in Bulgaria, Romania, and Ukraine. At the end of 2000 acquired a 60% stake in Getty Petroleum Marketing (1,260 retail outlets in 13 states) for US$71 m. In July 2001 acquired Canada's Bitech Petroleum, which operates in Russia, Egypt, Morocco, Tunisia, and Colombia. In 2004 signed a strategic alliance with ConocoPhillips (which owns a 7.6% stake) for joint development of oil and gas reserves in Russia and possibly Iraq (West Qurna field). In 2005 bought the second-largest oil station chain in Finland (Teboil) for US$270 m. and Canadian company Nelson Resources, operating in Kazakhstan. Thirty percent of reserves are located abroad
ONGC (Oil and Natural Gas Corporation) Videsh	Bought substantial interests in Russia (20% stake in the Sakhalin 1 field), Sudan (25% stake in Greater Nile from Talisman and is in talks to build a 750 km pipeline from Khartoum to Port Sudan), Ivory Coast, Iran,

Continued

Table 3.2 Continued

Company	Comments
	Angola, and Vietnam. Has an agreement with a Russian research body and works with Lukoil. In February 2005 signed a wide-ranging agreement with Gazprom allowing the two groups to bid jointly for global energy assets. Signed a memorandum of understanding with National Iranian Oil Company to participate in Yadavaran (20% participation) and Jufeyr fields through service contracts. In September 2005 inked a memorandum of understanding with Norsk Hydro to cooperate in third countries, particularly in West Asia, Cuba, and Iran. In April 2006 bought a 15% stake in Brazil's block bc-10 from Royal Dutch/Shell for US$170 m.
Pemex	Holds a 4.81% stake in Repsol YPF and a 50% stake in a Shell-operated refinery in Texas, but Mexican law does not allow the company to form such alliances in Mexico
Pertamina	In May 2005 won a deal to develop three blocks in Iraq's Western Desert and in October 2005 placed successful bid in Libyan auctions
Petrobrás	Has concentrated E&P in Latin America (Perez Companc acquisition in 2002, long-term contracts with Venezuela), Gulf of Mexico, and Africa (Nigeria's Agbami and Akpo fields, block 5 off Tanzania's Mafia Island, Libya's Area 18); integrated downstream operation (second-largest retail network in Argentina and 130 stations in Paraguay); and strengthened gas business in Southern Cone (Bolivia pipeline). Aims to access refining capacity abroad to add value to Petrobrás crude (acquisition of 50% stake in Texas's Pasadena for US$370 m. in early 2006 and planned construction of a lubricants factory in Cuba through a joint venture with PDVSA and Cubapetroleo). Reserves outside Brazil were less than 12% in 2002; to rise to 17% by 2010 (14% of future investment will be overseas)
PetroChina	Concluded a deal in April 2005 for half the capacity of proposed Gateway pipeline from Calgary to the West Coast

Continued

Table 3.2 Continued

Company	Comments
Petroliam Nasional Berhad (Petronas)	With business interests in 35 countries, undertakes E&P activities in Sudan (with CNOOC and Sudapet), Chad (with ExxonMobil), Myanmar (Yetagun field in the Gulf of Martaban), Iran (with Total), and Central Asia. In 1996 acquired a 30% shareholding in South Africa's Engen, eventually buying a controlling stake for US$775 m. The Engen purchase gave Petronas control of 18% and 27% of South Africa's refining capacity and retail-fuel market, respectively. Engen's operations now contribute almost 20% to total annual revenue. In November 2004 Engen and Sasol combined their LNG operations in a new joint venture, Uhambo. Petronas and BP Energy plan to develop an LNG terminal and facilities in Wales, to become operational in 2007. Reserves outside Malaysia were 22% in 2002; goal of 30% of revenues coming from overseas by 2005
Rosneft	In June 2001 signed a contract with Colombia's Ecopetrol to launch oil extraction. In Algeria, has a production-sharing agreement with Sonatrach. In Kazakhstan, has an oil and gas extracting holding in cooperation with Itera and American First International Oil Corporation. In Iraq, had signed an agreement to develop oil fields, but this was cancelled following the regime change
Saudi Aramco	Created Motiva Enterprises LLC in the United States (a joint venture in marketing with Shell-Texaco) in 1997. Its effort to acquire a stake in state-run Hindustan Petroleum was thwarted after India's parliament suspended plans to allow such foreign investments. Holds a 14.9% stake in Showa Shell. Together with ExxonMobil and Sinopec is pressing ahead with a US$3.6 bn. expansion of a refinery venture in China's Fujian province. In return for guaranteeing crude supply to China, may get a 20–40% stake in the 200,000 barrel-per-day plant in Shandong province that is due for start-up in the first half of 2007

Continued

Table 3.2 Continued

Company	Comments
Sinopec	With Iran, signed an exploration agreement for Zavareh-Kashan block in 2001 and a contract in October 2004 to buy LNG for an estimated US$70–100 bn. over 30 years and develop the Yadavaran oil field. In May 2005 paid Can$105 m. for 40% of the Northern Lights oilsands project in Alberta. In 2006 concluded two deals with ONGC Videsh in Syria and Colombia
Sonatrach	Purchased a minority stake in Peru's Camisea gas field in 2003. Is also looking to expand oil and gas production in Niger and Mauritania, and farther afield in Nigeria. Is seeking refining and petroleum marketing opportunities in Asia. Already the world's largest LNG producer, it owns half of a £130 m. terminal on the Isle of Grain in Kent. Targets foreign reserves of 30% by 2015
Yukos	Has had drilling operations in Peru since 1995. Took a 53.7% stake in a Lithuanian refinery, Mazeikiu Nafta, from Williams of the USA, which it later sold to PKN Orlen

Sources: *Petrobrás Strategic Plan 2015*; "Petronas: a well-oiled money machine," *Far Eastern Economic Review*, March 13, 2003; *Financial Times*, various dates; *Petroleum Intelligence Weekly*, various dates; *Reuters*.

made economical only by the rise in crude oil prices) and so-called juniors that control sizeable oil and gas reserves in Central Asia, Africa, and Latin America.

The corporate activities of the national oil companies cannot be analyzed without taking into account the complex interplay of political, diplomatic, and economic factors. In the Middle East, in particular, "oil (and gas) is simply too important to the politics and welfare of these countries [and] their societies will be closely linked to the state and always suffer from lack of clarity of roles, functions, responsibility and decision power" (Sandvold 2004: 12). China's activism has fanned direct rivalry with the United States and other Asian powers such as India and Japan. In Iran, for instance, in the face of tough competition from China, authorities scaled down significantly the amount of liquefied natural gas (LNG) a year that a consortium of Indian companies will purchase for 25 years from the second half of 2009–10. The Angolan government rejected plans by Shell to sell its half of the Greater Plutonio project to ONGC when China offered a US$2 billion loan at conditions that India could not match. Section 7.4 examines the geopolitical impact of these trends.[5]

3.3 EMNCs in non-financial services

The rise of FDI in services is an important but often neglected area of research and policy action in the context of development (UNCTAD 2004a). Services FDI, especially in intermediate and infrastructure services, affects the economic performance of a host country in all sectors. Cross-border service investment was initially concentrated in trade and finance, but since the 1990s, privatization, GATS (General Agreement on Trade in Services)-induced liberalization, and the rise of global manufacturing value chains have all contributed to a steep increase in FDI in public utilities (telecommunications, electricity and gas, and water and sanitation) as well as in business services (third-party provision of tailored software application packages such as payroll and book-keeping).[6]

The productivity gap between developed and developing countries is particularly wide in services (van Ark and Monnikhof 2000). This is therefore not an area where EMNCs might *prima facie* expect to have a competitive advantage over their established competitors. Moreover, the high reliance on non-equity forms of investment, such as franchising, management contracts, concessions, partnerships, and turnkey, build-operate-and-transfer (BOT), and build-transfer-and-operate (BTO) projects, might also put EMNCs at a disadvantage insofar as they do not fully master such contractual forms, which are often more complex and sophisticated than standard forms of investment. Nonetheless, developing countries' OFDI flows in services have risen dramatically during the past decade, and their global share went from 1 percent in 1990 to 10 percent in 2002 (UNCTAD 2004a).

In certain service industries, EMNCs have been long present and operated outside of their home countries. The construction industry is covered elsewhere, as an example of a mature sector where EMNCs have gained a global prominence that corresponds to the predictions of the product-cycle framework. Since the 1960s, hotel chains such as India's Oberoi and Taj (part of the Tata Group) and Hong Kong's Peninsula and Shangri-la have appeared prominently in listings of the largest EMNCs. Dusit Thani, the Thai group that bought 83 percent of Germany's Kempinski in 1995 and operated in 22 countries when the Asian crisis hit, has transformed itself into a small niche player focused on the ASEAN market.

New operators are now emerging in regions with large tourism potential where few foreign investors have ventured so far because of the difficult investment climate. Protea Hospitality Corporation, the largest hotel management group in Africa, is the 21st-largest hotel group worldwide according to *Lodging* magazine (July 2005 edition). Hungary's Danubius Hotels run the principal accommodation complex in the spa town of Sovata in the Carpathian mountains in Romania's Transylvania. Kerzner International, a publicly traded group headed by a South African entrepreneur, capitalizes on "its reputation of building landmark properties in somewhat unproven markets."[7]

Wealthy individuals from emerging economies, especially in the Gulf region, have also long shown a penchant for property investment in hotels. Possibly the best example is Kingdom Holdings, the investment vehicle of Saudi prince Alwaleed bin Talaj, which owns 23 percent of Canada's Four Seasons and 33 percent of Switzerland's Mövenpick chains, as well as a substantial number of their hotels. Another example is the Dorchester Group, established in 1996 as an independent UK-registered company to manage the collection of luxury hotels belonging to the Brunei Investment Agency in Europe and the United States.[8] While primarily financial in nature, these investments have also allowed the participating companies to sell off their property portfolios and transform themselves into management companies. Now Dubai-owned companies are buying, developing, and managing their own hotel operations, not only in Arab countries but also in the Americas, Asia, and Europe. Luxury hotelier Jumeirah, best known for its opulent sail-shaped Burj Al Arab Hotel, has about 15 properties currently under contract or under construction set to open by 2008 and aims to increase its worldwide portfolio from 9 to 40 within five years.[9]

In other non-financial services, EMNCs are a more recent phenomenon. Given their relatively low penetration of fixed-line telephony and large populations, emerging economies have become the world's fastest-growing markets. In sub-Saharan Africa, in March 2006 Vodacom (a joint venture between Telkom and Vodafone of the United Kingdom) and MTN together had more than 17 million subscribers outside of South Africa. Orascom is one of the Arab world's largest MNCs (Box 3.1); in the same sector and region other operators are also raising their investment profiles – UAE's Etisalat (in Saudi Arabia, West Africa, and Pakistan), Kuwait's Mobile Telecommunications Company (in the Gulf and Africa), Qatar Telecom (in Oman), and Dubai Tecom Investments (in Malta and Tunisia). América Móvil was transformed in just over two years, from 2003 to 2005, from a Mexican company with some presence

Box 3.1 The Orascom Group: an Arab multinational

Orascom, owned by the Sawiris family, is one of Egypt's largest groups, covering everything from construction, to mobile telephones, to El-Gouna, a glitzy tourist city located on the Red Sea near Hurghada. Founded in 1950 by family patriarch Onsi Sawiris (who flourished in cement and contracting in pre-revolutionary Libya and in the United States, where he established security connections), it now comprises four main subsidiaries: Orascom Construction Industries (OCI), Orascom Hotels and Development (OHD), Orascom Telecom Holdings (OTH), and Orascom Technologies (OT). OCI, OHD, and OTH together account for 40 percent of the value of Egypt's stock market. The group has alliances with numerous multinationals, including Volvo Penta, Alstom, and British Gas, and acts as local agent for IT giants including HP, Microsoft, Oracle, Lucent Compaq, and Motorola.

OTH was established in 1998, to own a 24 percent stake (later increased to 31.26 percent) in the Egyptian Company for Mobile Services (MobiNil), the country's largest cellular telephone service provider, jointly with France Telecom. In September 1999, OTH bought a controlling stake in JMTS-Fastlink in Jordan, and in February 2000 an 80 percent controlling stake in Telecel, which then held licenses in 15 sub-Saharan African countries. The aim was to combine high-volume telecom services in the domestic market with high-priced services in countries such as Congo. In July 2001 OTH won the mobile phone network license in Algeria with a bid of US$737 million, to be paid in two installments five years apart, but investors' worries about the method of finance caused the stock to fall. OTH announced it intended to raise money through a bond and possibly a rights issue, and decided to look into expressions of interest to acquire most of its sub-Saharan licenses (which it did between May 2003 and December 2005). OTH then expanded to cover Tunisia, Pakistan, Iraq, and Bangladesh in 2004, while exiting Kuwait and Syria. In Iraq, where it first provided services in the central region before going south in November 2004, OTH is serving more than 480,000 customers on its network. Two major milestones achieved in July 2004 were surpassing 2 million subscribers in Algeria (where Djezzy has a market share of 86 percent) and 3 million subscribers in Pakistan. In December 2005, OTH acquired a 19.3 percent interest in Hutchison Telecom. By January 2006, the company's international subscriber base had reached approximately 30 million people – from 3.5 million in September 2001 – and it had nearly 10,000 employees. OTH lost to Telenor in a public auction for Serbia's Mobi63 and is currently bidding for Saudi Arabia's third license.

Becoming the primary GSM network operator in the Middle East is OTH's main mission. This includes providing GSM support operations to act as a backbone for its operations. At the same time, OTH faces the risk that if the Egyptian regulatory body, NTRA, comes to the conclusion that a disruptive force is needed to revitalize the Egyptian mobile market, a third mobile operator may enter in the medium term. This prompted its decision to diversify into fixed-line networks. In February 2005 OTH announced that its consortium with Telecom Egypt had won a 15-year license to build and operate the second network in Algeria for US$65 million. The Algerian market provides an attractive growth opportunity, given its relatively low fixed-line penetration of less than 10 percent, and a large population of more than 32 million.

Furthermore, in April 2005 OTH chairman and chief executive officer (CEO) Naguib Sawiris signed the €12.1 billion (US$15.65 billion) buyout of the Wind telecommunications business of Italy's power company Enel. Italy's third-largest mobile phone company and a major provider of fixed-line telephone service, Wind was losing money and had a high debt load. Enel preferred the offer by Sawiris over that of another consortium led by the Blackstone private equity group because it promised the utility a stake in the new company. Eventually, the Wind assets are expected to become part of Orascom. The new owners will need to invest big to increase the entertainment content of Wind's broadband and cable businesses.

OTH owes its success to several factors. First, it has been able to leverage brand name recognition, technologies, and financial means to operate in contexts where local players are often too weak to compete. The advertising campaign to launch MobiNil was the largest Egypt had ever seen. Naguib Sawiris was also appointed to the board of the GSM Association (the world's leading wireless industry representative body). Second, OTH was able (although some say it was luck) to anticipate the 1999–2003 global slowdown and dispose of several non-core businesses, such as the McDonald's franchise, the Renaissance Company for Cultural Production, which had established and managed several movie theatres, and El-Gouna Beverages. Reducing corporate debt has helped a great deal in a declining market because of the high borrowing rates on the Egyptian pound. The third main reason is the management team, which is rather heterogeneous by the standards of the Arab business community. Of the 18 people who constituted the top management team at mid-2005, there were three Egyptian managers with previous foreign experience, three foreigners, and two women.

Regional expansion, however, has not been without difficulties. In Syria OTH had problems with its local partner, which apparently had a close connection to the regime, on the terms of the revenue-sharing agreements. When OTH made public accusations about illegal efforts by its partner to assume management control, a court froze its local assets in SyriaTel in order to keep Orascom from pulling out of the country. With no room to negotiate, OTH just wanted to get out of the business, which it finally did. In Iraq, the Pentagon's inspector general launched an investigation into the Orascom contract, in part because of allegations from a rival that failed to win one of the mobile licenses.

Source: Goldstein and Perrin (2006).

in Central America to the largest telecommunications company in Latin America. It took advantage of the liquidation of the emerging markets' assets of US operators such as AT&T, Bell South, and MCI to reach more than 100 million subscribers in March 2006, compared with 74 million for Telefónica Móviles, its Spanish-owned competitor. In August 2006, Telmex bought a 3.4 percent stake in Portugal Telecom (PT), which was defending itself from a hostile takeover bid by a local rival. Although Telmex has not discounted the possibility that it may raise its stake in PT, analysts believe Telmex may be interested in acquiring, indirectly, a stake in Vivo, Brazil's largest mobile phone operator, which is jointly owned by PT and Telefónica Móviles. Russia's number-two mobile service provider, VimpelCom, controls Kazakhstan's second-largest operator, KarTel; the second- and fourth-largest operators in Uzbekistan, Unitel and Buztel; and Ukraine's fourth-largest operator, URS.[10] In addition, Altimo (formerly Alfa Group), a Russian holding company and the majority owner of VimpelCom, controls 40 percent of the second-largest mobile service provider of Ukraine, KyivStar, and the only mobile operator in Turkmenistan, Bashar Communications Technology. In late 2005, Altimo announced its readiness to pay as much as US$3 billion for one of the largest Turkish mobile operators (Vahtra 2006).

An interesting case is that of air transport, a somewhat paradoxical industry that combines extensive cross-border activities with almost insurmountable obstacles to foreign investment (Findlay and Goldstein 2004). Under bilateral air service agreements, airlines from each country are nominated to operate on a given route on the basis of agreements on capacity and frequency. The agreements cover the terms according to which carriers are designated to operate routes, the methods for setting capacity on a route, and any regulation that applies to fares. The restrictions include limits on access to routes by airlines based in third countries. Generally, foreign carriers are not permitted to operate on domestic routes. One key feature of these arrangements is the ownership restrictions on airlines operating international services. Typically, the right to take up the market access available in the bilateral air service agreement depends on the designated airline being "substantially owned and controlled" by the nationals of the economy involved. Further restrictions on the extent of foreign ownership apply at the national level. Airline alliances and marketing arrangements have emerged as an imperfect substitute for consolidation through (cross-border) M&A.

While few OECD airlines have been successful in overcoming these obstacles through ambitious foreign investments – possibly the only large-scale attempt is the merger between Air France and KLM – there are some interesting examples in developing areas. Emirates and South African Airways have acquired from government controlling stakes in Sri Lankan and Air Tanzania, respectively, to boost traffic at their hubs in Dubai and Johannesburg. Lan, which owing to geographical constraints may find it more difficult to turn Santiago into a major hub, has set up its own airlines in Argentina, Ecuador, and Peru and invested in a mini-hub in Miami, also for cargo traffic.[11] Low-cost Gol, the third-largest airline in Brazil, is planning to enter the Mexican aviation market in partnership with a domestic investor. Royal Air Maroc has filled the void left by the liquidation of Air Afrique with the purchase of privatized airlines in Senegal, Gabon, and Mauritania.

The world's second-largest airline by market capitalization, Singapore Airlines (SIA), has also been a very aggressive foreign investor in OECD markets, buying a 49 percent participation in Virgin Atlantic in 2001 and 25 percent of Air New Zealand. The latter experience illustrated the difficulties of services FDI. When the Australian government reneged on a deregulation deal that would have let Air New Zealand compete in Australia, and ruled instead that to get into that market it had to buy into Ansett, the latter's losses and capital requirements nearly bankrupted both companies. SIA tentatively offered to come to the rescue, but the New Zealand government dithered, Ansett collapsed, Air New Zealand was effectively re-nationalized, and SIA booked a loss of close to US$500 million on its diluted Kiwi investment.[12]

In the seaport industry, the three largest global container terminal operators are Hutchinson Port Holdings, Singapore-based PSA, and DP World, owned by Dubai's Ports, Customs, and Freezone Authority. More broadly, in 2003 there were 11 companies based in emerging Asian economies among the 20 leading MNCs in the container terminal industry (Olivier *et al.* 2005). Their rapid global ascension has been made possible by the original strength of home ports, membership of conglomerates with broader logistics aspirations, and financial power that has allowed them to take the lead in M&A activity.

Other examples in transport industries include the Colombian companies Express de Santiago Uno and Inversiones Alsacia (which in early 2005 won the tender to operate trunk routes 4 and 1 as part of Santiago city's Transantiago urban transport plan) and América Latina Logistica (a regional rail and road transport company in Brazil that expanded into Argentina with the acquisition of two rail networks in 1999).

Retail trade is another service industry where FDI has grown recently as the sector is quickly emerging as the most important outlet for the commercialization of dry, fresh, and processed agro-food products in developing countries.[13] Large, modern OECD retailers – including large-format stores such as supermarkets, hypermarkets, warehouse and discount clubs, club stores, and chain convenience stores – faced saturation and intense competition in their home markets, while the revolution in retail procurement logistics technology and inventory management, together with the declining cost of information and telecommunication services, made it possible and convenient to amortize investment across a global network of subsidiaries. With an effective computerized management system, the lag between purchasing and delivery time is greatly reduced, inventory costs are kept under control, and large-scale retailers and agro-food producers can trade almost seamlessly around the globe.

Representative EMNCs in the supermarket business include

- Shoprite is Africa's largest retailer, with more than 700 shops in 16 countries. Opened in late 2004, its hypermarket in Mumbai is India's biggest. Shoprite was among the first foreign retailers to be let in by India's wary government.
- Chile's Cencosud recently bought the Disco chain from Royal Ahold, to become the second-largest food retailer in Argentina, where it is already the largest investor in shopping malls. With this deal Cencosud 2005 sales exceeded US$3 billion, split equally across the two sides of the Andes.
- Another Chilean company, Falabella, manages stores and supermarkets in Argentina and Peru, where it has issued more than a million credit cards. With foreign sales of US$196 million in 2004 (16 per of total turnover), it has recently targeted Colombia and Mexico.[14]
- Migros Turk, a Koç-affiliated firm, opened its first Ramstore Shopping Center in Moscow in 1997. It now operates more than 40 such stores in Russia, Kazakhstan, and Bulgaria and plans to spend US$150 million a year opening new ones.
- Slovenia's Mercator managed to transform itself from a small, debt-ridden, and struggling grocer in 1997 into the country's leading retailer, with 873 retail stores and a market share exceeding 45 percent. It completed 16 acquisitions to face the onslaught of foreign competitors effectively after Slovenia joined the EU in 2004. It then started building shopping malls in former Yugoslav states, where Slovenian retail trademarks and brand names are highly regarded. The group has become the third-largest food-product chain in Croatia, with 4 percent of the market and 139 shops. In 2005, the combined net sales revenues of the Mercator Group amounted to €1.745 billion. The acquisition of a 76 percent stake in M-Rodic in 2006 made Mercator the second-biggest retailer in Serbia, with annual revenues of €400 million. Over the longer term, the company intends to expand its operations to other southeastern European markets such as Romania, Albania, Macedonia, and Bulgaria.

Outside of supermarkets, emerging retailers are tailoring specific strategies. With almost 1,000 pharmacies in three foreign countries (Farmacias

Benavides in Mexico, Boticas Fasa in Peru, and Drogamed in Southern Brazil) and 2003 sales in excess of US$1 billion, Chile's Farmacias Ahumada is the largest business of its kind in Latin America. In Mexico it invested in a new distribution center to bypass wholesalers and banned tobacco sales in its stores to win favor among consumers and the general public. Gome, China's largest electronic appliances retailer, saw demand becoming more price-sensitive and challenged the tight grip of local chains on the congested Hong Kong market by selling mainland brands instead of foreign ones.[15] Hong Kong specialty retailers are reacting by going abroad – in particular AS Watson, a subsidiary of Hutchinson Whampoa, has bought major chains in Europe. Its latest and most significant acquisition, the takeover of France's Marionnaud in January 2005, is aimed at exposing the company to the perfumery business, which remains very underdeveloped in Asia, and in China in particular. Grupo Elektra from Mexico has almost 900 points of sale for electronics, including in Guatemala, Honduras, and Peru. As it is owned by the same individual investor that also controls TV Azteca and Banco Azteca, Elektra can cover the whole chain from marketing and advertising to customer credit.

At the other extreme of the pyramid, some service EMNCs focus on the world's 5 billion or so poorest people. The belief that this market has considerable untapped potential is gaining ground in management circles (Prahalad 2005). Firms cannot simply edge down-market the products they already sell to rich customers and/or tailor the transnational model of national responsiveness, global efficiency, and worldwide learning to weaknesses in the local environment (London and Hart 2004). Instead, they must thoroughly re-engineer products to reflect very different economics – small unit packages, low margin per unit, and high volume. It is this strategy that has allowed some of the most successful firms in developing countries to compete with established MNCs – for instance, during the 1980s Nirma surpassed Hindustan Level, the Unilever subsidiary, to become the biggest detergent brand in India (Ghoshal *et al.* 2001).

Some such firms have also ventured abroad and turned themselves into EMNCs – two of the strengths of Bimbo, for instance, are its distribution networks and the hiring of entrepreneurs from among the poor. Two pharmacy chains specializing in generic drugs – Farmacias del Dr. Ahorro and Farmacias Similares – have expanded from Mexico to the rest of Latin America. Emerging mobile telephony providers have built their multinational expansion on the ability simultaneously to market low-denomination prepaid cards and to keep costs under control. MTN's investment in Uganda is a very clear example of such advantages

(Goldstein 2004a). By the time it acquired the second license to operate cellular telecom services in Uganda, MTN had already developed "a unique body of in-house corporate knowledge for managing the risks involved [in operating in difficult economic and political environments] without seeking external cover at additional cost" (Mistry and Olesen 2003: 40). On the basis of superior local knowledge and greater ability to read market signals, MTN Uganda chose to market prepaid phonecards aggressively, whereas Celtel – the first licensee, a company controlled by Vodafone of the United Kingdom in association with the IFC, which had enjoyed a monopoly position for several years – had marketed cellular service as a luxury. As a result, in less than two years MTN Uganda developed a subscriber base 22 times larger than Celtel's.

In food catering, other EMNCs grew out of countries with large emigrant populations, with an initial thrust to target their nationals overseas. Eventually they started competing with Western chains, which are constrained by an obligation to remain faithful to their core products, by paying more respect to local tastes (Table 3.3). Worldwide operations consist of a mixture of company-owned restaurants, franchises, and joint

Table 3.3 Fast-food chains from the developing world

Chain	Comments
Nando's (South Africa)	Founded in 1987, the company became famous for its wacky advertising and Portuguese-style flame-grilled chicken. In the first decade of operations the group opened 103 stores in South Africa, Namibia, and Swaziland and 37 overseas (in Australia, Botswana, Canada, Israel, Mauritius, Portugal, the UK, and Zimbabwe). By 2004 Nando's had spread its wings to 30 countries and earned about 40% of turnover in dollars, of which three-fourths came from restaurant operations and the rest from product exports. In particular, it has 190 local restaurants in South Africa and also 100 in Australia and 95 in the UK. The group not only expanded its stores, but also branched out into branded retail products (peri-peris and marinades are sold in UK supermarkets) and non-food items. International interests are held by Nando's International, which exploits the brand and receives royalties, and Nando's International Investments, which invests in various Nando's operations elsewhere. Ultimate control is vested in fully owned offshore company Nando's International Holdings, which holds 100% of the two international companies

Continued

Table 3.3 Continued

Chain	Comments
Pollo Campero (Guatemala)	Part of Guatemala's Grupo Gutiérrez, which also controls banking and construction firms. After opening its first US store in Los Angeles in 2002, it now has restaurants in Houston, Washington, and New York, and 200 more in Mexico, Guatemala, El Salvador, Honduras, Nicaragua, Costa Rica, and Ecuador. Jointly with local partners, it plans to open 600 restaurants in China and Indonesia
Jollibee Foods (Philippines)	The largest Filipino food company, with 2004 sales of US$397 m. In 1993, it became the first fast-food service company to be listed on the Philippine Stock Exchange. It opened its first store overseas, in Taiwan, in 1986. In 1998, the first US store opened in Daly City, California, which has a large Filipino population. Today, Jollibee employs approximately 26,000 people in 1,186 outlets in nine countries, including more than 500 stores in the Philippines (where it commands 65% of the domestic fast-food market) and 120 in China. The only unsuccessful venture has been in the Middle East. Almost 60% of Jollibee stores in the Philippines are franchised. Tony Tan Caktiong, president and CEO, was voted the World Entrepreneur of the Year 2004 by Ernst & Young

Sources: "Nando's spice for success: wit, integrity and passion for the family," *Business Day*, April 5, 1997; "Negative effects of strong rand clip Nando's wings," *Business Report*, August 26, 2004; "The buzz behind Jollibee," *Philippine Business Magazine*, Vol. 11, No. 9 (2004).

ventures, with the choice depending on the country. In the case of Nando's, international expansion has been rapid, but not without problems, as the group lost some control over the brand. Stores were initially 51:49 joint ventures, but Nando's has bought back partners' interests in a move aimed at bringing about more effective administration and cost efficiency.

EMNCs' overseas activities may be fully based on business services provision. If the offshoring of corporate services is taking off rapidly (UNCTAD 2005a), the main business services companies still perform such activities in their home countries to exploit lower labor costs. It has been only very recently that Indian business process outsourcing (BPO) companies have made some timid FDI attempts (Table 3.4). First, amid a

Table 3.4 Selected foreign investments by Indian BPO companies

Company	Location	Description
In high-income OECD countries		
HCL Technologies	Belfast and London	Employs 3,000 staff in the United Kingdom for back office and help work
Infosys	Australia	In 2003 was one of the first companies to achieve CMMI(r) level 4 accreditation
TCS	Melbourne	Center of excellence
In China and other emerging economies		
Evalueserve	Shanghai	The first knowledge process outsourcing company to provide business and investment research services in China
Genpact	Dalian	Established in June 2000, Genpact Asia services clients from Japan, Korea, Greater China, and Southeast Asia. Genpact Asia operates out of two sites and employs close to 1,500 people
Infosys	Hangzhou	Is building a US$15 m. software center with space for 6,000 programmers
MphasiS	Shanghai	Bought a call center, employing 100 staff, from CapitalOne, the US credit card issuer, in October 2002
Sasken	Shanghai	Started in 2001 with joint development of handset technology with Huawei. Sasken employs 22 engineers in China, most from India with expertise in telecoms
TCS	Budapest	Inaugurated its 24th global (and the only European near-shore) development center in 2001, now employing 1,000 people
TCS	Hangzhou	Awarded the Management Innovation Award for being the first and only company in China to get assessed at both CMMI and PCMM level 5
TCS	Montevideo	Now employing 300 staff (15 in 2002), it is one of the largest companies in Zonamerica, the technology park

backlash against shifting jobs overseas, some have acquired call centers in the United States and the United Kingdom to support their argument that outsourcing does not necessarily equal offshoring.[16] Second, cognizant of the relative uneasiness of European firms and customers about working with BPO services in far-flung locations, they have invested in large facilities in Central Europe. Third, they have opened software development offices in China and other emerging economies.

4
The New Asian Multinationals

Summary

FDI outflows have accompanied the emergence of the so-called Asian Tigers and are now also on the rise from China. For the two largest Tigers, Korea and Taiwan, there is evidence of a "flying geese" dynamics, with the more labor-intensive stages of the production chain moving to the rest of Asia and, increasingly, China, while core corporate functions remain in the source countries. For Singapore and Hong Kong, the level of integration with China is even higher, although their MNCs have also invested in other developing countries to take advantage of preferential market access and Multi Fiber Agreement quotas.

4.1 Asian Tiger multinationals

Over the past three decades, four Asian economies of different size and location, and sharing relatively few characteristics in terms of trade specialization and business organization, have emerged as the paradigms of emerging economies. The large stock of outbound FDI originating in these four countries makes them a good starting point to analyze the existing literature on EMNCs and how their behavior may differ from that of long-established competitors. A relatively rich body of literature is available that attempts rigorous hypothesis testing on the basis of large datasets and well-established statistical methodologies (Pangarkar 2004).

Korea is considered the most successful among the large non-European developing economies. In 2001, Korean firms' world market share was 53 percent for code division multiple access, 42 percent for dynamic random access memory, 41 percent for thin film transistor–liquid crystal displays, and 32 percent in shipbuilding (Choi 2003). The history of

Korean investment abroad began in 1968 with a forestry development project in Indonesia, but outflows remained modest until 1986, with the exception of 1978, when a sharp rise was recorded in construction-project investment in the Middle East (Sakong 1993). Internationalization has taken on a completely new dimension since the late 1980s, when regulations were relaxed to manage the risks and opportunities of the burgeoning balance-of-payments surplus. In 1992, OFDI support measures such as financial and tax incentives became part of the nation's industrial policy (Dunning and Narula 1996). Large *chaebols* in machinery and electronics led the way, mimicking the "flying geese" strategy of Japanese MNCs in the 1980s, which consisted of setting up regional production networks across Southeast Asia. These *chaebols* were joined in the early 1990s by smaller firms operating in textiles and clothing, footwear, and electronics and auto parts, which have invested mainly in developing Asia. Delocalization helped the traditional labor-intensive industries, which were losing competitiveness as a result of increasing wages. In the 1980s, in particular, South Korean textile and clothing entrepreneurs began investing in Bangladesh. Finally, a small share of the mounting FDI in the 1990s was aimed at technology sourcing, in particular through acquisitions and minority participations in US high-tech companies. As part of a strategy of diversification away from the dependence on Japan and the United States, Korean MNCs also expanded to Europe – accompanying the maturing of the bilateral economic and political relationship, as reflected in several important declarations, agreements, and exchange programs.

Even before the Asian crisis hit, the government tried to curb rising foreign debt by imposing the obligation for companies to raise at least 20 percent of the funds for FDI projects above US$100 million in Korea. Most recently, it has been possible to detect a marked shift in Korean OFDI trends. On the one hand, the attraction of China has exploded, in particular for the more labor-intensive stages of the production of consumer electronics and other durable goods.[1] Since 2002, China has been the largest destination country for Korea's FDI, with the number of Korean MNCs having subsidiaries there rising from approximately 1,500 in the 1990s to approximately 4,000 in 2002. LG Electronics, for instance, has shifted some 35 percent of its production there, focusing on higher-end appliances in Korea.[2] This has raised fears of "hollowing out," which are discussed below. On the other hand, market-seeking investment in North America and Europe has increased rapidly, especially in the motor industry, where brands such as Hyundai and Kia are now acknowledged as among the most reliable in the market. To some extent mimicking the 1980s strategies of Japanese automakers, the Koreans have tended to invest in peripheral areas – countries such as Slovakia and states such as Alabama where unionization rates are low, land is widely available, and governments are keen on attracting FDI and offering special incentives and tax rebates (Table 4.1).[3]

Table 4.1 Major Korean greenfield investments in Europe and North America

Korean company	Company/location for investment	Description
Car assembly		
Kia	Žilina (Slovakia)	Production at €1.1 bn., 200,000 unit plant starts in late 2006
Hyundai	Montgomery, AL (USA)	Production at US$1.1 bn., 300,000 unit plant started in April 2005
Hyundai	Ostrava (Czech Republic)	Construction of €1 bn., 300,000 unit plant starts in 2006, to begin production in the second half of 2008
Car components		
Hankook	Dunaujvaros (Hungary)	First non-Asian plant, €500 m. investment and 1,600 jobs, production to start in 2007. Initially to be in Slovakia but government balked at €100m. incentives
SungWoo	Ostrava (Czech Republic)	Invested US$200 m. in a plant employing 1,500 staff. Serial production launched late 2006 and plant to be completed in December 2008
Consumer electronics		
Nuritech	Hurbanovo (Slovakia)	Plant has employed 450 people to produce basic boards for consumer electronics from June 2005
Samsung	Galanta (Slovakia)	Has invested US$60 m. since October 2002 to produce television sets and monitors and employs 2,200 staff
Samsung Semiconductors	Austin, TX (USA)	Invested US$500 m. in 2003–05 to expand and upgrade the memory chip fabrication plant
Humax Electronics	Newtownards (Northern Ireland)	Opened its digital set-top box operations in 1997; was awarded a Queen's Award for Enterprise in 2002

Singapore and Taiwan have followed two notoriously different trajectories of economic development, the main characteristics of which can be also identified in the foreign expansion of their major companies. In the city-state, as early as in 1985, in reaction to the recession, the authorities identified overseas investment and the development of offshore opportunities as a long-term solution to the nation's small scale and slow growth in demand and investment opportunities. Government-linked companies – most of them managed under the umbrella of Temasek Holdings (Box 4.1) – first spearheaded industrialization in the 1960/1970s and then regionalization.

Box 4.1 The role of Temasek in Singapore's regionalization strategy

Established in 1974, state-owned Temasek Holdings has stakes in 70 companies, including Singapore Telecommunications (SingTel), the DBS banking group, port operator PSA, Singapore International Airlines (SIA), shipping line Neptune Orient, logistics group SembLog, and Singapore Technologies (ST), another diversified holding with interests in semiconductors, defense, property development, and hotels. With 2005 revenues of US$44 billion and net profit of US$5 billion on an asset base of US$126 billion, the group accounts for a quarter of stock market capitalization and wields huge sway over the Singaporean economy. Temasek firms have traditionally enjoyed some of the best credit ratings in Asia owing to strong cash flow generated by local market dominance and conservative financial policies. However, while a few companies, notably SIA, have rewarded their shareholders well, others have disappointed.

Since the appointment of Ho Ching, a former head of Singapore Technologies and the wife of the current prime minister, Lee Hsien Loong, as executive director in May 2002, Temasek has tried to clarify its strategy. To simplify the financial structure, ST would be abolished and Temasek would take direct control of its companies. Cash-rich Temasek's top firms have to expand their tiny home market, regionally when not globally. Since unveiling its charter in July 2002, Temasek has gone about geographically diversifying its portfolio and placing big bets on sustained economic growth in Asia and rising consumer affluence and spending. The group's 2004 report, the first ever, revealed that Temasek had spent S$3.3 billion on acquisitions in 35 countries over the previous two years. In the 12 months to March 2006, Temasek made acquisitions totaling US$11 billion.

Over the next decade, Temasek wants to reduce local-based assets to a third of its total portfolio, from 52 percent currently. The weight of China is obviously expected to increase following Temasek's acquisition of 4.55 percent of Minsheng Banking, the country's largest private bank. Other targets remain Indonesia and Malaysia, where a 38.4 percent stake in Medco and a 5 percent stake in Proton, respectively, were bought in 2004. Cultivating business ties with the family of Najib Razak, the country's deputy prime minister, is meant to improve relationships between Temasek and Malaysia, which have been notoriously tense in the past. Temasek will also enter the regional fund management industry. The purchase of an 11.55 percent stake in Standard Chartered Bank is yet another reminder of its enormous acquisitive appetite. In a short span of three years Temasek created a commendable pan-Asian banking franchise with stakes in a dozen banks, together valued at US$20 billion.

Nonetheless, the international context has proven much more demanding, and Temasek's knowledge of new markets much weaker, than managers probably thought. Under pressure to rapidly acquire size when not additional competencies, acquisitions have often been made at a considerable premium; for instance, in the case of Optus, Australia's second telecom operator, SingTel paid 50 times earnings. Air New Zealand, in which SIA bought a 25 percent stake as a back-door entry to the Australian market, went bankrupt in 2003, forcing the group to write off most of the investment. A four-year alliance between SembLog and Swiss freight-forwarder KNI, in which the former held a 20 per stake, broke up in 2004 as constraints surfaced because of substantial differences regarding business approaches, industry focuses, and scope of services.

Sources: "Champions who do not find victory," *Financial Times*, April 12, 2002; "Singapore keeps firm hand on state groups," *Financial Times*, July 16, 2002; "Whither Singapore Inc?" *The Economist*, November 30, 2002; "Temasek sets itself high standards," *Financial Times*, October 14, 2004; "Temasek strengthens ties to Malaysia PM," *Financial Times*, November 12, 2004; "Temasek strikes again," CLSA, March 28, 2006.

The *modus operandi* that served Temasek companies remarkably well in domestic ventures, however, has often proved inadequate in managing Chinese investments. On the one hand, Singapore now has a contractual business culture in which deliverables, timelines, and the nature of risk sharing are fully specified. This has proved excessively formalistic in China's emerging business community (Kumar *et al.* 2005). On the other hand, China's political system has proven very complex to navigate, especially when compared with great predictability of Singapore's. However, this is not to say that government institutions have not been supportive of Singaporean MNCs, including SMEs. Research on firms doing business in Hainan, for example, reveals on the contrary that such bodies can play a role when they complement the business networks on which ethnic Chinese investors rely when returning to the mainland (Tan and Yeung 2000).

Industrial-township projects, Singaporean-run manufacturing facilities, utilities, and support services with low-cost labor and attractive incentives in various parts of Asia are the second pillar of this government-led strategy (Table 4.2) (Pereira 2004; Yeoh and Wong 2004). SembCorp Park Management (SPM)[4] is a separate organization that has undertaken the planning, marketing, and management of industrial parks since 1990.

Table 4.2 Singapore's industrial township projects

Industrial park	Location	Characteristics
Indonesia		
Batamindo	Batam, 20 km from Singapore	The park, which commenced operations in 1991, spans over 320 hectares, houses 82 companies, and is staffed by 70,000 workers. Japanese MNCs are numerous
Bintan	Bintan Island, 50 km from Singapore	Most investors are from Singapore and focus mainly on the electronics and resource-intensive light industries
Vietnam		
VSIP	Binh Duong, 17 km from Ho Chi Minh City	Investment commitments valued at more than US$500 m.; tenants from various Asian countries, in a wide range of sectors
China		
CS-SIP	Suzhou	The park, which commenced operation in 1994, has received cumulative investment of US$16.9 bn. (US$3.3 bn. in 2003) from 1,012 companies, and is staffed by 70,000 workers
WSIP	Wuxi, 130 km from Shanghai	The first ISO 9002-certified integrated industrial park in China
India		
ITPL	18 km from Bangalore	Approximately 100 confirmed tenants, mostly foreign high-tech MNCs, with 8,500 employees

To bypass the poor investment climate characterizing such locations, SPM supplements its own expertise with high-level political commitment. The Indonesian facilities, part of the Riau economic development cooperation framework agreement signed by the two governments, are joint ventures between government-linked companies and the Salim Group, Indonesia's largest and better-connected business empire. In Vietnam the collaboration with the government is more visible, as SPM is conscious of the difficulty of forcing an alien business concept on a country that is still largely in transition. The projects have succeeded in enlarging the industrial estate area for Singaporean investors and, to a more limited extent, in cementing bilateral ties between Singapore and lower-income ASEAN countries, but they have three limitations. First, the enclave nature of such projects makes them highly dependent upon the continuous support of the governments; second, Temasek's way of doing business, reliant on a combination of managerial skills and easy high-level political access, does not seem to travel easily; and third, the program never generated profits that could eventually supplement Singapore's domestic economy.

In the case of Taiwan, in contrast, the bulk of FDI has been undertaken by SMEs operating labor-intensive factories producing goods targeted at the low end of the market. Such enterprises were pushed to invest abroad by increasing wages at home, heated competition in the export market, and the monetary authorities' strategy of accumulating excess foreign exchange reserves (Lin and Yeh 2004). The government therefore allowed indirect investment in China in 1990, and direct investment after 2002. The year 1998 also saw the opening of a regular container trans-shipment route between Kaohsiung and two ports on the mainland. Later, conflicting pressures began to emerge.

On the one hand, the authorities obviously saw the enormous potential of the mainland economy and the role that Taiwanese firms could play. Large Taiwanese enterprises have invested in China to support their strategy of export competition and technological capability. More than half of Taiwan's ICT hardware manufacturing – the backbone of the island's economy – takes place on the mainland (Mattlin 2004). An estimated 68,100 Taiwanese companies operated on the mainland in 2003, approximately a third of all externally invested companies.[5] On the other hand, the authorities became afraid that once the floodgates were opened, the dynamics of hollowing out would be impossible to reverse. By the end of 2000, Taiwan's authorities changed the original policy of "refraining" to "promoting," but in implementing the policy, there are still many restrictions. In particular, certain investments, including semiconductor factories, are not allowed, and exposure to China is capped at 40 percent of a Taiwanese company's net worth.[6] New measures announced in 2006 will approve mainland investments larger than US$100 million, or those of any size that relate to sensitive technologies such as flat displays and petrochemicals, only if the company allows on-the-ground checks in China by Taiwanese state-appointed auditors, negotiates the remittance of profits, and undertakes also to invest in Taiwan. In order to close a loophole that allowed Taiwanese businesspeople to invest in China in their personal capacity, the new supervisory regime also requires executives and directors of listed companies to secure board approval for personal investments.

Across the Asian Tigers, corporate motivations have ranged from taking full advantage of host countries' different factor endowments and raw materials, to acquiring skills and technologies, to avoiding trade barriers. For Korea, empirical tests therefore support both the vertical (resource-seeking) hypothesis and the horizontal (market- and efficiency-seeking) one – for FDI outflows to developing countries and to industrial nations, respectively (Lee 2004). Singaporean MNCs seem to be "motivated by the lure of cheaper, abundant resources and larger, profitable markets. When these strategic motivations are important, Singaporean MNCs hold a higher stake in their foreign ventures, despite the higher potential agency cost, in the hope of reaping future revenues and profits" (Rajan and Pangarkar 2000: 60–61). However, after controlling for access to (more or less) protected markets, labor costs, and ASEAN membership, econometric testing to explain the determinants of Singapore's FDI in different countries leaves much of the variation unexplained, suggesting that national security considerations (as well as ethnic ties) may play an important role (Blomqvist 2002). Not surprisingly, companies from Taiwan invest in developing countries when they want to combine their existing assets with lower-cost labor, whereas they move to developed countries when they are seeking new assets (Makino *et al.* 2002).

Foreign investors from the Asian city-states have also taken early and significant advantage of the quota arbitrage opportunities opened up by trade restrictions, in particular by quotas under the Multi Fiber Agreement. This type of investment uses host economies as an intermediate production point or gateway to the third countries or the global market. From the early 1960s onward, Hong Kong textile and apparel firms relocated first to Singapore, then to Malaysia and Thailand after exports from Singapore were in turn curtailed by quotas, and later on to Mauritius. More recently, the driver has been preferential market access provided by some industrialized countries to African and Central American countries through such mechanisms as the African Growth and Opportunity Act (AGOA), the Central American Free Trade Agreement (CAFTA), the Everything but Arms initiative, and country Generalized System of Preference schemes (Box 4.2). For instance, at present approximately 20 Taiwanese companies are investing in Honduras, mainly in the spinning industry, and the Taiwan External Trade Development Council is setting up the Taiwan Trade Center in San Pedro Sula in Northern Honduras.[7]

Few studies exist that analyze EMNCs' performance. An early study on Indonesian firms found that those that had invested abroad saw performance improving dramatically in terms of management expertise, exports, quality, and costs relative to the past and relative to other firms in the sample that had not invested abroad (Lecraw 1993). Pangarkar

> *Box 4.2* Asian investors in the Southern Africa textile industry
>
> As of 2002, there were 60 Taiwanese companies operating in Swaziland, most of them in the textile industry. In 2001–02, Tex-Ray Industrial founded three factories – two garment factories and a spinning factory – to obtain benefits under AGOA. The company has invested US$20 in Swaziland and employs more than 3,000 locals, as well as 9 Taiwanese executive officers and 75 employees from China. Garments are exported to the United States, and the spinning products are sold domestically.
>
> With the average monthly salary at US$120, labor unions are requesting annual wage increases. Tex-Ray has established its own labor union in each factory and has forbidden its employees to participate in national unions in order to avoid conflicts and time-consuming negotiations. Tex-Ray has indicated that the government needs to increase its leadership with regard to labor unions and that an intervention by the government may be necessary to bring things under control.
>
> Swaziland also has a severe lack of middle management and skilled labor. According to a Tex-Ray officer, it takes three months to train new workers, which has a negative effect on production efficiency and cost effectiveness. More significantly, despite the existence of its spinning factory, most of Tex-Ray's raw materials must be imported from other countries, and Tex-Ray's local companies are no longer favored by AGOA since 2004.
>
> *Source*: World Bank (2004, box 7.5).

and Lim (2003) focus on the case of Singapore. In addition to their finding that performance is positively correlated with the host country's business environment – as expected, although their tests do not allow to say whether Singaporean investors perform better than OECD ones when the environment is difficult – another interesting result concerns the relative size of the subsidiary the MNC parent. The larger the subsidiary, the better the performance – although, again, it is not possible to determine whether there exists a sample bias. Using firm-level data for large Korean manufacturing firms, Lee (2003) finds that firms that engage in FDI outperform other firms in the future in all possible dimensions: they are larger, pay higher wages, and are also more productive. Sachwald (2001) analyzes how the record of Korean MNCs relates to the evolution of industrial structure and access to foreign technology. The most ambitious of these strategic moves met with managerial difficulties and generated mixed results. Firms that were already exporting from home, were protected from foreign competition, and had "internalized a large share of Korea's productive resources" (p. 361) found that they did not possess "the adequate assets and skills on which to build strong competitive advantage over local firms" (p. 5) when they invested in the United States and Europe. The timing of the acquisition also matters. Those undertaken during low market cycles exhibit better performance than other acquisitions for two key reasons: lower likelihood of overpayment as a result of hubris and ease in implementing restructuring initiatives such as retrenchment (Pangarkar and Lie 2004).

As regards the effect of OFDI on home economies, and in particular the possible trade-offs with domestic employment and investments, research findings remain inconclusive. After peaking in the late 1980s, manufacturing's share in domestic employment in the Asian Tigers has started to decline, raising concerns that this was largely due to the simultaneous increase in FDI outflows. It seems, however, that the structural shift is the result of the success of Asian industrial firms in raising productivity, and therefore national income, with a corresponding increase in wages and labor costs. In fact, for Korea, econometric tests suggest that the relocation of companies to China and other lower-wage countries is not associated with any weakening of competitiveness (Lim 2004). The time path of productivity, factor use, and employment differs depending on whether a South Korean multinational increasingly invests in low-wage countries or shifts its investments abroad more toward advanced countries (Debaere and Lee, forthcoming). The former approach results in an increase in capital intensity; the latter in the employment of less capital per unit of labor. The trade balance effect is also unlikely to be negative, as affiliates in China import a large share of their intermediate goods and materials from Korea (Nam 2004).[8] Similarly, Lin and Yeh (2004) study Taiwanese MNCs operating on the mainland and find that when it is motivated by market expansion and technology acquisition, their cross-channel investment has a positive impact on domestic investment, while the opposite holds true when labor-saving is the main motivation. Chen and Ku (2003) go a step further and distinguish between the substitution and the output effects on employment; they find that in Taiwan technical workers tend to benefit more from OFDI, trailed by managerial workers and blue-collar workers, who may even be adversely affected.

4.2 Nurturing and sustaining competencies in Chinese MNCs

Following the 1978 launch of economic reforms, controls on the overseas activity of Chinese companies were progressively relaxed as the government became cautiously interested in exploring new business opportunities. Permitting OFDI was indeed one of the Fifteen Measures of Economic Reform approved by the State Council in 1979,[9] although one reserved until 1985 only to trading companies and selected provincial and municipal economic and technological institutions (Taylor 2002). Speaking in 1994, then Vice-Minister of Finance Zhang Youcai stated that the authorities "vigorously encourage and support the relevant authorities and powerful large- and medium-sized enterprises to make investment and initiate operations abroad so as to diversify their business and become internationally operated conglomerates" (quoted in Wall 1997).

Early in the 21st century, the pressure of domestic overproduction and of rising international reserves on the fixed currency regime convinced leaders of the opportunities of launching the "Go Out" policy of encouraging overseas investment. The State Asset Supervision and Administration Commission was set up in April 2003 with the mandate of turning the country's top state-owned enterprises (SOEs) under its control into 50 global MNCs. Although every company that wants to invest overseas must obtain regulatory approval, in 2003 MOFCOM and SAFE introduced a program that allowed overseas investments of less than US$3 million to be approved at the local government level rather than through the lengthy and complex process of applying to Beijing. In October 2004 a further marked easing of controls on overseas investment by local companies was announced and application approval procedures were streamlined.[10] Under the new rules, the government will no longer judge the feasibility of overseas investments, leaving such judgments to the companies involved. Applications will require submissions on fewer topics and will be accepted via the Internet, while the number of investment destinations requiring approval by the ministry will be cut from 30 to 7. Investments in other destinations can be approved by local authorities. In 2003, the State Administration of Foreign Exchange allowed selected provincial authorities to approve overseas investments of up to US$3 million from US$1 million. In December 2004 it raised the ceiling for investment in natural resources from US$1 million to US$30 million.[11]

International expansion and global operations demand considerable investments to accumulate the three essential ingredients of dynamic capability – the so-called Chandlerian three-pronged investments in production (minimum-efficient-scale plants), distribution (forward integration into marketing), and management (managerial hierarchies for internal coordination). The expansion of China's MNCs into high-income OECD markets to foster product differentiation and powerful brand-name promotion is illustrative of this process. At an early stage, acquiring companies turned foreign targets into sources of technology for producing the high-specification models in demand in OECD markets. The China Bicycles Corporation, for instance, transferred the technology of an American bicycle company back to its Shenzhen plant, which now has a highly successful export market. Another form of technological transfer that is rapidly gaining relevance has to do with very intangible assets such as experience of managing a business in a deregulated environment. As the once-dominant State Power Corporation is broken up, this incentive was at play in Huaneng Power Group's acquisition of a half share in Ozgen, an important player in the deregulated Australian power market.

At a later stage, manufacturing facilities in OECD markets can serve as a means to jump over tariffs and non-tariff barriers. The world's second-largest tomato products company, Chalkis, has an annual capacity equal to a third of the European market. Facing significant tariff escalation, it bought the French leader in tomato transformation, Conserves de Provence, to which it now sells concentrate.[12] Yet another motivation is to secure sourcing, as certain Chinese investors did by installing a facility in the French region of the Lot to recycle used plastics for export to China, where demand for items such as shopping bags cannot be met locally.[13]

When Japan began its major period of M&A abroad in the 1980s, the country's main advantage was superior management techniques and more efficient manufacturing structures and processes. These advantages were transferable, but the key advantage of Chinese companies – cheap labor costs – relies on physically locating production in China. At the same time, the process of establishing a fully functioning market economy is far from completed. With surplus production capacity rapidly increasing, market deregulation, and heated competition, vanishing profit margins are a constant feature of the economic landscape.[14] Bankruptcy procedures remain primitive, however, and many large companies are heading abroad out of desperation rather than as the result of solid growth plans.

The broader point is that failure to keep pace along the three Chandlerian dimensions can inexorably drive companies out of business. Although it is far too early to tell, the long-term sustainability of the international expansion of Haier – an industrial group with more than 30,000 employees worldwide, regarded as the "GE of China" – remains in doubt (Box 4.3). Similarly, TCL has so far failed to turn around Thomson's and Schneider's loss-making television and DVD player operations, which it bought in 2002: they generated combined

Box 4.3 Making a Chinese global brand: the Haier case

Qingdao Refrigerator Factory (the former name of the company) was established in Qingdao, a port city south of Beijing and home of Tsingtao beer, in 1984 to manufacture refrigerators based on technology transferred from Germany's Lieberhaier. Haier's sales grew by 70 percent a year on average over two decades to reach US$1.84 billion in 2004 (US$583 million in 2000; *Fortune* data). Although that increase is mostly due to its big domestic production volumes, Haier has become the world's fourth-largest white goods maker behind Whirlpool, Electrolux, and Bosch-Siemens, and ahead of GE.

Chairman and CEO Zhang Ruimin played a pivotal role in the company's turnaround. Zhang gained government approval to buy the production lines of Libher, a German company, and expanded beyond fridges into a range of white goods by taking over other moribund state enterprises, including Qingdao Electroplating, Qingdao Air Conditioner, and Qingdao Red Star, and the controlling stake in the Wuhan Freezer Factory. By 1991 Haier was market leader in China and took the crucial decision to list in Shanghai and raise the necessary funds to build an industrial park to produce multiple products. Zhang's "militaristic" style of management is legendary: he once ordered the smashing of 76 faulty refrigerators with a sledgehammer – now preserved for its symbolism in the company's museum. From that day, "quality supreme and sincerity for ever" became the company slogan and has become a core value on which the company's new routines are formed. Today Zhang, rated one of the 25 most powerful business people outside America by *Fortune*, is an alternate member of the Communist Party Central Committee – a rare honor for a businessman.

The company currently has 89 product categories and 13,000 stock keeping units. Haier enjoys leading domestic market shares in washing machines (24 percent), refrigerators (23 percent), vacuum cleaners (18 percent), and air conditioners (13 percent). In addition, Haier has developed its own logistics capabilities to ensure efficient and cost-effective distribution throughout China, especially outside the major cities such as Beijing and Shanghai. As China's transportation and logistics infrastructure remains underdeveloped and plagued by bureaucracy, this is the only way for Haier to keep inventory levels low. Nonetheless, aggressively chasing large contracts and courting chain retail stores is putting pressure on margins. Although in 2004 Haier boasted higher margins on fridges and air conditioners than many domestic rivals and the appliance arms of Korean rivals, it still lags behind the 20 percent of the appliance arm of Philips Electronics. Haier has also moved beyond white goods into computers, mobile phones (where sales have badly disappointed), and even interior design and pharmaceuticals. It is in talks with the Charoen Pokphand Group to build a plant in Qingdao that will make eight-inch wafers used in computers and home appliances. The business logic is that of using production execution capabilities across a wide range of consumer durables, but the risk is spreading such resources too thin.

Haier realized early on that the benefits from economies of scale that derive from huge factories in China are often offset by the cost of being insufficiently responsive to fast-changing market signals – hence the decision to move to higher-cost locations, with the exception of telephone handsets. Revenues from overseas operations were US$314 million in 2004. The company has 22 overseas plants in the United States, Europe, Asia, and the Middle East; sales outlets in more than 160 countries; and a US$15 million American headquarters in mid-town Manhattan – the 1924 landmark Greenwich Savings Bank building. In 2000, Haier opened a US$40 million, 300,000-square foot plant in Camden, South Carolina, becoming the first Chinese company to operate a US manufacturing facility. One of the plant goals is to establish a supplier base in the United States, as opposed to using its parent company's Chinese connections. Haier is currently getting precoated steel from a major US steel supplier, and Morton Custom Plastics in St. Matthews, South Carolina, is doing most of Haier's injection molding work. Much of the company's extruded plastic sheeting material is also supplied domestically, although it also utilizes sources in Asia.

Haier also invested €80 million in Europe in 2002–04. It purchased the refrigerator plant belonging to Meneghetti Equipment in Padua, also buying Meneghetti-produced built-in ovens and hobs to market them in China under the Haier brand name. Haier saw this acquisition as providing the opportunity to develop new products from a European manufacturing base. Also in Italy, Haier Europe Trading opened a warehouse facility in Varese, core of one of the country's white goods districts, with a view to tap its rich availability of specialized suppliers and managers. In Japan, Haier is currently in talks with Sanyo and Samsung Electronics over the co-development of network-enabled digital appliance operations, rather than develop advanced products and enter the Japanese market on its own. Haier estimates that by 2009 the white goods market in India will be worth US$5 billion and it aims to take US$1 billion of that. After a disappointing experience in a 30:70 percent joint venture with Delhi-based picture tube maker Hotline, Haier now operates two leased factories in India and is planning to open a new US$3–5 million company-owned factory with a capacity of 1 million television units. In October 2004, Haier announced that it was opening an R&D center and factory in India, where it also has five Plant Haier showrooms.

Haier has so far concentrated on niches: it claims 30 percent of the market for small fridges and half the market for wine coolers in America, and a tenth of Europe's air-conditioner market. To continue to grow, Haier will have to penetrate larger and more established white goods markets, such as those for full-sized refrigerators (where its American market share is only 2 percent) and washing machines. Another of the problems that manufacturers currently face is the shift from conventional home appliances such as refrigerators and air conditioners to digital appliances. Haier lacks the R&D and design skills of rivals such as Whirlpool, GE, and Electrolux; although it spends 4 percent of revenues on research, it employs just ten researchers in the United States. In addition, competitors such as Kelon have filed patent design infringement complaints. Haier is now creating local product-development teams in Tokyo and the United States to differentiate its line and move upmarket. In Japan, for instance, Haier offers washers that use less water, are quieter, and are narrow enough to fit cramped Japanese homes. R&D activities have been subcontracted to other firms – two in Australia and in France for mobile telephony; one in Korea for televisions. Haier is also starting consumer advertising. Previously most of its ads were limited to brand promotion on billboards and airport luggage trolleys. Now it wants to reach shoppers directly, but the company's first effort, an ad in the September 2002 issue of *Good Housekeeping* for the Access Plus freezer, looked old-fashioned.

In the transition from original equipment manufacturer (OEM) to original brand manufacturer (OBM), access to distribution or service networks constitutes an additional problem. Haier sells products in Japan through a tie-up with Sanyo and sells in Taiwan through an alliance with Sampo. In Korea, on the other hand, it has so far failed to sell its goods to Himart, the country's biggest electronics chain store, which is worried by low brand recognition for Korean consumers, stiff competition with local giants Samsung Electronics and LG Electronics, and poor after-sales service networks. In France, Haier's sole distributor went bankrupt a few weeks after securing the right to use the trademark. Finance is an additional issue. In 2004 Haier injected the 40 percent stake in Qingdao Haier Refrigerator into CCT Holdings, a small listed firm in Hong Kong, to give it paper currency for overseas acquisitions. A related headache is hiring good managers, as Haier cannot pay as well as foreign rivals and cannot offer stock options.

Source: Bonaglia *et al.* (2006).

2004 operating losses of HK$246 million as against TCL's overall operating profits of HK$497 million.[15]

The strategy of Haier can be contrasted with that of Galanz, another Chinese company, which makes 40 percent of the world's microwave ovens. Galanz has gone global by sticking close to home. Established in 1978 as a textile company, Galanz began making microwaves in 1993 and soon started exporting as a contract manufacturer for other companies. It makes microwaves for 248 companies, including GE, Fillony, and Harvard, and exports 10 million pieces a year.[16] All production takes place in Shunde in Guangdong province, where cost and quality can be more easily monitored and any part can be supplied within 20 minutes. Galanz now boasts the world's largest microwave oven factory. Shunde is also ideally located in the industrial hub between Guangzhou and Hong Kong, and exporting is logistically easy. Nonetheless, Galanz is so dominant – it boasts a 70 percent market share in China – that it risks the ire of anti-trust authorities. It may be only a matter of time before it also starts investing abroad.

5
Multilatinas

Summary

For most of the 20th century, Latin America played host to the handful of then-existing multinationals from developing countries. Although such companies never reached a globally competitive position, those that survived two decades of structural adjustment and market reform policies started investing overseas in the late 1990s. Relative to new Asian multinationals, these multilatinas have tried to leverage their superior knowledge of policy innovations such as trade liberalization, privatization, and regulatory reform.

5.1 The early phase

Until the early 1970s, Latin America hosted a much larger number of MNCs than Asia, let alone other developing regions. Building on the country's incipient industrialization – according to the 1914 census, the GDP (gross domestic product) contribution of the manufacturing sector was approximately 50 percent already – Argentinean firms started investing in neighboring countries as early as in 1890 (Chudnovsky *et al.* 1999). Argentinean firms tried to deploy their superior production, management, and marketing skills in smaller and/or poorer markets, with the most prominent of them – Alpargatas and Bunge y Born – rather rapidly reaching a larger size in Brazil than in their home country. Indeed, it would not be inaccurate to suggest that the first (and for a few decades, the only) EMNCs were Argentinean. Uruguayan FDI outflows were also far from insignificant in the first few decades of the 20th century, to the extent that the country appeared relatively high in the ranking of foreign investors in its two much larger neighbors, Argentina and Brazil (Jacob 2004).

Recurring economic and political crises, however, took a heavy toll on the ability of Latin American firms to plan for the long term, while a number of macroeconomic shocks made entrepreneurs more risk averse. This translated *inter alia* into a domestic refocusing of major business groups, especially in the context of major privatization waves in the late 1970s and, much more deeply, in the early 1990s. Wealthy Venezuelans also invested massively in the United States in the 1970s, mostly in Florida (banking and real estate), but this was a form of risk diversification by means of portfolio investment and capital flight (Wilkins 1981).

The history of Brazilian MNCs is somewhat different, reflecting the country's development trajectory. On the one hand, the domestic market grew for more than seven decades at an average rate in excess of 4 percent, providing excellent opportunities for domestic firms to grow as well. On the other hand, a cautious approach to trade and FDI liberalization, combined with relatively constant government support to industry, allowed the formation of "national firm leaders" (Amsden 2001) capable of competing with OECD-based competitors, if not globally at least on third markets. In particular, a continuous public policy effort to improve infrastructure and invest in capital equipment reinforced Brazilian construction companies (so-called *empreiteiras*). Odebrecht – which, as mentioned before, is the single largest non-oil private investor in Angola – Camargo Corrêa, and Andrade Gutierrez gained a number of important contracts in Africa and the Middle East. State-owned Petrobrás, through its fully owned Bráspetro subsidiary,[1] entered into partnership agreements with oil majors and fellow national oil companies to explore offshore fields in various countries. From the late 1970s onward, it was the turn of manufacturing companies such as Copersucar (sugar), Gerdau (steel), Gradiente (consumer electronics), and Cofap (auto parts) to buy out existing firms in foreign markets. But these companies still accounted for a much smaller share of the stock of Brazilian FDI than the construction companies and Petrobrás.

5.2 The consequences of market reforms

Relative to Asia, the Washington Consensus reached Latin America much earlier – basically in the early 1990s, although some elements of it were already present in the so-called neo-conservative experiments of the 1970s (Foxley 1983). It has gone deeper – to include privatization of both utilities and pension systems, as well as trade liberalization and free trade agreements with OECD countries – and has been implemented over a longer time span. In the context of this research, it is a moot point to discuss whether the ingredients and the cooking have always been appropriate (e.g., Ocampo 2004). What is key, on the other hand, is to discuss the effects that "neo-liberal" policies have had on the ability of aspiring Latin American MNCs to enter the global marketplace in relatively high-margin businesses, and not to place themselves at the bottom of the value curve and then stay there indefinitely.

Compared with their Asian peers, which leveraged technological prowess and social capital in their foreign expansion, *multilatinas* have invested abroad on the basis of a superior ability to manage the process of economic liberalization. In their analysis of 14 firms of various sizes from three industries (energy, steel, and food/beverages) in four countries (Argentina, Brazil, Chile, and Mexico), Suarez and Oliva (2002) discovered that each organization responded to the post-reform competitive environments in essentially four stages:

1. *Turnaround and catch-up*. Recognizing that their efficiency and quality levels were far below those of world-class competitors, the firms initiated action plans to measure the gap and catch up. Often such change involved significant modifications in the structure, size, scope, and culture of the organization.
2. *Expansion*. Realizing that growth was imperative for survival against larger rivals, the companies expanded their operations significantly, usually joining with related businesses in the local market or even in other countries.
3. *Acquisition of new capabilities*. Becoming increasingly sophisticated as they competed with larger foreign rivals, the firms developed new capabilities in areas such as customer service, technological innovation, and brand management.
4. *Quest for industry leadership*. Having completed the previous stages, the companies concentrated on becoming dominant in a particular industry. As a result, some were able to compete with the best of their global competitors; others became top-class niche players in the region.

A policy area where domestic reforms have changed the behavior of domestic firms, in turn providing them with the incentive to internationalize via FDI, is trade liberalization. The case of the auto industry is particularly interesting. During the long period of import-substitution industrialization that basically lasted until the early 1990s, foreign assemblers invested in Latin America to jump border tariffs, but few of their suppliers followed them. Spurred by domestic content requirements and shielded by international competition, Argentinean, Brazilian, and Mexican producers of auto parts grew in size and indeed invested in upgrading their production capabilities. Brazil in particular developed what appeared to be a rather sophisticated industry (Goldstein 2004b). In the case of pistons and connecting rods, for example, Metal Leve held more than 60 percent and 98 percent, respectively, of the internal market, set up a research facility in Michigan, and opened production facilities in South Carolina.

Owing to FDI from OECD countries, automotive productive capacity has steeply increased since the early 1990s, first in Mexico and later in Brazil. Quite a few new projects are characterized by the attempt to involve components suppliers in the vehicle manufacturing process to a much higher degree than in traditional assembly arrangements.[2] The relationship between automakers and their suppliers now involves the interchange of information and engineering, as well as medium- and long-run work contracts (between three and five years). Once the removal of most trade barriers had led to the entry of OECD-based MNCs, infant industries failed to fully match world-class requirements and were almost wiped out. In Brazil, by 2004 the share of domestic capital in auto parts had fallen to 21.1 percent of fixed assets (from 51.9 percent in 1994), to 13.5 percent of sales (from 52.4 percent), and to 23.8 percent of investment (from 52 percent) (Sindipeças 2005: 12). Many local outfits – including Metal Leve and Cofap – were bought or merged with foreign companies.

A few domestic-capital stalwarts were restructured to meet customer demands and have survived and indeed learned to compete globally.[3] In addition to Sabó from Brazil (Box 5.1), examples from Mexico include San Luis, which has become the world's biggest producer of light-vehicle suspension springs, with foreign plants in the United States and Brazil; Condumex, which produces automotive cables for Delphi and others in Mexico and has opened small plants in Brazil and Spain; and Grupo Industrial Saltillo, a maker of iron and aluminum engine blocks and heads that is reportedly considering an investment in China at the request of its global customers. Following a different, and yet similar, strategy, Mabe, Mexico's leading appliance producer, scooped up depressed appliance makers in Latin America in 1993–95 filling orders for General Electric, which now lets Mabe manufacture all of its refrigerators, stoves, and ranges in the region (Bonaglia *et al.* 2006). "Follow-the-customer" examples can be found in other sectors, including in food (Box 5.1).

Box 5.1 Two EMNCs follow their customers

Sabó is a global supplier of oil rings, rubber hoses, and gaskets for Volkswagen. It has received seven times a General Motors' Worldwide Supplier of the Year award. A US$250 million business that is still owned by the founding family, it has been described as the "última moicana brasileira (The last of Brazil's Mohicans in the car components business)." In 1993, when foreign competitors began investing in Brazil to follow their global assembler customers, Sabó established its first foreign factory, in Argentina. Kaco, a three- factory German firm, was bought in 1995. Now the company operates three more (one in Hungary, one in Áustria, and a second one in Argentina), in addition to four in Brazil, the most recent one in Mogi-Mirim (São Paulo) mainly producing for the US market. Sabó's products are sold in 70 countries, and foreign affiliates account for 60 percent of total turnover and employ 1,260 people, almost half as many as those working in Brazil. Sabó invests US$15 million per year in R&D and maintains a center in the United States staffed by 18 engineers. The company is studying the viability of opening a new factory in China mainly to supply Volkswagen, one of its largest clients. To this end, it recruited from TRW a Brazilian executive who was in charge of installing TRW's plant in China.

Grupo Bimbo produces buns, sliced bread, snacks, tortillas, and gummy bears. The Servitje family, which established it in 1944, still controls and manages the company. Depending on the product, its market share in the late 1990s varied between 92 and 97 percent. Its success in fending off the arrival of foreign rivals such as Continental Baking was largely due to efficient backward integration: Bimbo manages 29,000 vehicles serving 30,000 routes to supply 1,300,000 different points of sale. As the Mexican economy slowly opened up in the second half of the 1980s, Bimbo invested a total of US$30 million to become a local supplier of hamburger buns, eventually progressing from being McDonald's preferred supplier in Mexico to its exclusive one. The first foreign acquisition took place in Guatemala in 1991, followed by others in Chile and Colombia (where it bought market leaders) and in the United States – a string of companies in Southern states with a large Latino population. In Latin America Bimbo replicated its domestic strategy of managing the whole supply chain and succeeded in competing with rivals that relied on less efficient third parties for logistics. Bimbo then set up new plants in foreign markets along with McDonald's: every sandwich McDonald's sells in Peru, Colombia, and Venezuela comes on a locally baked Bimbo roll. In 1995, Bimbo realized that its candy-making technology was obsolete, so it began to do contract work for Park Lane Confectionery of Germany. Then it bought Park Lane and invested in Eastern Europe to take advantage of cheap labor to make goods for sale in third markets. The company has been consistently ranked first or second among Mexico's most admired corporations. Foreign sales went from 4 percent in 1995 to 33 percent in 2004. Bimbo's global workforce is now 16,000 strong and the management is also increasingly globalized: the Czech candy factory in Ostrava is managed by an Indonesian Cantonese with a German passport who previously worked at Park Lane.

Sources: "Bimbo un gigante con hambre," Expansión, September 29, 1999; "The World's new tiger on the export scene isn't Asian: it's Mexico," The Wall Street Journal, May 5, 2000; "Ahí está el pan," Expansión, July 19, 2000; "Sabó avança na Europa e pensa na China," Valor Econômico, August 19, 2004; "Hacen hamburguesas con insumos mexicanos," Reforma, August 23, 2004; "O senhor dos anéis," Istoé Dinheiro, September 8, 2004.

The second policy area where firms have been exposed to major changes relates to the scope of state intervention and the structure and regulation of product markets. Nowhere has the privatization process advanced further than in Chile, and for this reason many Chilean managers believe that they know more about business in a recently deregulated and liberalized environment than their counterparts in other Latin American countries. Del Sol and Kogan (2004) study two such Chilean firms that have made successful investments abroad: Endesa, an electricity generator and distributor, and Provida, a pension fund. They show that the basis of their success was the capacity to redeploy the resources accumulated during economic reforms and confirm this finding by analyzing 165 foreign affiliates of public Chilean firms operating in Latin America during the period 1994–2002. Controlling for country, industry, year, and size effects, they show that Chilean affiliates have a higher return-on-earnings (ROE) and a higher probability of returning positive profits, evidence that Chilean participation added value in firms established during economic reform.[4]

In sum, removing trade barriers and exposing Latin American companies to head-on competition at home for the first time has produced considerable adjustment costs, but has also pushed many of the "survivors" to adopt more aggressive strategies, which have included overseas expansion. Nevertheless, risk diversification remains an important motive for both market- and resource-seeking OFDI (Tavares 2006). Demand growth has shown a high degree of volatility, exchange rate regimes have changed rather frequently, and international commodity prices have also fluctuated widely. Although much reduced from the past, when revolutions and coups d'état were very frequent occurrences, political risk in Latin America is also a concern for investors. In this situation, having a portfolio of business operations in different locations and sectors can be an effective hedge instrument even when considering the liability of foreignness, that is the problem of being an outsider and being blocked in access to resources that are crucial for conducting business successfully. In some cases, *multilatinas* that had built dynamic capabilities at home were almost obliged to deploy them overseas. To cover itself against exchange rate fluctuations, Marcopolo, a Brazilian bus manufacturer that has managed assembly lines abroad for more than a decade, had to reorient its international operations into a deeper manufacturing presence.

The fact that FDI is now becoming a strategic option is clearly shown by the increasing number of Latin American companies that take this route, by their differing nature, and by the broad range of sectors in which they operate. Lolita, a Uruguayan producer of womenswear, responded to the country's economic crisis in 2002 by aggressively chasing new business opportunities in the rest of the continent, Europe, and Asia, and now sells through franchisees in 15 countries. As fast product replenishment is the company's strategic advantage, in the process Lolita has re-nationalized production from China to Montevideo, where 60 percent of goods is now produced. In 2004, an example is Lolita's turnover exceeded US$9 million in Uruguay and Brazil alone. Another example is provided by two small oil companies from Argentina's Chubut province (Petrominera, owned by the local government, and Dragón) that in April 2006 signed an exploration and production contract in Ecuador.

6
Existing Theories and Their Relevance to EMNCs

Summary

The various social sciences, including economics, management, and sociology, have studied the internationalization patterns of corporate entities in developed economies. Each of them has contributed rich insights into our understanding of emerging multinationals, but none offers a fully satisfactory account. The so-called eclectic paradigm, with its emphasis on the categories of ownership, localization, and internalization, remains useful, but it, too, must be adapted to the different realities of EMNCs.

Corporate internationalization, through export and/or overseas investment, is studied both in the business organization literature and in economics. In economics, the so-called eclectic paradigm has emerged as the most influential perspective. Based on transaction costs economics, it tries to conceptualize the decision to invest abroad in terms of market, product, and industry characteristics. This approach may look similar to – but is intrinsically different from – the view that OFDI is likely to be a substitute for exports as it is driven by differences in rates of return and capital abundance. Administration sciences take a behavioral approach and visualizes internationalization as a gradual and evolutionary process, focusing on the root causes and main features of such gradualism. In what follows, I present the main hypotheses advanced by each school and their relevance to the study of emerging multinationals.

6.1 The monopolistic advantage and the product lifecycle

Theorizing the modern multinational firm as one that has its home in one country but also operates under the laws of other countries dates from 1960, when David Lilienthal first distinguished between portfolio and direct investment (Kobrin 2001). In his seminal dissertation in 1960, Stephen Hymer was the first to use industrial organization categories and market imperfections to analyze the MNC (Pitelis 2002). Different or unfamiliar laws, linguistic and cultural barriers, and possible discrimination increase the risks of foreign firms compared with domestic rivals. Therefore, in order to invest directly in a foreign country, spurn arm's-length transactions, and assume the liability of foreignness, MNCs must have some advantages over competitors or other reasons. Firm-specific advantages such as economies of scale, cost or knowledge advantages, product differentiation, and credit access allow MNCs to invest abroad and increase market power. In fact, according to Hymer, FDI was a way of perpetuating the monopolistic role of the MNC in the international market. An MNC would use foreign subsidiaries to remove competition between the foreign affiliate and domestic operations already present. Increasing market power was the ultimate goal of the MNC, and FDI was one means of achieving that goal.

Vernon (1966) describes the process of internationalization across countries by building on the concept of the product lifecycle developed in marketing. The model argues that sales and production of a new product move around the world following the four stages of the product's lifecycle: introduction, growth, maturity, and decline. Firms generate a new product designed to satisfy the needs of high-income consumers locally. They then start exporting to countries that are similar to their home market in terms of consumers' income and needs, and later expand into countries that differ in terms of income and consumer needs. Once process and product technologies have been established and matured and margins start falling owing to increased competition, firms are pushed to invest in overseas production in low-cost locations. Finally, in the decline stage, production in developed countries stops because it is not economically viable, and instead is concentrated in developing countries. Demand in developed countries is served through imports from developing countries.

Vernon's "genuine product cycle" differs from the so-called catching-up product cycle developed by Kojima (1960). The most important characteristic of pro-trade-oriented FDI is that it is an investing country's comparatively disadvantaged industry that invests overseas, to achieve a stronger comparative advantage through providing appropriate capital goods and technology (i.e., a borrowed technology from the viewpoint of the host country) to its production subsidiary in the foreign country. As long as this type of FDI is promoted, a "flying geese" stimulus for industrialization is transmitted sequentially from a lead goose to follower geese, bringing about enlarged trade and co-prosperous economic growth. The model appeared to provide a very suitable description of the process that saw Japanese MNCs transfer stages of their production to the rest of Asia and the latter acquire in turn the means for accelerated industrialization. Nonetheless, Buckley (1991) argued that the Japanese experience was *sui generis*, and therefore inappropriate for extrapolation. He also criticized Kojima's model for emphasizing plant- as opposed to firm-based economies of scale and for ignoring the development of dynamic capabilities and the role of culture and politics in the geography of FDI flows.

Industry-level trade patterns conform to the product lifecycle model (for references to the empirical literature, see Cuervo-Cazurra 2004). The model's ability to explain the internationalization of individual firms, however, is more limited, especially in light of changes in the environment of international business, such as the shortening of lifecycles, the reduction of income gaps among developed (and some previously developing) countries, and the increase in the speed of imitation of innovation. Moreover, the type of MNC portrayed by Hymer is largely ethnocentric and fails to recognize that systematic differences exist among different types of MNC on the basis of corporate structure, the level and type of control mechanisms, and the extent of interdependence among organizational units (Tolentino 2002).

Nevertheless, in mature industries such as construction Vernon's theory maintains its relevance. The 2003 *Engineering News Record* ranking of the world's 100 largest contractors includes 18 firms from emerging economies, of which 16 have international sales in excess of US$100 million (Table 6.1). This is obviously well above the weight of EMNCs in other industries. No fewer than 43 of the top 225 firms by sales hailed from China. These firms have built up a particularly formidable market presence in Africa. In Algeria, for example, China State Construction & Engineering Corporation (CSCEC) has recently built the new Algiers airport, various five-star hotels, and the main hospital in Oran. In fact, price competition from Chinese contractors can be stiff, sometimes along dimensions other than cutting-edge technological skills. In particular, such companies have access to a low-cost workforce in China that they post overseas as required.[1] The size of the domestic market, the obstacles that foreign companies face there,[2] and the *de facto* monopoly they enjoy in Hong Kong also provide Chinese construction companies with an advantage. Moreover, economic diplomacy is often used: not only is China's increasing development assistance tied to the

Table 6.1 The world's 100 largest contractors (country ranking by average firm revenue in 2003)

Country	Average revenue	Average internationalization	Number of firms
France	14,380	58.76	3
Sweden	14,056	81.84	1
Netherlands	8,625	52.14	1
Germany	6,719	52.72	3
Austria	6,468	72.58	1
Spain	6,364	18.50	5
Japan	5,363	20.78	19
UK	3,882	52.30	5
China	3,868	15.33	12
Australia	3,709	18.55	1
Korea	3,608	28.92	2
USA	2,555	14.96	35
Italy	2,245	51.67	5
Greece	1,824	100.00	1
Norway	1,644	63.36	2
Brazil	1,576	81.28	1
Egypt	1,318	14.51	1
India	1,228	6.60	1
South Africa	1,174	50.84	1

Source: Author's elaboration on *Engineering News Record* data.

use of Chinese services, but this is often extended to countries that agree to sell oil and other natural resources. Finally, tighter controls over corruption in OECD countries, especially since the Convention on Combating Bribery of Foreign Public Officials in International Business Transactions was signed in 2001, are also reportedly benefiting competitors from countries that are not parties to this legal instrument. Chinese contractors, at any rate, insist they had to work hard to establish reputations, especially in Africa, where the work and the working conditions are demanding.

6.2 Behavioral models

The so-called Uppsala model deals with knowledge acquisition, that is, how organizations learn and how such learning affects their investment behavior. Firms handle the problem of risk through an incremental and rather slow decision-making process, where information acquired through foreign investment in one phase is used in the next phase to take further steps.[3] Through this incremental behavior, the firm can keep control over its foreign venture and gradually build up its knowledge of how to conduct business in different foreign markets. The model corresponds to the past behavior of Swedish and other Nordic firms, which "often develop[ed] their international operations in small steps, rather than by making large foreign production investments at single point in time. Typically firms start[ed] exporting to a country via an agent, later establish[ed] a sales subsidiary, and eventually, in some cases, [began] production in the host country" (Johanson and Vahlne 1977: 24). Interestingly, this process did not necessarily correspond to sequential entry into progressively more distant markets. Swedish corporations' patterns of international expansion initially focused on distant markets "as a means of building strength prior to meeting strong competitors closer to home in Europe" (Mathews 2002a: 98). What is relatively more important in the Uppsala model is "psychic" distance, approximately corresponding to proximity in terms of cultural or institutional norms.

This strand of the literature has a number of very useful implications for the study of EMNCs, as shown by the fact that in the 1970s in the overwhelming majority of cases, firms from developing countries investing abroad did so only after testing the waters by exporting there (Wells 1983: 67–73). Moreover, for EMNCs geography remains a strong predictor of bilateral FDI flows, especially in East Asia. Indeed, when Japan itself was a *sui generis* emerging economy in the 1960s, the "flying geese" framework for analyzing its OFDI flows was closely connected with the emergence of a network of Japanese MNC activities in Southeast Asia. While headquarters remained in Japan, production bases progressively moved to other Pacific locations where labor costs were lower. As modularization is the main feature of the Asian production model, and as this is particularly suitable for cross-border outsourcing, a similar pattern of geographically proximate networks of production characterizes Korean and Taiwanese MNCs.

Finally, psychic distance is connected with the density of ethnic ties. In many cases, for instance, Mexican MNCs have entered the US market by establishing a presence in Arizona, California, and Texas, Southern states with a strong presence of Mexican migrants. Not only did this coincide with physical proximity, but it also provided market opportunities to cater to the specific demand of the Mexican population (Vasquez-Parraga and Felix 2004). Casanova (2004) argues that when a firm focuses on its "natural markets" – defined as those markets with a common history or language or physically close to the country of origin of the MNC – its probability of success increases. Physical proximity, low language barriers, and previous personal contacts make Latvia the first choice for Estonian investors, although this does not prevent them from being as disappointed as others with the host economy's business environment (Mägi 2003).

The main limitation of the behavioral approach is its determinism – firms may fail to evolve, or they may jumpstart to higher stages without necessarily going through intermediate ones. So-called born-global firms operate in international markets from the earliest days of their establishment and seek to derive significant competitive advantage from the use of resources and the sale of outputs in multiple countries (see Rialp-Criado et al. 2005 for a review). Although selected small, technology-oriented EMNCs can be analyzed in these terms (Hashai and Almor 2004), for most companies based in emerging markets the risks/opportunities trade-off between meeting the pent-up demand of the domestic market and venturing abroad is still biased against early foreign expansion.

Another phenomenon that is difficult to reconcile with the Uppsala model is the decision to establish a direct presence abroad *despite* a lack of success in exporting from the home country, possibly through a local agent (for Colombian cases in neighboring Venezuela, see Franco and De Lombaerde 2000: 74). The term "leapfrogging MNCs" has been proposed as a definition of companies that jump over the various stages predicted by the Scandinavian model. OECD-based MNCs respond to the new opportunities opened up by liberalization in emerging markets with a set of offensive moves that can give them a salient position in the newly liberalized economies. Successful domestic firms may respond to these offensives by achieving preemptive market position, attaining a critical size, creating national brands, exploiting national competitive advantages, adopting best international practices, and altering core values.

6.3 The eclectic paradigm – ownership, location, internalization

The eclectic theory of FDI, or OLI paradigm, was introduced by John Dunning and represents a mix of three different FDI theories, each with a different focus (Table 6.2). "O" refers to the ownership, firm-specific advantages – core competencies in production differentiation or entrepreneurial and managerial capacity – that allow an MNC to overcome the costs of operating in a foreign country. "L" are the location, country-specific advantages that determine where an MNC sets up shop. A firm will move offshore to combine its competitive advantage with factors of

Table 6.2 The eclectic framework of different industrial typologies

Category	Ownership advantages (Why?)	Localization advantages (Where?)	Internalization advantages (How?)	Products/industries
Resource-based	Capital, technology, market access, complementary assets	Control over natural resources, good infrastructure, skilled and abundant workforce	Stable supply sources at predictable prices, market control, technology mastering	Oil, copper, bauxite, bananas, cacao, hotels, export-oriented production of skilled labor-intensive goods
Market-based	Capital, technology, information, organizational and administrative skills, oversupply of R&D, scale economies, trademarks, and goodwill	Input, labor, and transport costs, market characteristics, public policies	Reduce transaction and information costs and buyer uncertainty, protect property rights and quality	ITC, pharmaceuticals, motor vehicles, tobacco, insurance, advertising
Rationalized specialization (efficiency): (a) products, (b) processes	As above, plus market access, economies of scope, and geographical diversification	(a) Economies of specialization, (b) low labor costs and local content incentives	(a) As localization advantages, plus economies of governance, (b) economies of vertical integration	(a) Motor vehicles, electrical equipment, business services, and R&D, (b) consumer electronics, textiles and clothing, pharmaceuticals
Trade and distribution (import and export trade)	Market access, distribution products	Input sourcing and local market, importance of client contact, post-sale servicing	Protection of inputs quality, sales guarantee, and avoidance of agents' misrepresentation	Many products, especially those for which close contact with subcontractors or final consumers is needed

Source: Dunning (1979 and 1980).

production that are available in a foreign country and earn a rent as a result. Finally, "I" refers to the internalization advantages of choosing a given organizational structure among various alternatives, ranging from the market (arm's-length transactions) to the hierarchy (wholly owned subsidiary). If markets are missing or function poorly, transaction costs can be kept in check through internalization, that is, by keeping multiple activities within the same organization.[4]

The OLI model, owing to its eclecticism, improved measurability, and great explanatory power, has become the basic reference in the literature on MNCs and it can be useful as a way to categorize the international operations of business in emerging economies, especially when the framework is augmented by including differences between vertical and horizontal diversification. Among the few studies that apply the eclectic paradigm to EMNCs, two by Cuervo and Pheng (2003a, b) focus on 22 Singaporean construction MNCs. The authors examine which location factors are viewed as the most significant for these construction MNCs, relative to other ASEAN contractors and contractors from developed countries, and the significance of ownership advantage and disadvantage factors. Firms identify their most important ownership advantage factors as coming from (1) information, knowledge, technology, and R&D capability; (2) the firm's name and reputation; and (3) management and organizational capability. In other Southeast Asian countries, the most important host location factors are the host governments' attitude, policies, and regulatory framework; social, political, cultural, and geographic factors; and the cost of doing business. Relative to established international competitors, Singaporean contractors have a significant size disadvantage in certain project types.

In the case of EMNCs, however, the OLI framework suffers from two major limitations. First, rarely do enterprises based in developing countries possess significant monopolistic advantages. If they invest abroad, it is not on the basis of "O," and the parameters that determine the degree of "I" in their foreign operations are different. Nevertheless, regardless of the investor's origins, the "L" decision follows the same broad criteria. Second, the OLI model is basically static. It is intended to explore all important factors impacting entry-mode decisions, but in practice it neglects strategic factors, characteristics of the decision maker, and situational contingencies (including competition) surrounding the decision-making process.

Dunning responded to these criticisms in a later paper with Narula (1996) presenting the contours of the investment development path (IDP) model, which dynamically connects an economy's structural features (i.e., its production structure, technical infrastructure, mix of tangible and intangible resources, and institutional set-up) with patterns of FDI. In particular, an economy's net outward investment position (NOIP) depends on its level of development, and the relationship between FDI, on the one hand, and the OLI factors that underpin foreign investment decisions, on the other, changes according to the country's stage of economic development and sophistication (Table 6.3). Thus, the rate of structural change and the development of the NOIP have common determinants, and the expectation is that there is a U-shaped relationship between economic development and a country's NOIP, which will first grow and then decline as economic development proceeds. In other words, the relative weights and roles of the three elements of the eclectic approach to international production vary as countries (and their firms) become richer and more embedded in the world economy and shift from natural to created assets (Dunning 1979, 1981).

Nonetheless, Dunning and Narula (1997) emphasize the idiosyncratic nature of the IDP. With regard to country (market) size, small countries record an above-average NOIP in earlier periods because the lack of economies of scale more or less inhibits inward FDI and indigenous firms are pushed to international markets in order to achieve economies of scale.

The IDP framework has indeed proven very useful for smaller European economies.[5] It can also be applied to non-OECD economies, especially when additional factors promoting the agglomeration (e.g., scale economies, learning effects, externalities) or dispersion (e.g., congestion externalities, certain market structures, increases in factor mobility) of firm activities are included (Bellak 2000). Unfortunately, the scarcity of consistent time-series data on outflows from emerging economies makes it virtually impossible to evaluate the IDP hypothesis empirically on total FDI stocks or flows.[6]

It must also be borne in mind that some emerging economies, despite their large size and potential, may suffer from a unwelcoming investment climate and therefore register relatively low inflows at the same time as their companies invest abroad. In other words, multinationalization may emerge as a defensive strategy to escape a harsh business environment. This may explain the paradox of a positive NOIP for countries such as Russia and Turkey (Andreff 2003 and Erdilek 2003, respectively). Bonaglia and Goldstein (2006) similarly highlight how in Egypt – a country which as a result of poor investment climate and broader geopolitical motives receives limited FDI inflows – two MNCs

Table 6.3 The investment development path (IDP) model

Stage	Outward FDI flows	Inward FDI flows	Net outward investment position	Comments
1	Almost zero	Also low	Negative but of insignificant value	The country's localization features (bad governance, poor infrastructure, lack of skilled labor) are inadequate to support even vertical ("low labor cost seeking") inward investment. Domestic firms lack ownership advantages
2	Few firms	Rise considerably	Increasingly negative	Economic development (higher disposable income, better physical and human capital) makes the country a more attractive venue for MNCs, which engage in more sophisticated operations (with a resulting trend increase in real wages). Firms slowly accumulate the firm-specific assets that would allow them to engage in OFDI, initially in countries that are close either geographically or culturally
3	Grows rapidly	Grows slowly	Converges more or less rapidly to zero	As domestic firms become more competitive, foreign MNCs find it more difficult to deploy their ownership advantages solely for the host economy market, although they will be attracted by its human capital. Over time, learning-by-doing will allow this process to evolve and OFDI will emerge. The country's absolute cost competitiveness is eroded, reducing the incentive for vertical internal FDI
4	OFDI overtakes internal FDI		Becomes positive	Domestic and foreign companies are by now able to compete on an equal footing. The country's localization advantages are now fully based on the availability of sophisticated assets. In their overseas investments, domestic companies are driven by horizontal ("market-seeking") and technology-sourcing motives. As technological progress and human resource development proceeds, OFDI sectoral orientation shifts toward "created asset"-intensive sectors

Source: Dunning (1981 and 1986).

have successfully expanded abroad, following different strategies. Socialist countries in the 1980s provide an earlier similar example. While inward FDI was very limited, firms used internationalization as a way to escape from the home country system (Svetličič and Rojec 2003). Far from invalidating the IDP scheme, however, these exceptions confirm the importance of heterogeneity and idiosyncrasies in examining countries' FDI paths.

6.4 Dynamic capabilities and the resource-based view

The process of expansion abroad through the creation of subsidiaries and their management is a manifestation of the phenomenon of the growth of the business firm (Penrose 1955). The theory of firm-level growth – according to which, to the extent that managers can find ways to coordinate increasingly sophisticated and widespread bundles of resources, there is no upper limit (i.e., equilibrium) to the process of growth – provides a key insight into the origin of scope economies and informs issues in the study of MNCs. Intra-firm knowledge generation gives rise to "excess" resources that can be deployed by management at a zero marginal cost. Firms are social communities that specialize in the creation and internal transfer of knowledge, and MNCs arise not out of the failure of markets for the buying and selling of knowledge, but out of superior efficiency as an organizational vehicle by which to transfer this knowledge across borders (Kogut and Zander 1993).[7] Moreover, and contrary to standard economic theory, firms are heterogeneous insofar as they do not all possess the same capabilities.

Strategic management theory, with its focus on performance differences among firms, provides a useful complement to the OLI framework in understanding the activities of the modern multinational. In particular, global competition and the management of a firm's global stocks and flows of knowledge merit closer attention. If firms specialize in the internal transfer of tacit knowledge, the less codifiable and the harder to teach is the technology, the more likely the transfer will be to wholly owned operations. This result implies that the choice of transfer mode is determined by how efficiently the MNC transmits knowledge relative to other firms, and not by an abstract market transaction.

A widely held view is that the profound economic metamorphoses in emerging economies in the 1990s resulted in dramatic changes in the competitive environment, compelling firms to develop new strategies and capabilities in order to compete. Bartlett and Ghoshal (2000) studied 12 EMNCs and argued that the reason for their global success is that they treated global competition as an opportunity to build capabilities and move into more profitable segments of their industry.[8] All of the companies in the study overcame the same core challenges. They broke out of the mind-set that they were unable to compete successfully on the global stage. They adopted strategies that made being a late mover a source of competitive advantage. They developed a culture of continual cross-border learning. And they all had leaders who drove them relentlessly up the value curve.

Yet, for its extension to EMNCs, the resource-based view finds its limitations in the emphasis it places on first-mover advantages, endogenous barriers to entry, and the definition of resources as rare, non-imitable, and non-transferable. Keeping the main points of the dynamic capabilities approach, Mathews (2002b) departs from the most stringent assumptions to develop a strategic account of the late-comer firm, which is seen as good at "linking with various kinds of contracting or licensing arrangements, and leveraging resources (knowledge, technology, market access channels) from such linkages" (p. 468). Insofar as this linkage, leverage, and learning framework is consistent with the extended resource-based perspective, it provides clues to understand what can account for the extremely rapid appearance of global players given their scarcity of resources and international experience (Mathews 2006). The case of Cemex is described in Box 6.1. EMNCs may hence be particularly prone to engaging in non-sequential internationalization across countries, which

---

Box 6.1 Cemex: linking, leveraging, and learning

Cementos Méxicanos (Cemex) was founded in 1906 in Monterrey and spent decades consolidating its grip on the Mexican market. From its base in Northern Mexico, it started to export to the Southern United States, the Caribbean region, and Central America only in the mid-1970s. The acquisition of smaller firms, construction of new production plants, renewal of existing ones, and opening of commercial firms in export countries supported growth in the 1980s. Cemex also developed arbitrage skills and became a large cement trader.

Cement is mainly local. On land, it cannot be affordably transported farther than about 400 km, so plants must be near construction hotspots. Moreover, anti-dumping regulations are rife, for instance in the United States. For these reasons FDI is a substitute for trade. In 1992 Cemex sank US$600 million into Valenciana and Sanson, two underperforming cement plants in Spain. In a competitive, albeit more mature, market, Cemex could master new efficiencies such as inventory management, just-in-time delivery, and how to access customers in third countries. These learnings served when domestic construction collapsed during Mexico's 1995 recession, as Cemex thrived by channeling offshore production into markets such as Puerto Rico and Florida. It used the dollar revenue as a guarantee to raise money for scooping up cement mixers in Trinidad, Panama, Venezuela, Colombia, and the Dominican Republic. The 1997 Asian crisis gave Cemex another opportunity to buy assets on the cheap in Indonesia and the Philippines. Without overseas listing, Cemex largely eliminated the country risk associated with being a Mexico-based company. By the late 1990s Cemex had become the world's third-largest producer (trailing only France's Lafarge and Switzerland's Holcim) and the largest cement trader. In 2004 it made its largest acquisition so far, gobbling up RMC of the United Kingdom. Breaking from its traditional emphasis on bags of high-margin cement in developing countries, this investment is aimed at raising Cemex's presence in, and exposure to, ready-mix concrete in continental Europe.

Cemex, unlike its European rivals, concentrates on developing countries, where profits are greater because most cement is sold in bags for small-scale building, rather than in big ready-mixed quantities. In order to enlarge the pool of potential customers in Mexico, it launched the Construcard project in association with GE Capital, offering revolving credit at below-market rates for the purchase of building materials, and opened 1,300 Construrama distribution centers.

Most important, Cemex had developed its information systems before it started expanding abroad, whereas Holcim and Lafarge have had foreign subsidiaries for decades and have found it much harder to overcome institutional inertia. Not long after taking the helm in 1985, the company's chief executive, Lorenzo Zambrano (the founder's grandson), set up a small team of programmers to come up with ways to generate automated plant reports. At the end of the 1980s, Cemex set up a satellite network to transmit all the internal data to its headquarters in Monterrey. Cemex has never had a big mainframe, relying instead on distributed, interconnected systems that share information across the company. The company's pilot e-mail system was launched in 1991. All Cemex trucks are equipped with a computer and a global positioning system receiver, and their positions are combined with the output at the plants and the orders from customers. This enables dispatchers to redirect the trucks en route, reducing the window of time for delivery from 3 hours to under 20 minutes, even with the chaotic traffic and the last-minute cancellation of orders that are typical of emerging economies. A new subsidiary, Cemtec, was set up to train high-ranking executives in this field, both from Cemex plants and from other companies within the region, at international levels. In 2000, the company merged with four other Spanish and Latin American firms to create Neoris, an IT consultancy. Neoris is now part of CxNetworks, a Miami-based subsidiary that Cemex wants to use to turn itself into an e-business in every way possible. Also parts of CxNetworks are Construmix, a construction-industry online marketplace, and Latinexus, an e-procurement site.

Sources: "The Cemex Way," *The Economist*, June 14, 2001; Barragán and Cerruti (2003); Mathews (2002a).

Cuervo-Cazurra (2004) defines as "the selection of countries that are very different from the country of origin for the firm's first international expansion" (p. 2). Three explanations are advanced: the variation across firms in terms of their resource bundles, particularly in their ability to manage complexity and diversity; the variation in firms' ability to transfer and use their resources across countries; and the inclination that given firms have to acquire externally the resources needed to operate across countries, rather than to develop them internally.

EMNCs use different competencies to challenge Western firms' dominance in an industry. The consolidation of the global brewery industry provides an example. As in other sectors where advertisement spending is huge and can be used as the most effective means to erect barriers to entry (Sutton 1991), among the corporate objectives is to build global brands and maximize the return on advertisement outlays. So far, SABMiller has followed a different strategy, building a portfolio of local premium beers instead of trying to sell its core Castle lager – which dominates in Southern Africa – across different markets.

6.5 Conglomeration and internationalization

Implicit in Hymer's work is the presumption that capital, management, and a highly skilled workforce are all scarce resources. Large monopolistic firms that access them have an advantage and possibly an incentive to diversify geographically and functionally. In developed countries, however, broad diversification, by diverting resources and providing alternative avenues for growth, has been argued to deter firms from actively seeking international expansion. Moreover, business diversification demands that managerial centralization be sustainable, but this hinders organizational and technological learning across subsidiaries (Wright *et al.* 2004), *a fortiori* when they are located in different countries. Finally, if diversification is no more than a risk-hedging strategy – in fact a rather appropriate one in environments characterized by a high degree of political and economic instability – then portfolio investment is probably more adequate than FDI.

In the case of late industrialization in developing countries, foreign technology acquisition capability became a necessary condition for corporate success. In the best-performing diversified business groups, this capability was transformed into organizational know-how that provided a key resource in the effectiveness of corporate growth through diversification (Amsden and Hikino 1994). Instead of creating new products, these business groups leverage domestic and foreign contacts to combine foreign technology and local markets, sequentially entering new, unrelated markets (Leff 1978). But as the selection environment changes with the opening up of the national economy to increased world competition, the business groups evolve, sometimes to the point of making the transition to independent product innovation (Kock and Guillén 2001). The burden of managing a variety of unrelated business lines in subsidiaries located in multiple locations is made lighter by the long-established practice of resorting to a network architecture, which is more conducive to information sharing than the traditional hierarchical structure.

In this context, business groups may diversify internationally either to capitalize on existing resources and capabilities or to acquire and develop new ones in host-country environments (Hoskisson *et al.* 2000). The first strategy (i.e., international exploitation) is likelier to happen in other, similarly endowed emerging markets, while the second one (i.e., international exploration) leads groups to invest in more developed OECD markets.[9] The more efficient and competitive firms, which are also the most likely to undertake international expansion, may have been led to diversify to avoid the costs of inefficient capital markets (Khanna and Rivkin 2001). Moreover, family-owned conglomerates may find it easier to make a long-term financial commitment toward internationalization than Western competitors that act under the more immediate (although possibly value-enhancing) pressure of financial markets.[10]

Absent a large dataset, suggestive evidence of the strength of conglomeration/multinationalization links is provided by the experience of developing countries where diversified groups have a particularly high weight.[11] With economic liberalization, many emerging economies' conglomerates have adopted the "focus on core competencies" imperative that is currently fashionable in the West. Nonetheless, conglomerates with an international reach remain pervasive. Building the kind of institutions that can support well-functioning markets for capital, management, labor, and international technology takes many years, if not generations (Khanna and Palepu 1999). Spreading out businesses and management talent can overcome the distortions and red tape common in developing markets. In addition, traditional MNCs prefer to work with trustworthy conglomerates rather than venture alone into difficult markets. Later, as the MNC "acquires sufficient familiarity with the local environment, it will need [the local partner] and its ilk less and less. Thus the problem for [the local firm] becomes, not whether to compete, but how to learn as much as possible from the MNC" (Khanna and

Palepu 2004b: 38). One, if not the main, competence that local firms can acquire is the project-execution capability (Amsden and Hikino 1994) that, more than proprietary technology, serves to establish activities such as banking, public utilities, telecommunication services, and construction. Once it has been acquired in one sector and country, often at a non-trivial cost, such capability can be replicated in other sectors and/or countries.

The early history of Indian MNCs suggests that diversified conglomerates were the first to advance into foreign markets, deploying their execution skills. In the 1960s groups such as Tata, Birla, and the Kirloskars began expanding to East Africa and Sri Lanka, regions with strong cultural and ethnic links to India. As an example, by 1995 Birla was operating in 15 countries. These inroads, however, did not really respond to strategic planning, as ties among different independent-minded parts of the corporate empires were often tenuous at best. In contrast, in the 21st century the Tata Group has ambitious globalization plans "to move Indian manufacturing to a world class-level and a useful place to start is subassembly or key component manufacturing by setting up plant overseas" (see Box 6.2).[12] Reliance Industries, India's largest conglomerate, with sales equaling 3.5 percent of the country's GDP, also has its "sights on becoming a world-beating company."[13] Its strategy is nonetheless much more focused on the domestic market: it completed its first overseas deal only in 2004, when Reliance Infocomm acquired London-based FLAG Telecom, a bandwidth supplier with intercontinental undersea cable, for US$211 million.

In other emerging economies results are similar. In Chile, the hypothesis that group-affiliated firms are more profitable than independent ones in their foreign investments cannot be rejected (del Sol and Duran 2002). Moreover, these investments are more likely to generate profits when they are made with partners from a developed country than when they are made with partners from the host country (del Sol 2005). The largest individual investor in China is Thailand's Charoen Pokphand (CP) Group (Box 6.3). Two highly diversified conglomerates, Koç and Sabanci not only continue to dominate the Turkish economy, but have also developed internationally. For example, Koç-controlled Arçelik, currently Europe's fifth-largest white goods company, plans to double its sales in the next five years on the back of acquisitions in Britain, Germany, and Romania (Bonaglia et al. 2007).[14] Tunisia's Elloumi Group, with activities in three core industries – cables and wires (Chakira-Câble and COFICAB), auto parts (COFAT), and food products, each directed by one of the France-educated (at Polytechnique and Centrale) children of the founder – operates three wire plants in Portugal, Egypt, and Morocco. In 2001 COFICAB Portugal was awarded the APMEI excellence prize as one of best companies operating in the country.[15] In Russia, all major MNCs are conglomerates controlled by one of the oligarchs (Guriev and Rachinsky 2005). Metal company Severstal, for instance, is also involved in auto manufacturing (Ulyanovsk Automobile Factory [UAZ]; the Zavolzhskii Automobile Factory in Nizhnii Novgorod, which supplies engines to PAZ and GAZ; and ZMA in Naberezhye Chelny, where it manufactures the Rexton sports utility vehicle as part of its strategic partnership with SsangYong Motor Company) and finance (Metcombank and the Sheksna insurance company). Other financial industrial groups with foreign operations include AutoVAZ, Lukoil, Norilsk Nickel, Alfa, and Sistema/MTS.

Box 6.2 Tata: from Indian to global conglomerate

In its transition from a collection of business units to a truly global conglomerate, Tata has very ambitious plans. Each of the group's businesses will in the future be judged on its potential to be among the world's top three in the sector and on its ability to generate higher returns that the cost of capital. The 2000 buyout of Tetley of Britain by Tata Tea, to create the world's largest tea company, was followed by a cooperation agreement between Tata Motors and MG Rover, the setting up of a software center in Shanghai by Tata Consultancy Services, and the purchase of the truck division of Daewoo by Tata Motors (production has already risen by 10 percent since the ownership change) and of the steel division of Singapore's NatSteel by Tata Steel. Plans also exist to open hotels in Beijing and auto plants in South Africa and Thailand. In 2004, overseas markets accounted for a fifth of Tata Group sales of US$14.25 billion.

Bangladesh, where Tata is committed to investments totaling US$2 billion for projects in power, steel, and fertilizers, is the group's biggest overseas market by value. South Africa has been identified as the next frontier in Tata's globalization strategy. Tata plans investment of ZAR1.5 billion (US$245 million) on new projects in South Africa, where VSNL holds a controlling 26 percent stake in SNO Telecom, the second network operator, and is bidding for IT services group Business Connexion (BCX). Very positive sales of the group's trucks and passenger automobiles could also accelerate a decision to launch a local assembly factory, allowing Tata Motors to take advantage of South Africa's free-trade agreement with the European Union to access European markets.

Sources: "Tata Motors looks to widen investor base," *Financial Times*, September 27, 2004; "India's largest group faces end of an era," *Financial Times*, September 29, 2004; "Tata identifies South Africa as car assembly hub," *Financial Times*, March 23, 2005.

Box 6.3   A Thai conglomerate in China: the Charoen Pokphand Group

Since its founding by immigrants from southern China in the early 1920s, the Charoen Pokphand (CP) Group has grown from a seed supplier in northern Thailand to one of Asia's largest conglomerates. CP went through a major restructuring on the eve of the Asian financial crisis, offloading its shares in the Lotus convenience store chain to Tesco and the KFC chain, merging its cable television operation with the Shinawatra Group, and simplifying its corporate structure. Still led by the founder's son, Dhanin Chearavanont, the group is a diversified conglomerate active in agribusiness (it is the world's largest producer of animal feed and tiger prawns) and services – telecommunications, logistics, and retailing – and had sales of US$15 billion in 2004. The rising number of free-trade agreements between Thailand and potential trading partners has prompted CP Trading Group Co. Ltd. to step up its overseas business expansion. CP wants to set up seed-manufacturing plants in India by forming a joint venture with government agencies, while another two plants in Turkey (where it is now the largest poultry producer) and Burma will focus on size and capacity expansion.

Drawing on its Chinese ethnic origins, the CP Group was the first foreign investor to enter the Shenzen special economic zone in 1979. Thanakorn Seriburi, a long-time CP employee, has been supervising business development and investment in China since 1979. By 1997 Chia Tai, the CP Group's name in China, was the biggest foreign investor there, with nearly 130 joint ventures ranging across a wide gamut of businesses, including some such as motorcycle manufacturing (under the Dayang brand), television production, and herbal remedies in which it does not operate in Thailand. In 2003 it employed 70,000 people in China, where it generated almost a quarter of global sales.

The CP Group is credited with having a network of high-level contacts in China that is both extensive and deep. Nonetheless, its opportunistic behavior – the belief that it could operate businesses peripheral to its core competencies through partnerships with those with experience and/or contacts – often landed CP Chinese affiliates in financial trouble. Its overall performance has been lackluster, especially in the retail sector, where the Lotus Supercentre venture faces increasing competition and the group wants to move to a leasing model from being currently wholly owned. In feedstock, the group expects to reduce the number of mills as better infrastructure would allow investment in larger plants, with improved economies of scale, and the ability to transport feed to customers farther afield. CP has ambitious plans to expand capacity at its motorcycle manufacturing operation to 3 million units within five years and further diversify into the Thai fast-food business. The CP Group also signed a memorandum of understanding with Krung Thai Bank, the country's largest state-owned bank, to co-invest in Business Development Bank in China. A subsidiary, CP Consumer Products, started importing Guizhou Tianan Pharmaceutical's Jin Tianan brand dietary products into Thailand.

Sources: "Radicalism, Asian-style," *The Economist*, March 22, 2001; "China: firms looking to Thailand trade," *The Nation*, July 26, 2004; "Optimism in the face of history," *Far Eastern Economic Review*, August 26, 2004; "Economy of scale key to CP's success in China," *The Nation*, March 3, 2005; Pavida (2001, 2004).

Box 6.4 D'Long Strategic Investment: a multinational conglomerate

Founded in 1986 in Shanghai as a photo-processing business by Mr. Tang and his three brothers, D'Long Strategic Investment has grown into one of China's largest private conglomerates, with an annual turnover of US$4 billion and 15,000 employees. Through size and wide diversification, the group aims in its words "to create new values for China's traditional industries" – for instance, helping local farmers participate in establishing large enterprises for fruit, vegetable, and meat production with all the necessary infrastructure for storage, transport, and export. Its structure includes six group companies and participation in various other ventures. One of the six, Xiang Torch Investment builds trucks and produces automotive parts, machinery, electrical equipment, and industrial gases. Xiang Torch claims that in 2002 it built 30,000 trucks, 100,000 heavy-duty gearboxes under license from Eaton, and 50,000 gearboxes under license from Germany's ZF. Another group company, Xinjiang Tunhe Investment, makes noodles and 85 percent of China's tomato paste. Among its more exotic activities is the Minsk project, a military theme park built around the former Soviet aircraft carrier Minsk, moored near Shenzhen City on the South China Sea.

D'Long, rather than build up its own name abroad, concentrated on buying well-known but ailing foreign brands, retaining their marketing, distribution, and R&D operations, and transferring the bulk of the manufacturing to China to cut costs. D'Long opened offices in Detroit and Munich in the mid-1990s to foster technology exchange with foreign firms such as Eaton in the United States and MAN in Germany. In 2000, it bought Murray, an American lawnmower and bicycle maker, once owned by Britain's Tomkins, with US$400 million in financing provided by GE Capital. It closed two of Murray's three factories, fired top management and some 650 workers, and moved the manufacture of low-end mowers to Jiangsu province. It pressured engine suppliers in America to cut prices, threatening to transfer their contracts to Japan's Suzuki. It also bid for Grundig, a German television and home appliance maker, but in January 2004 lost to a Turkish/British consortium. In 2002, its strategy moved to a different scale when D'Long announced it would pay bankruptcy administrators US$10 million to buy the Fairchild Dornier 728 development program (including both prototypes and all the program's fabrication and assembly tooling). D'Long established a new subsidiary called Fairchild Dornier AeroIndustries, which carried out a series of power-on tests in February 2004 and proclaimed the first prototype would fly by late in the year. D'Long expected production to start in 2006.

Concerns were long aired that the group was overreaching itself and that it was quietly assuming control of financial institutions. Many questioned the little-known company's ability to raise the estimated US$1 billion investment needed for certification and serial production. In April 2004, three domestically listed firms controlled by D'Long issued statements noting that D'Long had been using the shares it owns in them as collateral for loans. The share price of the three firms plunged, leading to real financial problems, as worried banks cut off cash and demanded hard collateral on loans. D'Long then entered into debt restructuring, the biggest since the 1998 collapse of Guangdong International Trust and Investment Corporation.

Sources: "Spreading their wings," *The Economist*, September 4, 2003; "D'Long caught short," *The Economist*, April 22, 2004; "Enigmatic D'Long in race to fund flight of relaunched 728," *Aviation International News*, April 25, 2004; "Beijing tackles Delong's wreckage," *Caijing*, August 5, 2004.

The 1997 Asian economic crisis demonstrated the risk of investing with no apparent regard for economic return and running up debts far in excess of the amount of equity. Nonetheless, in economies such as China in which business groups historically have never been strong, positive incentives and suasion from national and regional governments have encouraged firms to form, or at least call themselves, business groups. The experience of D'Long, a big Chinese conglomerate with sizeable overseas interests that went bankrupt in 2004, is indicative of the fact that corporate diversification may have negative and far from negligible consequences in terms of resource allocation (Box 6.4). Other Chinese investors have also widely diversified, although mostly on the domestic market – Wanxiang, for instance, into securities, banking, property, and consumer goods.

7
The Role of Governments

Summary

Policies and politics play a key role in emerging multinationals' decisions to invest overseas, as well as in the modalities and location of their expansion. Another issue that remains insufficiently analyzed is the emergence of developing country investors in non-financial services.

The preceding chapter showed the extent to which research on MNCs from emerging economies has developed since the mid-1980s, following a methodological framework similar to that used for analyzing international business in a developed country context. Nonetheless, the existing literature has largely left unexplored the role of institutions in affecting the competitiveness of firms and the development strategies of countries. As authors such as Pavida and Weung have underlined in their analysis of emerging Asian MNCs, corporate strategies are embedded in the political economies of both host and home countries – if not in the global political economy. Similarly, since the mid-1990s *multilatinas* have reacted to the new market incentives and opportunities opened up by government policies (Chudnovsky *et al.* 1999; Goldstein and Toulan 2006), as have South African businesses in the context of the post-Apartheid transition (Chabane *et al.* 2006). This chapter analyzes the external environment – the role of policies and politics – and the next chapter studies the dense network of ethnic contacts within which MNCs operate.

7.1 The role of support policies

Although the debate on the role of the state in spurring industrial competitiveness, and by extension economic development, remains one of the most heated in the social sciences (e.g., Lee *et al.* 2005), there is no denying that in emerging economies government actions play a key role in compensating indigenous firms' lack of ownership and internalization advantages (Yeung 1999). Government strategic interventions in the form of large-scale public investment in skill formation, establishment of public research institutions, fiscal incentives for innovating firms, and a "soft" patent system to legalize reverse engineering have all contributed to strengthening indigenous technological capabilities and have allowed firms continuously to recombine foreign technology and indigenous R&D.

Multinational expansion is a new phase in the growth of the firm, and EMNCs, no matter how important the fresh competencies they possess, still start from a weaker competitive position than their established rivals. In fact, to the extent that overseas investments by these countries' firms serve primarily the purpose of augmenting the assets they possess, public policies must accompany and sustain the process of development and structural transformation. This has prompted many governments to develop new tools to assist them in gaining international presence and prestige. To some extent, the same risks of capture and misplaced priorities in policy action that often plagued 20th-century industrial policy may present themselves. Nonetheless, the very fact that, by definition, EMNCs operate in foreign markets makes it much easier to exert discipline on them and prevent firms from receiving subsidies they do not rightfully deserve (Rodrik 2004). At the same time, the lack of appropriate policies may hamper internationalization – especially when informational and financial bottlenecks are major hurdles that companies have to clear when investing abroad. To the extent that such policies are likely to be less developed in those countries that have a poor record of facilitating corporate competitiveness in general, the situation may be further worsened (Franco and De Lombaerde 2000).

At the general level, changing policy regimes have important effects on outward investment. Obviously, full convertibility (liberalization of both current and capital account transactions) is the most important factor, at least insofar as controls discourage transparent FDI outflows and leave room only for capital flight. An illustration of progressive liberalization to accompany the internationalization of domestic companies is provided in Box 7.1.

Table 7.1 presents a range of restrictive measures on OFDI in a few emerging economies. The experiences of China, Korea, Singapore, and Taiwan have been presented above. Indian authorities similarly recognized that to promote the growth of firms and businesses into strong,

> *Box 7.1* Recent policy changes in South Africa
>
> In November 2002 the South African Reserve Bank, in recognition of the important role South African business has to play in regenerating the continent, eased capital controls on local companies wishing to invest in other African countries or wanting to expand existing ventures. The limit was raised from US$79 million to US$216 million with immediate effect. This limit was raised again in 2003 to ZAR2 billion per project in Africa and ZAR1 billion per project outside of Africa. The 2004 Medium-Term Budget Policy Statement abolished exchange control limits on new OFDI, although application to the South African Reserve Bank's Exchange Control Department is still required for monitoring purposes and for approval in terms of existing FDI criteria, including demonstrated benefit to South Africa. The South African Reserve Bank reserves the right to stagger capital outflows relating to very large foreign investments so as to manage any potential impact. South African corporates will be allowed to retain foreign dividends offshore. Foreign dividends repatriated to South Africa after October 26, 2004, may be transferred offshore again at any time for any purpose.
>
> *Source*: SA Reserve Bank.

India-based multinationals, they should be accorded increasing flexibility to undertake capital account transactions, especially for acquisitions of businesses abroad (Sinha 2000). Between 1978 and 1992, companies registered under the Companies Act 1956 could finance overseas direct investment in the form of the export of indigenous (not second-hand or reconditioned) plant, machinery, and equipment (Pradhan 2003). The Inter-Ministerial Committee could also permit *ad hoc* equity participation by way of capitalization of fees, royalties, and other entitlements, but cash remittances were strictly limited to "hard and deserving" cases. At the same time, anti-trust regulations limited the scope for organic growth at home and pushed Indian companies to find better business opportunities abroad. The guidelines were first updated in 1992, removing all screening requirements for any equity investment below US$2 million, of which US$500,000 could be in cash and the rest could be used to finance Indian exports of plant, machinery, equipment, and know-how. The regime was further relaxed in August 1995, when the permitted value of direct investment under the automatic route was increased to US$30 million in the case of SAARC (South Asian Association for Regional Cooperation) countries and Myanmar, INR120 million in Nepal and Bhutan,[1] and US$15 million in all other cases. Since 2000, Indian companies have been allowed to issue American and global

Table 7.1 The regulation of outward FDI in selected countries

	Authorization	Permission	Prior approval	Foreign borrowing	Taxes on remitted overseas income
Argentina	Unrestricted			Up to US$2 m. per month	World income[a]
Brazil	Unrestricted	Above US$5 m. per group, per annum	Banking sector only		World income[a]
China	Since 2005 MOFCOM does not require feasibility studies	To seven destinations only	US$3–30 m. depending on sector		
Estonia			No restrictions		
India			Above 100% of company's net worth	Up to 100% by ADR/GDR proceeds	
Mexico			No restrictions		
Russia			Above US$10 m.		
Singapore			No restrictions		
South Africa	Unrestricted. Application still required for monitoring purposes	Above ZAR2 bn. per project in Africa and ZAR1 bn. Per project outside Africa	Obligation to demonstrate benefit to South Africa		Complete freedom to transfer foreign dividends repatriated
Thailand	Unrestricted under US$10 m. per year, from the Bank of Thailand (BOT) for larger amounts	From the Bank of Thailand (BOT) for portfolio investment (1–9.99%) of any amount			World income unless there is a double taxation treaty

[a] To avoid double taxation, residents are given a credit for foreign-paid income taxes equal to the value of the additional tax burden generated by the foreign-earned income.

depositary receipts without prior government approval. Up to 50 percent of the proceeds can be used to acquire foreign companies.[2]

Enterprises interested in investing abroad may receive institutional support through various channels, varying from information services covering investment conditions and opportunities to facilities that provide financing and guarantees. As shown in Box 7.2, Malaysia was a pioneer. Similarly, in 1996, Thailand's prime minister established the Thailand Overseas Investment Promotion Board to support the investing activities of Thai MNCs abroad (UNCTAD 1997). Nonetheless, policies toward OFDI remain at a very rudimentary stage (Pavida 2004). Two government bodies have put in place some measures in this area – namely, the Board of Investment and the Export–Import Bank of Thailand – but there is no consistent framework.[3] In Brazil, the national development bank, BNDES, created in 2002 a special credit line to support OFDI, which is granted on the condition that within six years the beneficiary increases its exports by an amount equal to the credit. This instrument was first used by Friboi in 2005 to buy Swift in Argentina.[4] Among the measures of the new Política Industrial Tecnológica e de Comércio Exterior launched in March 2004 is the creation of 38 multidimensional external trade units within the Banco do Brasil to support the internationalization strategy of national firms. In November 2005, the Programa de Incentivo aos Investimentos Brasileiros na América Central e no Caribe was launched to stimulate Brazilian investment in Central America and benefit from CAFTA. Long-term investment guarantee schemes also exist in Central and Eastern Europe to cover equity participation, advisory services, and both commercial and non-commercial

---

Box 7.2 The Malaysian South–South Corporation Berhad (MASSCORP)

The Malaysian South–South Corporation Berhad (MASSCORP) was conceived to promote and enhance both trade and investment joint ventures. MASSCORP was incorporated in 1992 following the successful trade mission to Latin America by Malaysia's prime minister, Dato' Seri Dr Mahathir Mohamad, and his entourage of Malaysian business entrepreneurs in 1991. It is a consortium that comprises 85 Malaysian shareholders, most of whom also subscribed to the formation of a business association – the Malaysia South–South Association (MASSA). MASSCORP acts through business forums/ dialogue sessions between MASSA members and visiting Southern Heads of State and their business delegations; fact-finding, trade, and investment missions to Southern countries; and a library of economic information on trade and investment opportunities in Southern countries.

Source: www.masscorp.net.my

risks (Kalotay 2003). Worried that Korean companies have concentrated too many of their overseas subsidiaries in China, Kang and Lee (2004) suggest that the government collect information on issues such as market demand, labor market conditions, custom, and government policies and pass it on to companies that are willing to invest in more distant locations but hesitate because of a lack of reliable information.

In China, governmental measures aimed at facilitating investment abroad are more modest. Exports of equipment, machinery, and raw materials for overseas Chinese firms are exempted from export taxes. Enterprises investing abroad in natural-resource projects can enjoy the same tax incentives and subsidies as domestic producers. More recently, the China Export and Credit Insurance Corporation (Sinosure) – China's first wholly state-owned policy insurer – launched a campaign to promote its investment insurance products covering economic and catastrophic risk to Chinese companies overseas.

7.2   The role of competition policies

Links between OFDI promotion and domestic polices are complex. Policymakers may be justifiably worried about the ability of their countries' corporations to compete in international markets, but they should first and foremost be responsible for preserving and enhancing market competition and preventing the emergence of powerful monopolies. As Wilkins (2004) notes in her history of foreign investment in the United States before 1945, Franklin Roosevelt's administration had decided that illegal international cartel arrangements and the immense patent holdings of large domestic and foreign corporations represented a threat to an American recovery based on rapid technical change. A good deal of the energy of the 1939–41 Temporary National Economic Committee, its hearings, and its reports was focused on these phenomena. This obviously made it increasingly difficult for foreigners to invest in the United States, and the terrain was further altered by the commandeering during World War II of German patent assets, which were made widely available to American corporations for war and postwar production.

In contemporary times, countries have shown different attitudes. South Africa, when it revamped its competition law to attune it to post-Apartheid needs, agreed that a merger that lessens or restricts competition may be defended on public interest grounds. In determining whether a merger can be justified on such grounds, the Competition Tribunal (or Competition Commission, as the case may be) may specifically take into account the ability of national industries to compete in international markets. In the Tongaat-Hulett and Transvaal Suiker case, the tribunal found that the parties were actually "sizeable" enterprises by world standards – one firm was larger than the second-largest European miller and refiner and larger than the third-largest Australian refiner in terms of refining capacity. The smallest of the South African companies was also generally recognized to be the lowest-cost producer in South Africa, by a significant factor. This supported the inference that productive efficiencies had little to do with the size of the firm. The tribunal displayed a general skepticism toward arguments that insisted that a precondition for successful international competition was domination of the domestic market. Although scale economies and rationalization of production units may support this argument in select instances, the tribunal is generally inclined to the view that the most aggressive and successful international competitors are those that face robust competition at home. Similarly, the competition authorities vetoed in February 2006 a plan to merge the liquid fuels business of Sasol, South Africa's largest locally domiciled company and the world's largest producer of synthetic fuel converted from coal and natural gas, with Engen, a subsidiary of Malaysia's Petronas. The merged company, Uhambo Oil, would have controlled about half of South Africa's refining capacity and one-third of the retail market. Two listed health-care groups, Netcare and Medi-Clinic, announced significant foreign acquisitions to create platforms for further international expansion. Netcare is focusing on developed economies, starting with the United Kingdom. Medi-Clinic is moving into the developing markets in the Middle East. Both enjoy good returns, with returns on capital employed of more than 28 percent in 2005, despite persistent government intervention in their domestic market.[5]

Brazilian authorities took an almost diametrically opposed position in 2000 when they cleared the merger between the Antarctica and Brahma breweries to create American Beverages (AmBev). Management presented consolidation as necessary to create "national champions [able] to occupy spaces globally and compete equally in international markets" and argued that "this is what Brazil wants."[6] The authorities accepted the argument that the firms – although they then controlled more than 90 percent of the local market – were small by international standards and that the merger would enhance economies of scale. Whether subsequent evidence supports this stance is not clear. AmBev set itself ambitious goals – to be a Brazilian MNC – and took over Argentina's leading brewery and Uruguay's second-largest one, effectively living up to its corporate name. Some conditions on the merger, combined with more effective competition from domestic rivals, saw AmBev's market share dip to approximately 68 percent in 2003. The success of the strategy to turn Brahma into a global brand remains to be proven.[7] On the one hand, AmBev eventually combined with Belgium's Interbrew in March 2004 to create InBev, the world's largest beer company by volume. The very complex financial link-up saw the controlling shareholders of AmBev (which will have an equal say on the combined company's board for at least 20 years) emerge as the very clear winners.[8] On the other hand, the Brazilians are credited with infusing InBev with a cost-cutting, efficiency-obsessed management culture that is new for the Belgians, who prided themselves on their marketing savvy.[9] In December 2005 a Brazilian manager was appointed as the new chief executive officer (CEO) to replace the Belgian executive who had steered the reverse takeover.

Russian authorities appear well disposed toward the consolidation of different industries and the emergence of domestic monopolies. A dramatic example is the planned combination of RusAl and Sual to create a Russian national champion in aluminum and acquire the aluminum assets of Swiss metal trader Glencore. While all companies are ostensibly private, the Kremlin has actively supported this and similar deals, and the federal anti-monopoly agency does not seem interested in investigating their consequences.

The interplay between the orientation of competition policies and the accumulation of corporate skills and resources is also very apparent in the case of services. On the one hand, a tough regulatory regime may contribute to making companies more efficient and also more willing to invest abroad in order not to assume excessive market power.[10] On the other hand, when companies can accumulate extra profits on the domestic market, they have the necessary funds to invest abroad, possibly with lower hurdles.

Telecommunications is an industry where such factors have come into play. While multi-country operators largely come from countries that reformed early and where privatization and competition forced them to become more efficient, their exposure to competition was still limited as they were generally protected from full market liberalization (Guislain and Qiang 2006). Telmex, Mexico's state-owned monopolist, for instance, was privatized in 1990, but full modernization of the regulatory framework occurred only in 1995–96. According to the OECD (2004), "the regulatory framework that had been put in place presented many deficiencies … local, mobile, long distance and international rates have fallen, but still need to decrease further [and] the overall recent trends show that in spite of recent improvement, Mexico still lags behind in several significant dimensions of market development" (pp. 109–10). This has not impeded América Móvil, the cellular telephone services provider that was spun off from Telmex in 2000 and is also controlled by Carlos Slim Helú, from growing steadily across Latin America as global telecom companies left some national markets.[11]

7.3 The role of international policies

It is well known that cross-border investment activity is not protected by any international regime comparable to those of the World Trade Organization (WTO) for trade. Bilateral investment treaties (BITs) aim to protect and promote foreign investment flows. Double taxation treaties (DTTs) aim to avoid having the same income taxed by two or more states. Preferential trade and investment agreements (PTIAs) – both bilateral and regional in nature – aim to create preferential market access and other forms of economic integration among the signatory states.

South–South investment agreements (SSIAs) have grown rapidly in number, geographical coverage, and policy width (UNCTAD 2004b). In 2004 there were 653 BITs, 312 DTTs, and 49 PTIAs among developing countries. The first BIT between two developing countries was signed in 1964. By 1990, their number had reached 44, and it has more than quadrupled since then to rise to figure of 653 by July 2004, or 28 percent of the 2,300 BITs worldwide. Of these, half have been ratified and have thus entered into force. In total, 113 developing countries have entered into BITs with another developing nation. China, Egypt, and Malaysia have each signed more than 40 such agreements, and have also signed more agreements with other developing countries than with developed countries. Asia accounts for 68 percent of South–South BITs, followed in terms of number by Latin America. As a rule, South–South BITs deal mainly, with investment protection and promotion (i.e., they do not grant free access and establishment, unlike the Western hemisphere BITs), they refrain from explicitly prohibiting performance requirements, and they limit transparency requirements to the stage after the adoption of laws and regulations. Data for nine developing economies that report OFDI stock by destination indicate that as of 2003 roughly 20 percent of South–South FDI stock was covered by South–South BITs in force.[12]

A similar, though less pronounced, trend emerges for South–South DTTs. Since the first-ever such South–South treaty was signed in 1956 between India and Sierra Leone, the number has grown slowly, reaching 96 by 1990. During the 1990s, 172 new DTTs were signed between 73 developing countries. The growth continued through 2006, by which time 312 DTTs had been undertaken between 94 developing countries, and 14 percent of all DTTs were between developing countries.

The first South–South PTIA was signed in 1970 (by seven Arab countries), and the number grew rather slowly in the decade that followed. By 2004, however, the total number of PTIAs among developing countries had risen to 49, and slightly less than one-third of all current PTIAs have been concluded between or among developing countries. Latin America and Asia are the most active regions, with 25 and 14 such agreements, respectively. Some South–South PTIAs are rather modest in content: they simply establish frameworks for promoting FDI and mandates for future cooperation. Other agreements are substantive in nature, and may include development-related provisions on the establishment of an institutional framework, the granting of flexibility through provisions for special and differential treatment, the provision of technical assistance and capacity building, and the promotion of home-country measures.

While South–South BITs do not explicitly mention development aspects in their preambles, some 81 percent of the PTIAs reviewed by UNCTAD refer in one way or another to the development objective set forth in the preamble. Two-thirds of South–South PTIAs include institutional set-ups that allow for modifications in light of the (developmental and other) experiences that arose out of their application. Some 62 percent of these same agreements contain provisions dealing with technical assistance, either generally or with regard to certain subject areas.

Some regions also have cooperation schemes that aim to establish regional enterprises by promoting joint ventures (Te Velde and Bezemer 2004). The ASEAN Industrial Cooperation Scheme assisted more than 100 projects through special tax and tariff incentives. The ASEAN secretariat has also begun various activities in the area of investment facilitation, by providing information through portals, databases, publications, and statistics. The Andean Community has promoted regional MNCs (*empresas multinacionales andinas*, EMAs) through Decision 292, which introduces freedom of profits transfer, avoids double taxation, grants employment advantages through national treatment of Andean expatriates, and extends national treatment to EMAs, including for purposes of public procurement and investment incentives.

Another example of regional cooperation is the Islamic Corporation for the Insurance of Investment and Export (ICIIE), a subsidiary of the Islamic Development Bank, which provides insurance facilities in accordance with the principles of sharia. Owing to its cooperation with the

Table 7.2 EMNCs' participation in the MIGA portfolio (June 2005)

Country	Total	%	Number of Contracts	Number of Countries	Number of Companies
South Africa	248,170,229	4.67	16	6	6[a]
Egypt	78,981,154	1.49	1	1	1
Singapore	73,700,000	1.39	6	4	3
Mauritius	58,141,939	1.09	6	3	4
Tunisia	31,052,407	0.58	3	1	1
Czech Republic	24,548,950	0.46	6	1	1[b]
Senegal	23,409,478	0.44	2	1	1
Slovenia	22,371,335	0.42	4	3	3
Turkey	6,389,170	0.12	4	2	3
Lebanon	6,300,000	0.12	2	1	1
India	5,150,000	0.10	2	1	2
Costa Rica	1,407,379	0.03	2	1	1
Total	801,244,505	15.09	47	n.a.	n.a.

[a] Barlows Tractor International Limited.
[b] Raiffeisenbank.
n.a. = not available

Multilateral Investment Guarantee Agency (MIGA) of the World Bank, ICIIE had a end-2005 investment insurance applications pipeline of close to US$1 billion. Finally, in the absence of political risk insurance instruments developed by their own countries' institutions, EMNCs can access multilateral ones, although a very minor portion of the MIGA portfolio corresponds to South–South FDI (Table 7.2).

7.4 The political economy of EMNCs

The importance of political factors, as opposed to policies, in determining the geography of international investment and the differential success of firms in foreign markets has long been recognized in the international political economy literature. Susan Strange (1992), in particular, highlighted the fact that the increasing activism of firms in world politics constitutes a major structural change in international relations, with important consequences for state–firm and firm–firm bargaining. She hinted at the emergence of triangular diplomacy: (traditional) state–state diplomacy has been joined by state–firm and firm–firm diplomacy in the international political economy. In addition, she noted how difficult it has become to link MNCs with specific nations, not least as a result of the decreasing centrality of territorial considerations of power. Another dimension that is often overlooked is the possibility that firm-specific political resources may constitute a form of first-mover advantage in international business – especially "in a new market where early entry is restricted by the government or where economic success is influenced by linkages to government officials" (Frynas *et al.* 2006: 21).

Political considerations have traditionally played a key role in driving deals and determining contractual conditions in extraction industries, which account for an important share of OFDI from emerging and developing countries. In countries with important raw material endowments, host governments first welcomed foreign investors, then became increasingly attentive to the question of the division of risks and rewards, and finally exerted pressure for heightened control (Vernon 1970). Western governments have traditionally used a wide variety of means to counter these factors and protect the interests of their MNCs. As Wilkins (1974) notes, in the 1910s "oil and politics became intermixed, US and host nation politics" (pp. 13–14), and American government did everything to defend the interests of its companies, even when they did not fully comply with national regulations.

In the 1970/1980s, "solidarity" was an important motivation for 3WMNCs' South–South investment decisions (Warhurst 1994). Host governments showed a strong preference for MNCs from other developing countries: in Peru and Colombia, for example, the authorities preferred Brazilian firms for deals in copper and coal, respectively, expecting them to be more sympathetic to requests for technical assistance and technological transfer. Sometimes the common technological and developmental challenges faced by developing country producers of similar types of minerals, particularly in neighboring countries, justified these tie-ups. The risk also existed, however, of forfeiting the benefits that Western corporations could possibly provide in terms of superior technology, management, and market access. In fact, Wells (1983) noted that governments may prefer to deal with experienced firms from OECD countries rather than with up-and-coming competitors from poorer countries.

Modern oil companies from emerging economies have been described as "a new breed of second-tier transnationals with business models premised on their comparative advantage in unsavory markets where more socially responsible companies fear to tread" (Pegg 2003: 93). So far, it is the aggressive international search for oil and gas supplies by Chinese companies that has received most attention (see Table 3.2). While more competition on the demand side is welcomed by oil- and gas-producing countries, and may in theory contribute to making the bidding process for exploration and production rights more open, the risk exists that companies that are based in emerging economies may follow looser business practices. Oil revenue flowing into government coffers without appropriate safeguards "has a particularly pernicious effect, encouraging corruption and lack of accountability and fostering systems based on patronage rather than popular representation" (Ottaway 2005: 27). Legal texts such as the OECD Convention on Combating Bribery of Foreign Public Officials in International Business Transactions, stock market disclosure requirements, codes such as the OECD Guidelines for Multinational Enterprises (a revised version of which was issued in 2000), and initiatives such as the British-led Extractive Industries Transparency Initiative and the Publish What You Pay coalition of civil society organizations have combined to increase the transparency of revenue payments in OECD countries – and more broadly for firms listed in OECD financial markets. In a sector where, overall, transparency is still poor, Chinese energy companies sit at the bottom of the table in the company of Petronas and Lukoil (Save the Children 2005).

Moreover, to the extent that they look to markets where competition is less intense to cut deals with regimes that are politically isolated, China's and India's expanding diplomatic and economic involvement with energy-rich countries raises important issues for the West. In Sudan, the China National Petroleum Corporation (CNPC) has emerged as the country's largest foreign investor, reflecting China's diplomatic philosophy, which preaches non-interference in other countries' internal affairs. In April 1999, CNPC planned to make an IPO on the New York Stock Exchange designed to raise US$10 billion, and its support to the Sudanese government came under heavy fire. CNPC had to withdraw the offer and refashion it because of the negative publicity suggesting that the proceeds would be invested in projects that could lead to human rights abuses.[13] The depth of Chinese interests in Sudan and Beijing's principle of non-interference in the internal affairs of other states have made it hard for the United States to get the humanitarian crisis in Darfur onto the UN Security Council agenda.

In Angola, the 2005 decision to transfer two concessions from Total to Sinopec, another Chinese oil company, was widely thought to reflect the worsening of Franco-Angolan relations caused by prohibited arms sales during the 1990s.[14] China signed a memorandum of understanding with North Korea in December 2005 to explore offshore oil possibilities jointly. Democratic India has also forged close relations with Myanmar's military regime as ONGC Videsh (also present in Sudan and Syria) and IOC-OIL scout for opportunities in offshore and onshore blocks. Myanmar is emerging as a possible critical source of energy for Thailand, too.[15] In January 2005, a meeting of ministers from India,

Bangladesh, and Myanmar in Yangon put forward the idea of a pipeline to India via Bangladesh.

While state ownership per se does not necessarily make enterprises oblivious to the need to ensure high standards of professional management, some governments may be inclined to pressure SOEs into acting as foreign policy instruments. The case of PDVSA is particularly interesting insofar as this firm has long been a leading EMNC. Its international strategy has changed over the past two decades, partly reflecting changes in the relationship between the company and the Venezuelan government (Box 7.3).[16] On a more positive note, 30 years of economic partnership through foreign investment by state-owned KPC in neighboring countries as well as the developed West proved crucial when Kuwait was invaded by Iraq in 1990. According to Tétreault (1997), "the success of the Kuwaiti appeal [to provide military forces to fight the occupation] depended on the unique access that Kuwait had to decision-makers in key host countries" (p. 381).

> *Box 7.3* Economic diplomacy and corporate internationalization: the case of Venezuela
>
> Petróleos de Venezuela (PDVSA) was created in 1976, when the government nationalized the oil industry. With US$46 billion in revenues and US$3.8 billion in profits in 2003, it is South America's largest company and the seventh-largest from a developing country, accounting for a third of Venezuela's GDP, 80 percent of its export income, and half of the government's revenues. The United States consumes approximately 1.5 million barrels of Venezuelan oil a day, out of 2.6 million the country produces.
>
> The project to turn PDVSA into a world-class major through international investments was first aired in the early 1980s, as a means to diminish the volatility in the demand for Venezuelan extra-heavy crude and secure a long-term downstream outlet. The idea was shelved as world prices recovered, but became a priority again around 1983. That year, building on an existing cooperation, PDVSA and Germany's Veba Oel established a joint venture that in 1988 absorbed almost a third of Venezuelan oil exports. On top of access to Europe's largest market, Veba contributed its cracking technology to refine high-sulfur crude. Later in the decade, additional joint ventures were concluded with Sweden's Nynäs Petroleum and in the United States (50 percent of Citgo and of the Champlin refinery, both later to be turned into wholly owned subsidiaries). Citgo, based in Tulsa, is the fifth-largest US gasoline producer, with eight refineries, one of the largest gasoline distributors (13,000 stations), and the largest asphalt producer on the East Coast. It normally gets only half of its raw crude (about 400,000 barrels a day) from PDVSA. All in all, PDVSA has a shareholding (or, in a single case, leaseholding) participation in 19 refineries located outside Venezuela with refining capacity close to 2 million barrels per day.

PDVSA has long had a reputation for being one of the country's most meritocratic institutions. Its foreign-trained executives stayed aloof from politics, and politicians were loath to meddle in the company's affairs for fear of ruining Venezuela's money machine. Since his election, President Hugo Chávez – who often talks of uniting South America economically and politically – has been trying to wrest control of PDVSA from the technocrats, increasing the amount the company has to turn over to the government by 30 percent with a view to using the cash for social programs. State ownership was enshrined in the 1999 Constitution and legislation prohibiting private control of joint ventures for oil exploitation was passed in November 2001. Alí Rodríguez, a former secretary general of the Organization of the Petroleum Exporting Countries (OPEC), was put at the PDVSA helm in 2002 to mend the fractured company after an oil strike led to a coup that ousted Chávez for two days. A close relative (Asdrúbal Chávez) was appointed as director of the PDVSA Comercialización y Suministros division. Government loyalists have also been put in charge of Citgo, replacing American executives.

The Venezuelan president is also promoting a plan to integrate South America's oil and gas companies under his country's leadership as a way of joining regional energy suppliers and consumers to provide energy more cheaply and more efficiently, bolster the region's influence in energy, and counter Washington's influence in the oil industry. Under a 2001 accord that sweetened a deal Venezuela already had with Central American and Caribbean countries, Venezuela offers approximately 30,000 barrels more a day at bargain-basement credit rates. The country also provides fuel oil to Argentina in a complex barter exchange and has offered assistance to Bolivia as it embarks on a plan to strengthen its state-owned energy company. In June 2004 Venezuela and the 13 small, scattered countries in the Caribbean agreed to start up a regional energy company, PetroCaribe, that would receive Venezuelan oil under preferential terms. The plan's cornerstone, to create a transnational oil company for South America called PetroAmérica, has merit, but it is technically challenging and faces a host of bureaucratic and practical hurdles.

The future of Citgo is also being debated. Critics have long highlighted the fact that PDVSA allowed its affiliates in the Dutch Antilles to retain for reinvestment purposes practically all the cash flows generated by their operations and questioned the logic of this dividend policy. In effect, PDVSA could have taken advantage of the double taxation treaties between the countries where its refineries were located (chiefly the United States) and the Netherlands, on the one hand, and the Netherlands and its Caribbean dependencies, on the other, to avoid the payment of withholding taxes on repatriated dividends. In February 2005 Chávez said he planned to sell Citgo because it was in effect contributing tax (US$348 million in 2004) to the US government rather than to Venezuela, and in April the decision was taken to put on sale two Citgo refineries.

A third dimension of geographical diversification – away from Venezuela in the case of exploration and production, away from the United States in the case of final markets – is closer partnering with China. Part of China's effort (it already operates two oil fields in Venezuela) is to learn about the workings of heavy oil refineries. Much of the oil that will be exploited in the future will be tarlike, requiring an intricate and expensive refining process. The two countries signed accords in Beijing in December 2004 and Caracas in January 2005 to develop 15 declining oil fields in Zumano in eastern Venezuela and participate in much larger projects. In return, China is offering a US$700 million line of credit to build housing. Even more ambitious plans are being explored to rebuild a Panamanian pipeline to pump crude oil to the Pacific, where it would be loaded onto supertankers that are too big to use the Panama Canal. Another proposal would lead to the construction of a pipeline to carry Venezuelan hydrocarbons across Colombia and then ship them to Asia. Venezuela and India will also start a pilot project on heavy oil exploration in Rajasthan, where the Jaisalmer-Bikaner basin reportedly contains approximately 14.6 million tonnes of heavy oil reserves and 33.2 million tonnes of bitumen.

Sources: "PDVSA is stepping on the gas with Citgo," *Business Week*, March 11, 1996; "Venezuela pushes to lead regional oil economy," *The New York Times*, August 13, 2004; "Chávez to sell US arm of state oil company," *Financial Times*, February 3, 2005; "China's oil diplomacy in Latin America," *The New York Times*, March 1, 2005; "Venezuela venderá dos refinerías de Citgo," *El Universal*, April 18, 2005; "Venezuela, India to begin project on heavy oil exploration," *The Hindu Business Journal*, April 18, 2005; "The troubled oil company," *The New York Times*, April 20, 2005; Baena (2002); Boué (2002, 2004).

A slightly different case is that of South African parastatals, in particular Eskom Enterprise, which are expanding into the rest of Africa to further Pretoria's objective of regional integration in infrastructure. While there is an economic logic in this insofar as the "African Renaissance" would first and foremost profit South African companies, most of Eskom Enterprise's acquisitions are yet to come to fruition. The Africa Economic Development Strategy of the Department of Trade and Industry notes that "despite the current increased levels of South African investments in the continent, from a government perspective, those positive trends and interventions towards contributing to intra-Africa trade and economic development have been ad hoc and fragmented to a large extent, hence the need to develop a seamless and cohesive strategy" DPE (2006). The Continental Investments Project aims to develop an overarching strategy and a coordinated approach for SOE investments on the continent, taking full account of differences in risk profiles, limited funding mechanisms, and risk mitigation measures for infrastructure investments associated with investing on the continent, as opposed to domestic investments (DPE 2006).

Many governments and observers, especially in OECD countries, consider the political nature of SOE behavior a distortion of good business practices. In practice, however, the dynamic interdependence of economics and politics is very complex. Two examples from China suggest that simplistic stereotypes that paint firms as instruments of unethical governments simply fail to shed light on the reality of international business. In connection with the bid to win exploration rights in Angola, China's Eximbank offered a US$2 billion soft loan (1.5 percent over 17 years) as part of a longer-term aid package. In December 2004, a British transparency watchdog, Global Witness, announced that the money was in danger of being diverted to other uses. Only hours after a high-level Chinese delegation visited Luanda, Angola's president sacked Antonio Pereira Mendes de Campos Van Dunem from his post as secretary of the Angolan council of ministers – too striking to be a complete coincidence. In the case of Unocal, Chevron and CNOOC traded accusations of protectionism at the same time as they continued to collaborate on deals in other countries (Goldstein 2006b).

Moreover, while political support may be useful in some circumstances, the perception that a firm is under the control of a foreign government may also hinder the possibility of foreign expansion. In India, the chairman of ONGC, which is 70 percent owned by the state, threatened to resign amid attempts by the Minister for Petroleum to meddle in company affairs. The minister proposed appointing the Director General of Hydrocarbons, effectively the industry's regulator, to the board, and when ONCG lost the PetroKazakhstan auction to CNPC he publicly slammed the bank that was advising the Canadian company for "mov[ing] the goalpost while the bidding process was on."[17]

Finally, there are many examples to suggest that Southern investors are not immune to the dangers that are almost synonymous with emerging markets (Box 7.4; Appendix 2). Danger refers here to the high risk that business activity will be hampered by the lack of a legal system capable of passing and enforcing good laws, no less than by poor transport links and unreliable water and energy supplies. While certain modes of strategic governance may be appropriate in EMNCs' home countries, the different configurations of political, social, and institutional relationships that prevail in other emerging economies may easily turn out to be hostile, notwithstanding *prima facie* commonalities in the business systems (Yeung 2004). Moreover, although outright expropriation of foreigners' assets has receded as a risk, nationalist opposition to the sale of state assets to foreigners is another concern (Wells 1998). In India, the signing of the giant Posco steel deal in 2005, which is

Box 7.4 Cemex in Indonesia

In 1998 Cemex bought 14 percent of East Java-based Semen Gresik, Indonesia's largest cement producer, for US$115 million, with an option to increase its stake to 51 percent by the end of 2001, as part of an IMF-backed privatization program. Cemex later built its stake up further to 25 percent by buying shares on the open market and in late 2001 agreed with the government to acquire an additional 51 percent stake. Nationalist opposition developed quickly, prompting the government to propose selling Gresik but using the proceeds to buy back the Padang and Tonasa units in the provinces of West Sumatra and South Sulawesi. The dispute could not be solved, however, and the government asked Cemex to remain patient and continue negotiating. In frustration, in December 2003 Cemex filed a request for arbitration before the International Centre for Settlement of Investment Disputes (ICSID).

The new government of President Susilo Bambang Yudhoyono, reputedly willing to solve high-profile disputes with foreign investors as soon as possible as part of its plans to woo them, engaged in talks about a possible out-of-court settlement after taking office in October 2004. A deal was allegedly discussed in January 2005 to create a new Cemex-controlled joint venture that would take control of Gresik's production facilities in Tuban. Proceeds from the transaction would fund the building of a new cement plant by Gresik, which would also have an ownership stake in the new entity. However, negotiations broke down as the deal did not address key details such as how much Cemex would pay for the new facilities.

As most other cement plants in the country are controlled by foreign companies, including France's Lafarge, Germany's Heidelberg, and Switzerland's Holcim, Vice President Jusuf Kalla said that the government wanted local investors to acquire Cemex's 24.9 percent stake on the grounds that cement is a strategic industry. In May 2006 Cemex announced it had decided to sell for US$337 million to Rajawali, a local diversified business group founded by Peter Sondakh, the 19th-largest debtor of the Indonesia Bank Restructuring Agency (IBRA). To become effective, the deal must be approved by the government as the majority shareholder. Jakarta told Cemex it wanted to buy back its shares via a consortium of state pension funds and other government-controlled companies. The high-profile affair is being closely followed by the media amid rumors that people in high places are backing other investors to gain control of the Cemex stake.

Sources: "Govt fears Cemex may back down out of Semen Gresik purchase," *The Jakarta Post*, December 7, 2001; "Jakarta adds new twist in Cemex row," *Financial Times*, May 18, 2006; "Govt delays decision on Cemex-Rajawali share deal," *The Jakarta Post*, May 19, 2006.

expected to create 13,000 jobs directly, was delayed by the rise of "resources nationalism." Opponents were angered by the prospect of India losing the benefit of domestic beneficiation of iron ore. Peruvian presidential candidate Ollanta Humala in 2006 has stated his opposition to further Chilean investments and ruled out opening the ports business in Peru to companies from the neighboring country.

Host governments may find investors from small economies, which do not enjoy the luxury of a large captive market, less threatening than competitors from a larger country. Pangarkar (2004), for instance, mentions the case of Sri Lanka, where companies from Hong Kong were warmly welcomed, whereas those from India faced hostility. But, as two examples from similarly small city-states show, this remains a hypothesis, or rather something that may hold only in certain circumstances. In the case of Temasek, state ownership proved a major hindrance. SingTel's takeover attempts in Hong Kong and Malaysia, for instance, were turned down largely for that reason, as was PSA's ambition to buy into Hong Kong's port. Moreover, an ST Multimedia joint bid with Telekom Malaysia for a 48 percent stake in India's fifth-largest mobile operator was rejected by Indian regulators because ST already has a 28 percent stake in Bharti TeleVentures. In March 2006, Thai protesters, demanding the resignation of then prime minister Thaksin Shinawatra, targeted Singapore after Temasek paid US$3.7 billion for Shin Corp, Thaksin's telecommunications and media firm. What caused outrage was not only that Thaksin legally paid no tax on his capital gains, but also that a foreign company would now own a significant stake in the Thai telecom infrastructure. The affair played a not insignificant role in the decision by the Thai military to remove Thaksin from power in September 2007 (Goldstein and Pavida 2007). DP World met with opposition to the acquisition of P&O not only in the United States but also in India's Gujarat state, whose Hindu nationalist ruling party has a record of hostility to Muslims.[18] Hutchinson Port Holdings, the world's largest independent port operator, which is controlled by Hong Kong billionaire Li Ka-shing, was rebuffed twice in India on security concerns.[19]

Importantly, some of these episodes and associated risks resulted from clashes between foreign firms and domestic competitors, rather than between foreign firms and the host government (Wells 1998). Mongolian business, for instance, maintains an ambivalent attitude toward Chinese investors.[20] In one corner stand the obvious complementarities between a cash-rich country, hungry for natural resources, and a poor landlocked one that desperately needs investments in infrastructure and a diversification away from Russian dependence. In the other corner linger Mongolian cashmere producers' suspicions that Chinese factories, already larger and more efficient, are cornering the supply of raw feedstock by buying directly from herders in Mongolia itself.

The political goals that may motivate foreign investors cause a second set of inconveniences. These predicaments are commonest in natural resources, and developing countries' populaces may harbor particular hostility toward investors from neighboring countries. In the Baltic region, Russian oil and gas majors have acted as "patriots," executing the country's foreign policy through their overseas operations, and this has invariably provoked suspicions in host economies (Vahtra and Liuhto 2004). In Lithuania, where Yukos held a 54 percent stake and management rights in the Baltic state's only refinery (Mazeikiu Nafta), the *de facto* nationalization of Yukos by the Russian government raised fears that the plant might be at the mercy of the Russian pipeline monopoly, Transneft.[21] In Montenegro, the interest of RusAl in buying the KAP aluminum plant, which accounts for 80 percent of national exports, sparked fears that the latter's future might ultimately be decided by the Russian state. Podgorica had tried hard to court Western investors, without success, and inserted tough break-up clauses in the privatization contract, holding RusAl to high operational and financial standards.[22] In Thailand, Chinese state investors' interest in buying the largest integrated petrochemical company in Southeast Asia has met government resistance.[23] The prospect of gas exports – principally to India – has also been a sensitive political issue in Bangladesh. Bangladesh has proven reserves of 64 million tons of high-quality coal at Barapukuria, 450 km (280 miles) north of Dhaka. Tata announced a major investment that would add value to the country's natural gas and create jobs, but major opposition parties have said they will resist any move to sell gas without ensuring reserves to meet domestic needs for 50 years. Donors believe Bangladesh should export gas to generate funds for development, while the international oil companies said they could not produce gas as per installed capacities because of poor local demand.[24] As the example of Petrobrás's involvement in the Bolivian gas industry suggests (Box 7.5), expectations that bending over backward *vis-à-vis* host governments will guarantee smooth operations for EMNCs may evaporate rapidly. On a more general level, governments and firms may not equally master the intricacies of economic and business diplomacy. While Petrobrás was expecting the nationalization and had already prepared the response (no new investments) even before the Bolivian president made the announcement, there was probably a lack of communication among the Planalto (the Brazilian presidency), Itamaraty (the Brazilian foreign ministry), and Petrobrás in the days leading up to this.[25]

Box 7.5 Petrobrás in Bolivia

The opening of Bolivia's oil and gas sector to foreign investment in the 1990s was initially highly successful. The 1996 "capitalization" law brought over US$3.5 billion in foreign capital, with 12 companies exploiting 76 contracts and boosting proved and probable natural gas reserves from less than 227 billion in 1997 to 1.5 trillion at the end of 2004. Foreign investors saw the country as the upstream hub of a huge integrated gas market, covering Argentina, Chile, Uruguay, and southern Brazil, as well as feeding LNG export plants. In recent years, however, mounting popular opposition to its exporting to Chile – President Gonzalo Sánchez de Lozada was forced out in 2003 after protests left 56 dead – has slowed down exploration and production spending, from US$605 million in 1998 to US$190 million in 2004, or what is thought to be the minimum required to maintain production at contractual levels.

A new hydrocarbons bill has been the focus of widespread social and political unrest and prompted two resignation threats from President Carlos Mesa. The turning point was the July 2004 referendum that decided to raise duties and exploration levies to up to 50 percent of production values. The implementing bill put forward by the opposition parties would introduce a non-deductible tax at the wellhead (Impuesto Directo a los Hidrocarburos, IDH) of 32 percent on new oil fields, on top of existing royalties of 18 percent. In May 2005 the Senate gave its approval to the draft law. The bill also enhances the status of YPFB, the state-owned oil company, which was largely reduced to the role of a regulator under the 1996 law. YPFB may even recover some of its former upstream assets if provisions in the law calling for the renationalization of certain assets now in private sector hands are not reversed. The Cámara Boliviana de Hidrocarburos, which represents foreign investors, is threatening to scale back investment plans, arguing that this is a covered-up 50 percent royalty that would in effect confiscate investments.

Petrobrás is the biggest investor in Bolivian oil and gas: US$1.5 billion since 1996. Its partners have poured in a further US$2 billion to build a gas-chemical plant and the Puerto Suárez thermoelectric plants and to extend the pipeline to Argentina. Petrobrás has also been planning a 20 percent increase in the capacity of the 3,150 km Gasbol Bolivia-to-Brazil gas pipeline as part of its plan to meet the expected doubling of demand in Brazil by 2010. Once the political situation started to worsen, the company initially took a rather conciliatory stance. In late 2004, when RepsolYPF, British Gas, and BP first warned that they would sue the government if their contracts were not respected, Petrobrás announced its intention to remain in the country no matter what. In March 2005, however, Brazil's energy minister said that charging an excessive level of royalties would have consequences for the possibility of an expansion in Petrobrás's investments. Nevertheless, Petrobrás's president José Eduardo Dutra affirmed that the political situation was "not at all alarming" and posed no threat to the company's activities in Bolivia.

Bolivia's new president, Evo Morales, took over in January 2006 and soon started a rapprochement with Venezuela's Chávez that caused increasing concern in the West as well as in Brazil. On May 1, 2006, Morales declared a

> nationalization of the oil and gas fields, backed by Bolivian army troops. Foreign companies that did not transfer control of gas fields to YPFB and sign new contracts with the government within 180 days had to leave Bolivia. Although YPFB's president said compensation would be paid, perhaps in natural gas instead of cash, according to Morales there was no need to pay companies because they had already recovered their investments and had earned a significant profit from the fields. Petrobrás scrapped US$5 billion investment plans announced in February 2006 and threatened to seek international arbitration over the nationalization, but was eventually convinced by Brazilian energy chiefs formally to accept the decree and let the government start thrashing out new contracts with Bolivian officials. However, there have also been expressions of discontent within Lula's administration, in particular on the part of Foreign Minister Celso Amorim.
>
> *Sources*: "Les Européens sont 'très préoccupés'," *Le Monde*, October 7, 2004; "Petrobrás amenaza con no invertir más en Bolivia," *La Prensa*, March 24, 2005; "Risky business," *Petroleum Economist*, May 2005; "Oil companies not entitled to payment, Bolivia says," *New York Times*, May 12, 2006; Guedes and Faria (2003).

Finally, investors from emerging economies may suffer the consequences of political upheavals just as much as competing corporations from industrial countries. In the late 1990s, a number of Mauritian firms invested in neighboring Madagascar (in particular) and Mozambique. Much of the FDI was vertical in nature, the objective being to take advantage of very cheap labor available in those countries. To that end, the most low-skill labor-intensive processes were moved to Madagascar. This factor was strong enough to offset the negative consequences of an unfriendly investment environment, creeping political instability, the lack of rule of law, and poor institutional quality. However, following the political crisis in 2002, all of the firms closed down. It is only now, with the return of political stability, that some are considering returning there, although quite a few developed such an utter distaste for Madagascar that they will never again consider investing there.[26]

Moreover, home governments may react with hostility to the emergence of their own MNCs. This is far more than a theoretical possibility, as shown in Central and Eastern Europe, where most transition governments perceived OFDI as "unpatriotic" (Svetličič and Rojec 2003). On the other hand, to the extent that they worry about domestic business becoming too powerful, and therefore less amenable to political pressure, home governments may push firms overseas – with the possible unintended consequences of decreasing their own leverage. Orascom

Construction Industries invested in Algeria following the Egyptian government's refusal to buy a local cement factory on confused legal grounds that were interpreted as an attempt to rein in the increasing political independence of the Sawiris family (Goldstein and Perrin 2006).

8
Some Key Questions

Summary

Diaspora business communities play a key role in emerging multinationals' decisions to invest overseas, as well as in the modalities and location of their expansion. While the presence of an expatriate community may help companies weather foreign markets, multinational expansion still demands superior management skills and access to financial markets. The impact of emerging investors on the host economies is another issue that remains insufficiently analyzed.

8.1 The role of diaspora entrepreneurship in homeland FDI

Most existing theories of economic development ignore the dynamic role of interfirm interactions and, instead, stress state policies and macroeconomic forces as the decisive factors creating a country's industrial structure. This is inadequate insofar as mesoeconomic factors play such an evident role in creating the incentives that drive economic development, in decreasing the risk levels of international business, and in minimizing the liability of foreignness. The roles of government actions and "investment diplomacy" were analyzed in the previous chapter. At the non-government level, a parallel contributing factor to South–South FDI flows comprises ethnic ties, kinship, and the role of diasporas in homeland FDI. For individual firms and managers, the information costs of plunging into hitherto-unknown markets are very high and the possibility of resorting to trusted sources of information and social capital may therefore make all the difference between investing or not.

The extensive interpenetration of capital flows and business networks has received considerable attention in the literature, especially in the context of trading centers' specialization in matching buyers and sellers in different markets. Feenstra and Hanson (2004), for example, examine the role played by Chinese business communities ("bamboo networks") in East and Southeast Asia in the intermediation of a substantial fraction of trade between Asia and the rest of the world. Through their cross-border investments and global trade networks, these business communities have also facilitated the re-incorporation of mainland China and India into the global economy. In trade, expatriates command specific advantages over domestic producers because of superior knowledge of foreign markets and technology; they also score higher than foreign companies in their knowledge of local languages, adherence to shared values and norms of social behavior, and possible familiarity with the problems of managing low-wage unskilled labor.[1] Immigrants may also use their connections and superior market intelligence to exploit trade opportunities that non-immigrants ignore. A link between immigration, imports, and exports has been found by a number of papers that use the gravity equation to analyze bilateral trade patterns. Wagner *et al.* (2002) estimate immigrant effects for Canada using inter-province variation in international trade and immigration patterns, to find that the average new immigrant expands exports to his/her native country by Can$312 and expands imports by Can$944. Kugler and Rapoport (2005) show that through the formation of business networks, bilateral labor inflows and capital outflows can be characterized by contemporaneous substitutability and dynamic complementarities.[2]

In investment, Western MNCs cannot use hiring to internalize expatriates' specific skills, which are unobservable and non-contractible, while corporations that share ethnic ties can overcome this (Guha and Ray 2000).[3] Slightly modifying the OLI framework, Chen and Ku (2002) further argue that, in the presence of market imperfections, ethnic ties may provide privileged access to location-specific advantages that in turn reinforce the competitive position of EMNCs *vis-à-vis* other firms based in third-party countries. One illustration (out of many) is provided by the 1995 offer by Thai-Chinese businessman Albert Cheok to buy 38 percent of Philippine Airlines (PAL). Cheok, who had a close connection to Bangkok Bank, owned by the Thai-Chinese Sophonpanich family, was asked to make the offer by PAL chairman Lucio Tan, who controlled the rest of the carrier's shares. Tan, himself of Chinese origin, had at first asked Bangkok Bank to submit the offer.[4] On the basis of a gravity model of bilateral FDI, Gao (2005a, b) finds that cultural ties with Hong Kong, Taiwan, and Singapore alone are responsible for 60 percent of total FDI into China.[5] Empirical analysis also shows that in the early stages of South Korean

FDI, firms targeted areas with large populations of emigrant Koreans in the United States, Northeast China, and Central Europe.

The fact that EMNCs often enter foreign markets at an early stage in their lifecycle, possibly before they have accumulated improved and internally derived technological capabilities, suggests that the internationalization process is not incremental but rather driven by networking capabilities – the ability to draw from the complementary resources of different partners and to turn them to the firm's benefit (Pavida 2001). The rapid pre-1997 growth and international expansion of two nascent Thai multinationals, CP (see Box 6.3) and Siam Cement, was led by industry-specific factors, such as scale and scope economies, as much as by their networking capabilities. Three types of network relationships that were crucial to both these firms' domestic and international development were the ability to draw on the financial resources of different partners, links with foreign technology partners, and political connections. The practice of drawing on both technological and networking capabilities continued in their international expansion activities, thereby accelerating their diversification.

The Asian economic crisis, moreover, seriously undermined the social and institutional foundations of Chinese business communities in Southeast Asia. Confronted with increased hostility – when not outright riots as in the case of Indonesia – Chinese business communities increasingly recognize the limitations to their "home country"-based accumulation strategies and turn to globalization as an alternative growth strategy (Chua 2003). It must also be borne in mind that for many overseas Chinese business firms international diversification, *in primis* on the mainland but also to other locations such as Australia or Canada, was made necessary by the fact that in their home country new business opportunities were denied by state regulations of different kinds. For instance, according to Digal and Goldstein (forthcoming), the Sy Group invested in China to counter the restrictions of the Philippines' 1954 Retail Trade Nationalization Law, which protects Pinoy business. The emergence of Chinese business communities in Southeast Asia cannot therefore be solely conceived as an indigenous evolutionary process of social and institutional change. Outside forces obviously play a key role. In the above-mentioned Thai cases, the strategy of replacing internal sources of corporate capability with powerful networking skills worked well in booming regional markets, but proved unsustainable in the long term.

The case of India is different, insofar as many members of the diaspora have built large, diversified conglomerates in host countries in the developed world, *de facto* severing business (although often not personal and social) ties with India. The three Hinduja brothers, for instance, have created a multi-billion-dollar international business trading empire with interests in communications and media, automobiles, financial services, oil and lubricants, and pharmaceuticals. Not only do their headquarters remain in London – where they have made large donations to the Victoria and Albert Museum and the Prince's Youth Trust – but their Indian investments are limited to IN CableNet, a multi-systems operator.[6] Prominent Indian companies established by non-resident Indians include Jet Airways and Zee Television, but the financers behind these deals reside in the West. The Comcraft Group, owned by the Chandaria and Shah families of Kenya, represents a different case. With business interests in steel, aluminum and non-ferrous metals, plastics, chemicals, engineering, electronics, and industrial components, in India it owns Steelco Gujarat, makers of paper-thin steel, and Dexcel Electronics Designs in Bangalore. CEO Manu Chandaria is a member of the advisory board of the Federation of Indian Chambers of Commerce and Industries, which is overseeing an action plan to bring about a tenfold increase in FDI inflow from the Indian diaspora to US$5 billion by 2008. Sino-Mauritian firms have also started to invest in the mainland (Bräutigam 2005).

Italy also hosts considerable investments by Argentinean companies established by Italian emigrants in the late 1940s. The case of Techint is described in Box 8.1. The second example is Carlos Bulgheroni, whose Bridas oil company gained its share of world fame when it planned to build a controversial pipeline from Taliban Afghanistan to Pakistan.[7] Bulgheroni bought Torno, one of Italy's largest contractors, and then merged it with Fiat Engineering. Another group is Aeropuertos Argentinos, which runs 33 airports across South America and is controlled by Argentinean-Armenian businessman Eduardo Eurnekian. In December 2001, Aeropuertos Argentinos took control of Yerevan's Zvartnots international airport, and Eurnekian recently told President Robert Kocharian of his intention to invest heavily in Armenia's agriculture.[8]

Although on a smaller scale, diaspora investors can be found in other countries as well. The Mohammed International Development Research & Organization Companies (MIDROC) is Ethiopia's largest private investor. It groups the extensive and multifaceted business interests of Sheik Mohammed Hussein Al-Amoudi, born in a town located some 400 km north of Addis Ababa to an Ethiopian mother and a Saudi Arabian father. The sheik started business as a young man in Saudi Arabia, and in Ethiopia alone MIDROC has investments covering all sectors of the economy and employing around 15,000 people. Gulzar

> *Box 8.1* Ethnic ties and FDI: the case of Techint
>
> Techint, Argentina's largest conglomerate following the absorption of oil company YPF by Spain's Repsol, was established by Agostino Rocca, one of the fathers of Italy's steel industry, in 1945 with support from a number of well-off Milanese families. At the time Italy had barely emerged from World War II, while Argentina was still flourishing. Huge investments in R&D and other assets allowed the Siderca subsidiary to become the world's leading producer of seamless pipes. Prompted by increased competition, the company pioneered an integrated service in the steel tube industry that included installing the tubes in customers' oil wells and charging only for non-defective tubes after installation (tubes represent 15 percent of the total cost of an oil well). On the basis of the successful response to this new customer service strategy, it pursued it even further and was the first company to offer its customers the option to manage their tube inventory. CEO Roberto Rocca received the 1999 Willy Korf Award, the global steel industry's most prestigious. Its first investments abroad took place very early in the company's history, between 1947 (Brazil) and 1952–54 (Mexico), and by 1997 foreign subsidiaries accounted for 50.5 percent of its assets and 56.9 percent of its staff. In 2002 flat-steel subsidiaries Tamsa (Mexico), Dalmine (Italy), NKK (Japan), Algoma (Canada), Confab (Brazil), and Tavsa (Venezuela) merged to create Tenaris.
>
> This emphasis on dynamic capabilities notwithstanding, the group also diversified into other businesses, both to reduce its vulnerability to demand shocks and to leverage its networking and project-execution capacities across different sectors. In particular, Techint took advantage of its origins to enter into a number of joint ventures with Italian corporations that invested in Argentine privatizations in the early 1990s. Drawing on this experience in restructuring state assets and managing services as varied as railways, toll highways, telecommunications, gas transportation, and distribution, Techint expanded aggressively in Italy in the second half of the 1990s. It bought glass maker SIV from the state jointly with Britain's Pilkington, took over state-owned steel maker Dalmine, and ventured into private hospitals management. The group has more than 5,000 employees in Italy and maintains two headquarters, in Buenos Aires and Milan.
>
> *Source*: Goldstein and Toulan (2006).

International, a Dubai company set up by an Afghan refugee, is constructing a US$25 million Coca-Cola bottling company in Kabul, the first big-ticket investment by the diaspora since the end of the Taliban regime.[9] In Lebanon, the late Rafiq Hariri – who was prime minister in 2000–03 – made major investments through the Saudi Oger Group, which he bought in the early 1970s. Two groups founded by members of the diaspora in Ivory Coast (Mustapha Khalil's Eurofind and Najib Zahr's Africof) have also invested since the country achieved political and economic stability in the late 1990s. Africof is also active in neighboring countries where the Lebanese community has a strong presence, in particular in Guinea, where it jointly owns Banque Islamique de Guinée. Zouk, a Brazilian chain of "love motels" set up by Galician migrants, opened its first property in Madrid in 2004.[10]

In the zoology of international business, yet another species is exemplified by Hong Kong's Jardine Matheson, constantly ranked among the largest EMNCs, which can be best described as an expatriate MNC.[11] Founded by William Jardine and James Matheson as a commission business in 1832, it is the biggest of the British-owned *hongs*. Jardine Matheson owed its success to the strategic decision to eschew speculation and concentrate on building a pattern of relationships within and outside the business that would foster the flow of information, the knowledge with which to interpret it, the ability to influence others, and a reputation for probity that would attract and retain trading partners (Matheson Connell 2003). The British-based Keswick family, descendants of the firm's opium-trading founders, remain Jardine's principal shareholders.[12] In 1984 the *hong* moved its legal domicile to Bermuda, and in the 1990s it shifted its stock market listings out of Hong Kong to London and Singapore.

8.2 The challenge of multinational management

First-generation EMNCs were for the most part either family- or state-owned firms. Although in the latter there were some cases of crass political interference, by and large the managerial skills that had proven adequate to lead the process of import-substitution industrialization in the home economies were also adequate to manage the still modest set of resources deployed in foreign-based operations. Foreign subsidiaries of firms from developing countries paid managers strikingly low salaries, and additional savings were made by posting them without their families and housing them in modest offices and residences (Wells 1983: 32–34).

Nowadays, on the global stage, this situation no longer holds true. The complexity of managing far-flung, multi-plant, and multi-product operations is much greater than in the past. A growing number of managers are being sent on overseas assignments to transfer know-how from headquarters to subsidiaries abroad, compensate for a shortage of qualified local personnel in a given host country, standardize routines across organizational units, and create shared values. In addition, competitive pressures of various kinds oblige MNCs to have a multinational workforce, capable of balancing the often conflicting imperatives of globalization and local embeddedness. Human resource strategies such as targeted and rigorous recruitment and selection procedures, performance-contingent incentive compensation schemes, lifelong workforce development, and flexible benefits and training activities are necessary to compete, and, to the extent that they are successfully tailored to align with companies' characteristics and strategic goals, they can become inimitable resources (Chew and Horwitz 2004).

Challenges come in different forms. EMNCs may find it difficult to recruit capable and competent middle management and to offer staff career paths that are comparable to those of their OECD-based competitors. Even in developing countries, foreign MNCs are very often the preferred career choice for the best graduates, and for domestic business to find capable middle managers is often complex. To compound this, foreign investors in many developing countries complain that recruiting and retaining workers, particularly skilled ones, is raising the cost of doing business.[13] Moreover, the persistence of family ownership means that out-of-the-family managers still face a glass ceiling in their career. The US operations of Wanxiang, one of China's rising producers of auto components, are headed by the founder's son-in-law Pin Ni. Many second-generation tycoons, even those who have been educated in the West's most prestigious business and engineering schools, may share with their forefathers a proclivity to work hard and resistance to delegate, characteristics that may not bode well for efficient management of geographically spread businesses.

Even when EMNCs might *prima facie* benefit from cultural and ethnic proximity, they may fail not only because doing business abroad is generally difficult, but also because of the intrinsic limitations of management based on kinship and personal relationship. To maintain a minimum level of coordination even when decision makers are not located in the same place, international expansion often requires high degrees of socialization based on implicit values and mores. For established MNCs operating in developing countries, employing an expatriate manager is usually far more expensive than recruiting a local manager – *a fortiori* when due account is taken of indirect costs such as individual and family adjustment problems, difficulties in maintaining satisfying social relationships with local people, poor job performance, and a high rate of premature return. On the other hand, foreign suitors may find it particularly difficult to retain senior management in acquired firms. All such issues played a notoriously important role in Japanese OFDI in the 1970s and 1980s (Black 1990; Nicholson and Imaizumi 1993), although it is too early to quantify their impact on EMNCs' performance.

There is an intuitive agreement that charismatic leadership, investments in aggressive training, and new incentive schemes are common features in companies that expand abroad (Goldstein 2005; Suarez and Oliva 2002). Case studies such as SABMiller (Box 8.2) and Arcor (Kosacoff *et al.* 2001) also suggest that human resources play a key role in building corporate success. Nonetheless, few studies compare the management processes of traditional and emerging MNCs. Martínez *et al.* (2003) find that Latin American MNCs make less extensive/intensive use than established MNCs of processes such as formalization of corporate relationships, strategic planning and budgeting, and corporate control and reporting as vehicles to integrate, coordinate, and control operations of subsidiaries located in different Latin American countries. In fact, MNCs show a higher increase in regional coordination among their subsidiaries than their local counterparts. In other instances, EMNCs may incorporate managerial skills into the bundle of resources they buy in a takeover – following Lenovo's acquisition, the IBM PC business will continue to be based in the United States and will be run by an international management team in which each of the seven top positions is filled by a Chinese American pair.[14] Based on a study of international reward and compensation policies and practices in ten Chinese MNCs, Shen (2004) reveals that they adopt dual approaches depending on nationalities (host-country vs. expatriates) and managerial status (executive vs. non-executive). Similarly, Edwards and Zhang (2003) show that learning

Box 8.2   Human resource management at SABMiller

Founded in 1895, South African Breweries (SAB) was the first manufacturer to join the country's gold mines on Johannesburg's stock exchange. By the mid-1950s, it controlled most of the local beer market: of every 50 beers that South Africans drink, 49 are brewed by SAB and sold as different brands – Castle, Lion, and several others. Since the end of Apartheid, foreign brewers have considered trying to break SAB's near-monopoly, but decided that it would be too difficult. Facing little threat at home, but also little room to expand, SAB set itself the aspiration (rather than the plan) to be among the top five in the world. In the 1990s it bought up ailing breweries in other emerging markets, where beer consumption is growing fast. Its Plzeňský Prazdroj (Pilsner Urquell) and Tyskie brands are currently market leaders in the Czech Republic and Poland, respectively; in China it has acquired 27 breweries since 1994 in partnership with state-owned China Resources Enterprises and is now the second-largest brewer; in November 2001 it was the first major international brewer to invest in Central America when it bought Cervecería Hondureña;

and in Africa, following the purchase of Uganda's Nile and Lonhro Africa's operations and an alliance with Castel of France, it produces two-thirds of all beer. In 1999 SAB moved its prime stock market listing from Johannesburg to London to make it easier (and cheaper) to raise capital, although it still earns most of its profits in soft currencies.

SAB bought Miller Brewing for US$5.6 billion in July 2002 to create SABMiller. In its expansion into emerging markets, SAB had deliberately sought to replicate the operating skills – including the ability to improvise – it developed in Southern Africa to overcome challenges posed by eroded transport infrastructure, political instability, and poor communications. Moreover, the fact that South Africa does not try to establish a cultural hegemony made locals less resistant to South Africans coming in. All this mattered little in order to rescue Miller. For more than 20 years, the brand had been steadily losing ground to Anheuser-Busch, the world's largest brewer and the dominant US market leader, as a result of poor marketing and an uneasy relationship with independent distributors – America's arcane post-Prohibition rules separate brewers from distributors and retailers.

SAB has extensively used and refined its manufacturing team structures since the early 1990s. The first phase focused on substantial performance improvement, eliminating stocks, developing problem-solving skills and practices, identifying best operating practices, and structuring teams at four levels from shift through to region, focusing on situational, systemic, and strategic problem solving. A revision of team structures started in 1997 has achieved a step change in skill levels, so that teams have become self-sufficient and do not need assistance from quality control technicians and other specialists. Individual goals are reviewed monthly on an informal basis between managers and direct reports. The performance reviews cover the self-management practices. Nonetheless, as SAB management had no previous experience in the United States and brewing as an industry is tied to local tastes, observers expected American executives to be at the helm. CEO Graham Mackay, however, fired John Bowlin, Miller's CEO since 1999, finding him unsuitable to absorb enough of SAB culture and effect a dramatic turnaround at Miller. The new head is SAB's South African beer unit head, Norman Adami, who questioned Miller's way as being too pleasant to deliver results. Adami introduced SAB's exacting personnel rating system at Miller, under which 200 poorly performing executives were fired in 2002.

Sources: "Is Miller's time up?" *Fortune*, November 25, 2003; "The battle of big beer," *The Economist*, May 13, 2004; "Q&A with SABMiller's Graham Mackay," *Business Week*, June 28, 2004; Ashton and Sung (2002); Goldstein (2004a).

advanced management practices was one of the main aims of foreign investment by Chinese MNCs in the United Kingdom and that, in order to achieve it, a localization human resource strategy was adopted.

Board composition and corporate governance practices present additional challenges. Research on firms with headquarters in Norway or

Sweden indicates that, after controlling for a variety of firm-specific and corporate-governance-related factors, the presence of outsider Anglo-American board member(s) leads to significantly higher corporate performance measured in terms of firm value (Tobin's Q) (Oxelheim and Randöy 2003). Networking and signaling allow such companies to "break away" from small domestic capital markets by importing Anglo-American corporate governance systems and styles and enhancing their reputation. Internationalization, as manifest in the capital market (international cross-listing), the market for corporate control (foreign board membership), and the product and service market (export and foreign sales), contributes positively to the compensation level of CEOs (Oxelheim and Randöy 2004). Similarly, Khanna and Palepu (2004a) use the Infosys example to argue that the globalization of product and talent markets, rather than capital markets *per se*, is hastening convergence in corporate governance practices worldwide. This particular firm has emerged as the exemplar of good corporate governance in India, traditionally a backwater of corporate governance practices.

In Table 8.1, some evidence is provided regarding the presence of foreign directors on the boards of some of the world's largest EMNCs. Although the number of foreign directors increased from 35 to 52 between the late 1990s and 2003, their relative incidence has not changed dramatically (from 18.8 percent to 22.7 percent). As a matter of comparison, in 2003 there were 97 foreigners on the boards of 22 EU MNCs included in the world's top 100 (i.e., 33 percent). The only foreign CEO in the EMNC sample is Britisher Jonathan Leslie at Sappi, the South African paper and pulp company.[15] The only foreign director in the sample who also sits on the board of one of the world's 50 largest companies is DaimlerChrysler CEO Jürgen Schrempp. That the board on which he sits is that of another South African company, Sasol, is not fortuitous, given that many major companies from the country have moved their primary stock market listing from Johannesburg to London or New York.[16]

Nonetheless, at least in Asia, using nationality as the only criterion for separating local from foreign directors is not straightforward. Almost by definition, the overseas Chinese business community has ties that extend across national borders. So, for instance, in 2003 three of the four foreign non-executive directors on the board of directors of Shangri-La Asia – headquartered in Hong Kong and owned by the Kuok family from Malaysia – were overseas Chinese from Malaysia, the Philippines, and Singapore.

Table 8.1 Foreign directors on the boards of some of the world's largest EMNCs

Company	Late 1990s		2003/04	
	Executive directors	Non-executive directors	Executive directors	Non-executive directors
Hutchinson Whampoa[a]		3/15		3/14
Singtel		0/10	0/1	5/11
Cemex		0/12	0/6	0/6
Samsung Electronics	n.a.	n.a.	0/6	3/7
LG Electronics	0/4	0/4	0/3	0/4
Jardine Matheson[a]		4/12		4/11
Neptune Orient		3/9		5/14
Citic Pacific		1/14	0/10	2/5
Sappi	2/5	2/9	2/4	4/10
Shangri-La Asia	3/5	4/5	1/5	4/5
Sasol	0/4	1/6	0/3	3/11
Guandong Investment	0/9	0/4	0/8	0/4
Flextronics		4/7		5/6
Capitaland		2/10		3/11
Petrobrás		0/9		0/9
Anglogold	0/3	3/12	0/4	1/10
First Pacific[b]	3/5	0/8	2/4	1/8
CVRD		0/9		2/11
Gerdau		0/6	0/5	0/3
América Móvil		n.a.		2/10

[a] Permanent Hong Kong residents are considered as nationals.
[b] The company is registered in Hong Kong but belongs to Indonesia's Salim Group and its major assets are in the Philippines; only non-Asian nationals are considered as foreigners.
Sources: Own calculation based on annual reports. Own calculation based on company and stock exchange information.

8.3 Financial market issues

There is a distinct possibility that, insofar as they are inexperienced in M&A, EMNCs may overpay. They may either be unable to calculate a firm's value properly or fail to understand the true terms of business relationships and therefore commit excessive equity investments in order to prevent their partners from defecting to competitors. Moreover, to the extent that EMNCs have access to cheaper finance, for instance from state-owned banks, their hurdle rate (the rate of return in a discounted cash flow analysis above which an investment makes sense) may be lower. Such problems plagued the overseas expansion of Japanese corporations in the late 1980s (Shimizu *et al.* 2004).

At this stage it is probably premature to attempt a formal analysis, but the premia that emerging investors paid in 2005 for assets in two specific industries, energy and telecommunications, do not support the hypothesis of a tendency to overpay (Table 8.2). Still, the five memoranda of understanding signed in 2006 between China and India, which officially

Table 8.2 Major deals since 2004 in energy and telecommunications industries

Target (location)	Buyer	Date	Price[a]
Oil			
Spinnaker (USA)	Norsk (Norway)	September 2005	29.1
EnCana (USA)	Statoil (Norway)	April 2005	17.6
Kerr-McGee (UK)	Maersk (Denmark)	August 2005	15.7
Paladin (UK)	Talisman (Canada)	November 2005	12.4
Al Furat (Syria)	CNPC (China) & ONGC (India)	December 2005	12/13
Pogo (Thailand)	PTTEP-Mitsui (Japan)	June 2005	9.2
Vintage (Argentina)	Occidental (USA)	October 2005	8.4[b]
Nelson (Kazakhstan)	Lukoil (Russia)	September 2005	7.9
PetroKazakhstan	CNPC (China)	August 2005	7.3
Unocal (global)	Chevron (USA)	August 2005	5.8
EnCana (Ecuador)	CNPC (China)	September 2005	5.2
OML 130 (Nigeria)	CNOOC (China)	January 2006	4.6
Gas			
Caledonia (UK)	E.ON (Germany)	September 2005	10.6
Teikoku Oil (Japan)	Inpex (Japan)	October 2005	8.9[b]
Columbia (USA)	Chesapeake Energy (USA)	October 2005	5.1
Northwest (Australia)	CNOOC (China)	December 2004	1.98
Tangguh (Indonesia)	CNOOC (China)	May 2004	0.98
Telecoms			
PTCL (Pakistan)	Etisalat (United Arab Emirates)	July 2005	1.9
Celtel	MTC (Kuwait)	March 2005	1.7[c]
Investcom	MTN (South Africa)	May 2006	1.3[d]
Saudia Arabia (second license)	Etisalat (United Arab Emirates)	August 2004	1.1
Telsim	Vodafone (UK)	December 2005	1.0
Turk Telekom	Saudi Oger (Saudi Arabia)	July 2005	1.0

[a] In oil and gas, "price" refers to enterprise value per barrel of oil equivalent (proved and probable reserves); in telecoms, "price" refers to the margin over the next-highest bid.
[b] Proved reserves only.
[c] Price relative to the amount that Celtel's financial advisors had hoped to raise from an IPO.
[d] Price relative to the last GDS (Global Depository Share) closing price.
Sources: Credit Suisse January 2006 presentation; "Celtel accepts Kuwaiti offer," *Financial Times*, March 30, 2005; "Pakistan waives interest on Etisalat stake payments," *Financial Times*, January 10, 2006.

sanctioned cooperation between each other's state-owned energy companies when bidding for certain overseas assets, testify indirectly to the desire to depress auction prices when scrambling for energy sources.

There is also anecdotal evidence that Chinese managers fail to recognize that protracted negotiations with sellers, especially during an auction, may be customary business procedures and not a reflection of low trust or esteem.[17] In June 2006, China Mobile, which through its Hong Kong-listed subsidiary is already the world's largest mobile operator, with a claimed 264 million subscribers, tried to buy Millicom, a Swedish company that has more than 8 million subscribers in 16 countries. Although China Mobile's eventual decision to drop its offer was seen by some as evidence of reluctance to overpay, others saw it a confirmation that often Chinese managers cannot commit firmly to a deal.

A related question concerns the financing of international investments, especially as EMNCs become strategically more daring and bet big on acquiring increasingly large firms in OECD countries. Can domestic capital markets and institutions – not only commercial and development banks and the stock exchange, but also knowledge intermediaries such as merchant banks, business consultancies, and law firms – provide adequate macro- and microeconomic support? Or does the quest for global expansion necessarily require EMNCs to seek a secondary, if not a primary, listing in OECD markets, with all the development consequences that this move may entail?

Different models appear to emerge. In the case of China, the new global acquirer "is not necessarily doing the state's bidding, but is fostering the state's national sovereign desires around the world."[18] At the center of the anti-CNOOC allegations at the time of its unsuccessful offer for Unocal were in fact claims that it was funded by subsidized loans – although such arguments have been disputed by independent analysts.[19] Indian companies, on the other hand, raise funding for acquisitions from US private equity firms in transactions that effectively amount to foreigners hiring Indian managers to turn around companies in the foreigners' own markets. In the Middle East and in the Gulf more specifically, the emergence of new MNCs is accompanied by strategic moves to create well-functioning financial markets. In a regional environment characterized by unprecedented levels of liquidity, the Dubai International Financial Exchange (DIFX), which began operations in September 2005, intends to facilitate capital raising by regional MNCs. The first company to list on the DIFX was Investcom, in October 2005. The company, which is controlled by Lebanon's Mikati family, operates GSM (global system for mobile communications) networks, mostly under the Areeba brand, in Syria, Ghana, Yemen, Benin, Liberia, Cyprus, Guinea-Bissau, Afghanistan, and Guinea. Investcom was previously registered in Luxembourg, raised US$741 million in an IPO of global depository shares listed and traded on the DIFX and also on the London Stock Exchange, and was eventually taken over by MTN of South Africa. The Singapore Exchange (SGX) has also attracted interest from regional investors. As of May 2006 there were 100 Chinese listed companies (out of the 693 stocks traded on the SGX), and the launch of an IPO by Thai Beverage, the country's largest brewer, is the largest ever undertaken on the SGX and the biggest since Singapore Telecommunications' listing in 1993.

In other countries, MNCs have transferred their primary listing to overseas stock exchanges in order to decrease the cost of capital and to use foreign-listed stock as a means to finance acquisition. As noted above, this was the experience of South Africa in the late 1990s. The implications have been largely positive, although the growth in South Africa's gross national product was temporarily affected by a change in net dividend flows following the offshore listings (Walters and Prinsloo 2002). Since 2004 large Russian companies have issued shares on the London Stock Exchange, mostly in the form of global depositary receipts (Table 8.3). Although some observers have questioned the real motives behind these listings, hinting at the possibility of capital flight, Russian owners have been attracted to London by the possibily of establishing ownership rights, strengthening reputation, and investing in third countries. This trend accelerated in 2005 with the listings of Pyaterochka, the largest grocery retailer, and Evraz, the steel producer, which used their foreign-incorporated entities to circumvent Russian regulations that require a domestic listing before an international float. To fight the exodus, which raised concerns over the chances of developing a credible stock market, the Russian Federal Financial Markets Service has given the necessary authorizations contingent on the fact that these companies maintain their home listing and list no more than 70 percent of the stock registered on a foreign exchange.[20] This attitude contrasts with that of South African market regulators, which have concentrated on improving governance standards and developing the domestic institutional investor base.

8.4 The impact on the host economies

In recent years, topics such as spillovers, linkages, corporate responsibilities, and ethical and social standards have taken on increasing relevance in international economic relations and business. Knowing whether the

Table 8.3 Russian and CIS listings on London's main market

Company	Subsector	List date	Capital raised (percentage of shares)	Purpose
OMZ	Engineering – general	September 2003	n.a.	n.a.
Utd Heavy Machinery Uralmash-Izhora (INI)	Engineering – general	September 2003	£69.96 m.	n.a.
Efes Breweries	Beverages	October 2004	n.a.	n.a.
Sistema (INI)	Diversified industrials	February 2005	US$1,560 m. (19%)	Development of existing non-telecom businesses and telecom acquisitions
Pyaterochka	Food & drug retailing	May 2005	US$639 m. (32%)	The company received no proceeds from the sale of GDRs
Evraz Group	Steel	June 2005	US$422 m. (8.3%)	Acquisition of Palini e Bertoli and Vitkowice Steel
Novatek (INI)	Oil & gas	July 2005	US$966 m. (19%)	Debt restructuring
Kazakhmys	Other mineral	October 2005	US$1.4 bn.	
Kazkommertsbank	Banking	November 2005		
Amtel-Vredestein	Tyres & rubber	November 2005	US$201 m. (27.1%)	To pay down debt
Novolipetsk (INI)	Steel	November 2005	US$609 m. (7%)	n.a.
Kazakhgold	Gold mining	December 2005	US$197 m.	n.a.
Comstar (INI)	Telecoms	January 2006	£563.89 m.	n.a.
Rosneft	Oil & gas	July 2006	US$10.6 bn.	n.a.
KazMunaiGaz	Oil & gas	September 2006	US$2,255 (36.6% of ordinary shares)	n.a.

nationality of investors makes a difference is probably crucial, especially to the extent that the home country policy environment has a strong influence on corporate behaviors. Early work seemed to corroborate the expectation that EMNCs have a more benign impact on host economies than OECD peers because they have a better appreciation of local conditions, are culturally closer, and use "intermediate," small-scale technologies that directly substitute labor for capital. In the most rigorous such study, Lecraw (1977) controlled for industry composition and found that in Thailand foreign investors from other LDCs use more labor-intensive technology than either Thai firms or OECD investors. He concluded that, "on balance, LDC firms offered significant benefits to the Thai economy without many of the costs associated with other FDI" (p. 456). In their study of Sri Lankan manufacturing, Athukorala and Jayasuriya (1988) caution against simple comparisons and argue that firm attributes other than parentage can affect capital intensity. Differences between developed countries' MNCs and 3WMNCs were found to be marked in the textiles and apparel industries, "where the range of technological possibilities is wide enough to enable significantly different techniques of production to be utilized" (p. 420), but not in the chemical and metal product industries.

Unfortunately, empirical research has not caught up with the policy debate and only some simpler considerations can be given. The only study on the differential impact of ownership on technology transfer and technology compares South African and OECD companies in Tanzania (Kabelwa 2004). The results show that South–South FDI does indeed have a higher potential. Also on the positive side, Korea's Hyundai Motors set up its largest overseas assembly factory in the Indian state of Tamil Nadu, where it also operates an aluminum foundry and a transmission line. Major suppliers from Korea also invested in the Ulsan automobile cluster, often through joint ventures with Indian partners. Hyundai now has 85 percent domestic content, higher than any other foreign-owned automaker in India (Park 2004). However, a comparison of different foreign investors in Shandong province in China finds that Korean firms developed many fewer backward linkages with local firms than subsidiaries of US and Hong Kong firms (Park and Lee 2003).

A parallel issue is whether EMNCs, to the extent that they operate with essentially the same technology as their domestic counterparts, directly compete with them and eventually act to their detriment. In his study of Nigeria, Narula (1997) suggests that while the scale and industry of operations are similar, EMNCs use technology which, "although not necessarily proprietary, is 'different' in that it has been 'bundled' after being 'unbundled' in other locations. This results in a lesser need to adapt the equipment, and reduces the cost of operation, although this reduction in costs is probably partly offset by the cost of maintaining a larger expatriate staff" (p. 154).

In commerce, observers hold very different views on the consequences of modern retail trade formats introduced by foreign investors. For some, the previously highly fragmented nature of food retailing deprived consumers of quality food products, variety, and value-added services. Through increased efficiencies of purchasing, logistics, technology, and distribution, new retailing concepts will provide consumers with lower prices and wider access to quality food and consumer goods. In the case of Mexico, "the recent success of Wal-Mart, with its proprietary distribution sites and aggressive supplier price targets, has helped alter the retail food landscape and set new competitive standards in Mexico. With no value added tax on food, the efficiencies have had impact across the supply chain and have been passed on as lower prices to consumers" (McKinsey 2004). Others have argued that by taking the "easy" option of supermarkets shopping, consumers contribute to the destruction of smaller independent businesses and encourage unhealthy and unsustainable food production and attitudes (e.g., Blythman 2004). Moreover, although supermarkets' demand for large quantities of goods of consistent quality is good news for big farmers and efficient, well-organized farmers, for others it can be troublesome. According to Balsevich et al. (2003), "as supermarkets compete with each other and with the informal sector, they will not raise consumer prices in order to pay for the farm-level investments needed to meet quality and safety requirements" (p. 1153).

The evidence in the case of South African supermarkets such as Shoprite and Pick'n'Pay in Zambia, Mozambique, and other Southern African Development Community (SADC) countries, is mixed (Goldstein 2004a). Allegations are common that they source overwhelmingly from South African suppliers, bypassing local producers, sell goods that are past their expiration date, and treat employees according to lower standards than those prevailing in South Africa. Moreover, they do not yet have specific programs to help local suppliers access world markets.[21] While these companies are not infringing any laws – for instance, research on the behavior of Woolworths in Ghana does not suggest that it is attempting to undermine labor standards (Baah 2003) – they fail to contribute fully to the host economies' development in the way foreign MNCs are expected to in South Africa.

Finally, the evidence concerning Asian investors in the clothing industry in Lesotho, Namibia, and Swaziland is rather negative. International Labour Organisation (ILO) investigations have shown a general disregard for labor regulations, while the Ramatex case in Namibia (Box 8.3) has revealed the existence of serious environmental problems. The activities of Malaysian timber investors in the Solomon Islands, Guyana, and Suriname have been tainted by allegations of unethical behavior (Jomo 2002).

The arrival of EMNCs may also have an impact on product variety. In Vietnam, where frequent electricity outages and the lack of a broadcasting

Box 8.3 Ramatex Namibia

Ramatex is Malaysia's leading textile enterprise, with operations in Cambodia, South Africa, Mauritius, and China and 2004 turnover of US$300 million. Its investment in Namibia has been the largest ever by a foreign investor in manufacturing. Following six months of negotiations with the Ministry of Trade and Industry and the City of Windhoek, in 2001 Ramatex started construction of a fully integrated garment and textile plant in the Otjomuise area. Other stakeholders involved in the project include the Namibia Investment Centre, the Off-Shore Development Company, NamPower, NamWater, and Telecom Namibia. Authorities expected the Ramatex investment to add value to Namibian manufacturing, diversify exports, create opportunities for skills training and entrepreneurial development, promote SMEs, and stimulate economic growth. The city agreed to lease a 43 hectare portion of land at no direct cost and exempt Ramatex from land-use tax. As the site had already been earmarked for development as an industrial location, funding had been prearranged with the Development Bank of Southern Africa.

Given limited availability of skilled workers, Ramatex was expected to provide the necessary training. Talking about local staff, Malaysian investors said: "If they are prepared to work harder, if they are keen to learn, to be well-disciplined, if they are responsive to supervisors' instruction, they could be trained and become skilful sewers. The aim is to instill discipline, punctuality, high productivity, good quality and a culture of hard work. What we want is discipline, and hardworking Namibian people that can be equated to China when it comes to garment manufacturing." In February 2003 two of the four buildings started production, each housing more than 1,000 workers. By early 2006 Ramatex was employing some 4,000 Namibian workers and a further 2,000 foreigners.

The project, however, also raised various issues of concern. Ramatex had not released the results of an environmental assessment, although Namibian legislation requires it for all new projects before approval. Ramatex was at times allowed to bypass basic workers' rights, the Namibian Labor Act, the Affirmative Action (Employment) Act, as well as environmental and municipal regulations. Ramatex never increased workers' wages, despite signing a recognition agreement with the Namibia Food and Allied Workers Union (NAFAU) in 2002 that it would increase salaries after workers had been employed for three years. In May 2003 approximately 700 Asian employees, mostly from China, went on strike, demanding a salary increase and better working conditions. Separately, more than 400 Namibian workers were suspended after a spontaneous strike. In September 2004, the government deported more than 400 Bangladeshi workers after it was discovered they had been working without proper permits and living in unsuitable conditions.

Although President Sam Nujoma defended Ramatex, saying staff were still being trained, the Congress of Democrats, in opposition, and the International Textile Garment and Leather Workers' Federation (ITGLWF) expressed concerns about the treatment of workers. The ITGLWF further appealed to all US buyers of Namibian textiles to "intervene to bring pressure to bear on the company to put in place a corrective action program to address such appalling labor practices and workers rights' abuses." With the Multi Fiber Agreement withdrawal, the factory has experienced a 36 percent drop in exports since 2004. Rhino Garments, a subsidiary of Ramatex, closed in April 2005, citing NAFAU's connections to the ITGLWF as the reason for the closure. Ramatex is rumored to be considering shutting down its Windhoek operations completely.

Sources: "Rumours rattle Ramatex," *Namibian*, April 7, 2006; Goldstein (2004a); Jauch (2005).

network or satellite technology make television viewing rather unreliable in some remote mountainous and rural parts of the country, TCL from China developed a "powerful receiver" color television that provided much clearer reception than other brands (Yi 2004).

Finally, corporate citizenship can influence domestic policies differently. OFDI and active participation in global value chains make businesses in developing countries increasingly attentive to corporate social responsibility to convince investors and other stakeholders of their unspotted business credentials – although the speed of change varies widely, with Asia lagging behind Latin America and South Africa.[22] In the area of intellectual property rights and counterfeiting, when EMNCs start buying foreign companies and brands, they will develop a greater interest in stricter protection. In this sense it is possible that the emergence of a new geography of global FDI flows is accompanied by improvements in the business environments. On the other hand, the opposite risk is also present. As highlighted in Section 3.2, the increasing activism of oil EMNCs in Africa – especially when coupled with loans provided by countries that do not belong to the Paris Club and do not condition development cooperation on any policy requirements – might weaken the leverage of international financial institutions, derail efforts in the framework of the HIPC (highly indebted poor countries) initiative, and ultimately jeopardize its still flimsy achievements. This risk is particularly serious in those poor countries that depend on official aid to finance deficits on the current account.

9
Consequences for OECD Governments, Firms, and Workers

Summary

The rise of EMNCs introduces a wide range of new issues into the policy debate in OECD countries. These include the importance of nationality in determining corporate behavior, the adaptability of non-OECD investors to the policy environment and the informal norms that characterize business in OECD countries, the opportunity to tailor investment promotion to specific circumstances, and the consequences for national security.

EMNCs want – and indeed need – to establish a direct presence in OECD countries to access new markets, develop resources and capabilities, strengthen strategic alliances, and participate in global talent networks. Surveys conducted among companies in the Shanghai area, for instance, reveal that they are very interested in investing in Japan to access the market, tap into the country's substantial wealth of information related to leading technologies, and exploit the nation's highly skilled human resources (Matsuno and Lin 2003).

9.1 Motivations and entry modes

EMNCs may decide to invest in higher-wage OECD countries for a wide variety of efficiency-driven reason (Table 9.1). The deals can sometimes be described as aggressive – insofar as resources are acquired together with market access – and sometimes as defensive – in particular when they are made in anticipation of the imposition of tariff and non-tariff trade barriers.

Market-seeking has characterized acquisitions of firms in capital-intensive sectors such as metalworking (e.g., the takeover of Baton

Table 9.1 OECD countries' initiatives to attract Chinese MNCs

Country	Initiative
Australia	Invest Australia (IA) targets mineral processing, agricultural processing, manufacturing, and food/food-processing industries. The China team emphasizes proactive targeting of major companies, participation in key events, use of local media, cold calling, alliances with relevant local allies, and in particular an increase in the conducting of seminars, which are proven and cost-effective tools
Finland	The Ministry of Trade and Industry operates a small unit in Shanghai
France	AFII (Agence Française pour les Investissements Internationaux) has an office in Shanghai and its president visited China twice in 2004, once with President Chirac to launch the year of France in China
Italy	InvestinItaly organized the visit of a Chinese delegation to Italy in late 2005 to promote the country as an investment destination
Midwest US-China Association (MWCA)	Established in September 2004, aims to coordinate efforts to draw investment from China and Chinese companies. Core members comprise Illinois, Indiana, Iowa, Kansas, Michigan, Minnesota, Missouri, Nebraska, Ohio, and Wisconsin, expanding to local development associations, businesses, and universities. Areas of cooperation include agriculture, service, manufacturing, and energy conservation
Netherlands	Some 80 Chinese companies, mostly trading SMEs, have already established offices in the Netherlands. In January 2005, the Foreign Investment Agency opened a Shanghai office, with a focus on European distribution facilities, marketing, R&D, or headquarter activities
Think London	In the process of setting up an office in Beijing and likely to follow in Shanghai and Guangdong province; a small office already in New Delhi

Rouge Industries and Lucchini by Severstal) and auto components (e.g., the takeover of Carl Dan Peddinghaus and Federal Forge by Bharat Forge). In most such cases, the targets were going through serious financial difficulties, which made it easier for the EMNCs not only to bid but also to convince otherwise suspicious local communities and trade unions. Indian software and pharmaceutical companies such as Four Soft, Ranbaxy, and Wipro are investing in the United Kingdom and elsewhere to access EU markets. When Cemex bought RMC in the United Kingdom, it expected synergies to reach approximately US$200 million by standardizing some management processes, capitalizing on trading network benefits, consolidating logistics, and improving global procurement and energy efficiency.

In relatively more labor-intensive sectors, including the production of standardized electronics equipment, the logic is different. OEM firms have made a series of big-ticket acquisitions whose objective is simultaneously to acquire established brands, access existing distribution networks, and eventually transfer production from the acquired company back home to lower-cost locations. A notable characteristic of many such deals is that the Western company that is discharging divisions it no longer considers strategic acquires in turn a financial stake in the EMNC. This has been the case in the IBM–Lenovo, Thomson–TCL, Siemens–BenQ, and Philips–TPV deals. In many instances, after factories in the West have been acquired, they are shuttered and production is transferred to Asia. This has been the case with Moltech in Florida following the acquisition by the Shanghai Tyre & Rubber Company and for Eimo in Finland after the takeover by Taiwan's Foxconn. The need to acquire popular global brands also drives deals in light manufacturing such as beverages: SABMiller and Tata Tea provide excellent examples of this.

Greenfield investments are less frequent, although not absent. Examples from Korean automakers and Indian BPOs have been presented above. In R&D, a few EMNCs engage in catching-up FDI by setting up R&D centers in developed economies that serve mainly to acquire local technology and scientific knowledge (von Zedtwitz 2006).[1] Samsung manages an international network of 15 R&D and design centers, some of which are given considerable operational autonomy to offer heightened opportunities for international cross-fertilization. Chinese firms have much smaller R&D units abroad, mostly focused on technology monitoring and listening and other non-indigenous research activities (Table 9.2). Haier's decision to collocate its manufacturing and R&D sites in South Carolina, for example, serves to support product localization and process innovation.

Table 9.2 Selected Chinese MNCs' R&D centers in OECD countries

Company	Location	Description
Haier	Silicon Valley	Product design center
Haier	Germany	R&D center
Huawei	Silicon Valley	America Silicon Valley Research Institute (other research facilities in Dallas, Bangalore, Stockholm, and Moscow)
TTE	Indiana	Joint TCL–Thomson facility
Konka	Silicon Valley	R&D facility
ZTE	Silicon Valley	Product design center
ZTE	Poitiers	Product design center
3NOD	Southern California	Product design center

Source: von Zedtwitz (2006).

A further motivation is that geographical diversification of assets and sales shields global operations against the risk of political and economic uncertainties at home. South African financial services groups such as Investec, an investment bank, and Old Mutual, an insurance company, have reduced their exposure to the domestic market by acquiring important competitors in industrial markets, where growth rates are lower but much stabler. Nevertheless, the fact that South Africa still accounts for the largest, albeit declining, share of Old Mutual's operating profits was among the reasons for the frosty reception that Skandia shareholders gave to the 2005 deal, alongside concerns about the bidder's Zimbabwe holdings. The owner of Orascom bought Wind in Italy also with a view to merging the two companies eventually and listing shares on the Milan stock exchange, which is deeper and more liquid than Cairo's.

9.2 Performance

There are still far too few data points – with the exception of the foreign operations of Korean MNCs (see above) – to allow for rigorous analysis of the performance of foreign affiliates of EMNCs. There is nonetheless some evidence to suggest that, at least as far as relations with labor, suppliers, and customers are concerned, EMNCs – especially those from China and other Asian countries – find it relatively difficult to adapt to more developed countries' business environments. Haier's autocratic management style, for instance, was something of a culture shock to American workers.[2] In turn, the company's CEO has argued that the reluctance of Haier's American managers to adhere to his ambitious targets reflects "the cultural gap or the communication problem" (Zhang 2005).[3] Industrial relations at Haier Italy have also been very tense, with workers blaming Chinese managers for improvisation and the company firing a trade union representative.[4] Nonetheless, another Chinese-owned factory in the United States has had a very successful experience (Box 9.1).

Box 9.1 China International Marine Containers (Group) in the United States

China International Marine Containers (Group) (CIMC), based in Shenzhen in southern China, was founded in 1980 as a joint venture between China Merchants Holdings (a Chinese-Hong Kong investment bank representing mainland interests) and the East Asiatic Company Ltd. (a Danish firm). A downturn in shipping in 1986 forced the company to diversify into real estate and other businesses. In 1987 CIMC's largest customer, China Ocean Shipping (Group) Company (COSCO) – another state-owned group corporation – acquired more than 40 percent of the Danish share, injecting fresh capital into CIMC. CIMC reorganized and acquired another Chinese container builder in 1993. In 1994 it floated shares on the Shenzhen exchange, and currently a 55.44 percent majority of them are traded. Today the company is the world's top intermodal freight container manufacturer, with more than half of the world's ocean shipping container market – a relatively small industry that was not under as intense scrutiny as more strategic industries such as power or telecommunications. The company offers dry van, reefer, tank, and various specialty containers.

CIMC has 18 manufacturing plants along the coast and had 2003 total sales of US$1.67 billion, making it China's 39th-largest corporation (*Fortune* data). It employs more than 22,000 people. The operation produces a million of these steel boxes annually. The company is highly unusual in its ability to defy intense localism and make acquisitions in different geographic areas of China. CIMC typically offers local government fractional ownership – and dividends – in exchange for its votes in board meetings. This way, as ordinary shareholders, local governments get paid but the company is free of political peddling. Moreover, management has been able to install uniform business controls at CIMC acquisitions, even though they remained legally independent and had their own boards. CIMC is now diversifying into ground transportation equipment. Trailers are a key component of the expansion plans, as the market is far larger than that for containers. CIMC recently formed CIMC Vehicle, an operation that produces a wide range of equipment for both Chinese domestic use and for export. Factories in Yangzhou and Shenzhen have been expanded and equipped to manufacture products such as container chassis, tank trailers, vans, dump trailers, cement mixers, low-loaders, and auto carriers.

CIMC began looking for a way into the North American trailer market in 2001. At the time, US manufacturers were struggling through an extremely difficult economy, and several major plants were up for sale. In 2002, CIMC began an effort to purchase selected assets of HPA Monon (one of the largest US container manufacturers) out of Chapter 7. In June 2003, Vanguard National Trailer Corporation, a newly established CIMC subsidiary, took over the ten former HPA buildings in Monon, Indiana. CIMC spent US$4.5 million and another US$12 million on renovations and training.

A team of industry veterans manages the company, which imports fabricated steel parts made in China and mixes them with North American components to produce trailers designed for the American market. Monon's main assembly plant was first gutted. By November 2003, the building was completely empty, and Vanguard began equipping a plant that would produce trailers using automation and tooling designed by a team of Chinese and US engineers. As the plant was designed as an assembly facility from the beginning, a lot of design attention was paid to process flow. Engineers did not have to allocate space for fabrication equipment – those operations are carried out in China. Even the number of welding machines is minimal. About half of the fixtures came from China, primarily those that move material through the system. Some of the fit-up fixtures also came from China, but most are designed for conveyance and quick material flow. With the exception of the steel components that are fabricated in China, Vanguard trailers are equipped with familiar components produced by North American suppliers. And not all the fabricated steel parts are imported. Cross-members (which are hot rolled) and side posts (which are roll formed) are made in the United States. These products do not have much labor content.

According to Vanguard's managers, while the Chinese were not so familiar with the trailers that American customers demand, they had strong ideas about how to manufacture them. Vanguard created the design using the same engineering software program that CIMC has in China for its container engineering work. Drawings were transferred electronically to China. There CIMC engineers used ProMechanica, a high-level finite element analysis program, to make sure that the designs would perform as expected. The graphic basis of engineering has helped CIMC and Vanguard to bridge their language differences. In much the same way, a graphics system is making it easier for purchasing to order.

Projected employment was approximately 450 within two years, with annual production of up to 10,000 dry van trailers by the third year. Vanguard currently employs 300 people. The plant operates a ten-hour, four-day shift. The production technology department takes over the plant Friday though Sunday to perform maintenance and production upgrades without disrupting production. The company produced 4,900 dry freight vans in 2005 (+68 percent with respect to 2004, its first full year of operation) and expected to build 8,000 trailers in 2006.

Sources: "North-Central Indiana update," *Indiana Business Magazine*, August 2003; "Best of both worlds," *Trailer-Body Builders*, November 1, 2004; Meyer and Lu (2005).

The history of AmorePacific, a Korean cosmetics manufacturer, is also illustrative.[5] The company first tried breaking into the French market in the early 1990s, but its products, exported from Korea, failed to win over French consumers. Determined to escape the confines of the small domestic market, AmorePacific first unsuccessfully attempted to acquire small French cosmetics firms before setting up production lines at its factory close to Paris. The subsidiary hired local marketing, distribution, and production managers and was given a high degree of operational autonomy by the parent company in Seoul. Eventually it clinched an exclusive deal with French designer Lolita Lempicka to launch its own perfume brand, and AmorePacific has grown to be the 26th-largest company in the world in terms of cosmetics sales.

9.3 The risk of protectionism

In many OECD countries, EMNCs have received a pretty difficult reception, as a few examples show (Goldstein 2006b). In November 1995, the French government announced that it had reached an agreement with Daewoo to sell Thomson for the symbolic price of one franc. In addition to the polemic surrounding the decision to dispose of a firm that, despite making losses, still held very remunerative patents, what made many French people anxious was the prospect of seeing a national icon transferred to Korean owners. Nine years later, the situation had changed. It has changed in the sense that now the Koreans are resisting the acquisition of one of their firms by the Chinese (whereas 9 years earlier it was the French that resisted the Koreans). The first visit by officials from Bluestar – the first Chinese company to become, with no auto manufacturing facilities of its own, the owner of a foreign automaker – to Ssangyong, Korea's fourth-largest automaker, was accompanied by worker protests that blocked entrances and prevented the Chinese visitors from entering.[6] Similarly, in 2003 the fears raised by the attempt of Mahindra & Mahindra, the Indian vehicle maker, to take over Valtra, a Finnish tractor manufacturer, were such that Helsinki provided financial backing to a rival consortium of local investors.[7]

In December 2004 the landmark IBM unit purchase sparked fears in the United States that Lenovo could be acting as a screen for the Chinese government and army to transfer "advanced" and sensitive technology.[8] The deal was reviewed by the Committee on Foreign Investments in the United States (CFIUS), a multi-agency group that includes representatives from the homeland security, defense, justice, treasury, and commerce departments, to gauge any impact on national security. The IBM inquiry was a full investigation, which occurs in far fewer than 1 percent of cross-border deals. The committee's proceedings are secret, and IBM would not say what steps it took to address the concerns of the group. Information leaked to the press, however, indicates that IBM apparently made more in the way of commitments and assurances than concessions that might restrain its sales or product development.[9] The steps included agreeing to separate Lenovo's American employees, mainly in Research Triangle Park in North Carolina, from IBM workers there who work on other products such as large server computers and software. IBM also agreed to ensure that the chips and other parts in desktop PCs and notebooks were stamped with the name of their manufacturer and country of origin. Such labeling is fairly common among PC makers.[10]

Such heated debates reached unprecedented heights in June 2005 when CNOOC made a US$19.6 billion bid for the assets of Unocal, a second-tier American oil company.[11] The deal was hostile – Unocal's directors preferred a rival, although lower, offer from Chevron – and would have been the largest Chinese overseas takeover in history. The government-owned company, however, was effectively barred from the game by a hostile US Congress, which had the power to insert a clause into the energy bill that would make it all but impossible for the Chinese to buy Unocal.[12] In a similar episode in February 2006, a group of Washington lawmakers questioned the CFIUS decision to approve DP World's acquisition of P&O, the British operator that owns terminals at six ports on the East Coast. Eventually, the suitor agreed to insulate P&O's American operations from management control by DP World.

In these two cases, what was at stake was at least as much the power of Congress to diminish the power of the CFIUS as rather vague national security concerns. In a show of brinkmanship, President Bush responded that he would veto any legislation blocking the P&O deal, making a rare use of the threat.[13]

If security concerns are often advanced as a major justification for the screening of EMNCs, a parallel justification is the quality of industrial relations. It is argued that emerging investors are unaccustomed to dealing with trade unions and are prone to labor rights violations when pressured to reduce costs. For example, labor groups in Alberta have complained about proposals to enable foreign workers more easily to take up the slack in the oil sands.[14] European politicians opposing the takeover of Arcelor, the Luxembourg-based steel makers that resulted from the amalgamation of separate Belgian, French, and Luxembourg companies, by Mittal also cited concerns about corporate social responsibilities – even when trade unions themselves defended the record of the "Indian" company and in fact argued that Arcelor was less sensitive to their concerns.[15] In fact, according to the president of the Alberta

Federation of Labour, Labor leaders in some countries have argued that rather than ownership, the most important question is the treatment that a company gives to its employees and its willingness to sit down at the bargaining table and negotiate fair agreements. In other countries, very significant deals that saw EMNCs acquire sizeable assets hardly raised an eyebrow. In Italy, Severstal bought Lucchini, the country's second-largest steel maker, and Orascom's Sawiris acquired the second-largest telecom operator, Wind, without any specific government investigation or workers' opposition (Goldstein 2006a).

9.4 Proactive strategies

The counterpart to these problems is the frenzy that has erupted in industrial countries to promote inward FDI from China and other emerging economies. In official speeches during visits to Beijing, both the Italian president and the Canadian prime minister explicitly referred to this topic.[16] Tony Blair has encouraged Indian firms to invest in Britain.[17]

Nevertheless, stereotypes are hard to kill. In many cases, bureaucracies fail to understand why companies from emerging economies enquire about business opportunities in the West and suspect murky motives such as money laundering and illegal migration. When Comarch, a Polish banking software company, set up a representative office in Belgium, the salesman was given political refugee status so he could get a work permit.[18] Others have been less lucky: Tata Consultancy Services staff based in Europe could not enter Italy for three months to service Ferrari, an important client.[19] In fact, EMNCs consider bureaucracy the greatest obstacle to the establishment of their businesses and integration (see Bain & Company 2004 on Chinese MNCs), and therefore expect Western governments to provide them with institutional, legal, and operational support. In a sense, the situation is hardly different from the one that characterizes OECD investors in developing countries. Cognizant of this fact, OECD countries' investment promotion agencies are launching specific initiatives (see Table 9.1 for a summary of those targeted at Chinese investors).

The ongoing saga surrounding MG Rover also saw the multiplication of hopes and rumors that the failed UK automaker could be rescued by non-OECD investors (Box 9.2). What is important to acknowledge in this case is that false expectations may be raised and painful adjustments delayed when EMNCs appear as potential buyers of last resort to salvage troubled businesses. This is not a completely new phenomenon, however; already EMNCs had extended the operational lifetime of

Box 9.2 EMNCs to the rescue: the case of MG Rover

In 1994, BMW bought MG Rover, the remains of what was once the third-biggest auto producer in the world and the last major British-owned auto company, in an effort to become a mass-market manufacturer and achieve economies of scale. After it poured £4.5 billion (US$7 billion) into the deal, BMW sold the company in 2000 for £10 to a group called Phoenix, which also received a £427 million interest-free loan from BMW to take the problem off its hands. Already weak in every respect, the company failed to be re-ignited by the four investors behind Phoenix.

Rover has neither the volume of the giants nor the margins of a niche player. It has, however, a sports cars brand name (however battered), an EU manufacturing base, and experience in mass production. These factors can be important for automakers in emerging economies that either make or assemble automobiles under license in joint ventures with Western majors and are anxious to get their hands on technology of their own. Rover held talks with one Chinese firm and Malaysia's Proton to collaborate in the production of a new midsized model with Daastan to site assembly plans in Iran, and launched the Indian-built CityRover in 2003. In mid-2004 Shanghai Automotive Industry Corporation (SAIC) entered into exclusive negotiations to set up a development and manufacturing joint venture, with the British government reportedly ready to extend a bridging loan of £100 million. The two companies even contemplated a joint bid to take over Daewoo's Polish plant. The arrangement was welcomed by the financial community, and hailed as a "clever move" in a *Financial Times* leader. SAIC, however, walked away from the proposal in March 2005 because it feared that it would be landed with Rover's pension and other liabilities. Nonetheless, SAIC apparently acquired the property rights to the Rover 25 and the Rover 75, those to make the Rover 45 (which it sold on to another Chinese automaker, Nanjing), and the technology and the production equipment for making Rover's K-series petrol engines and for a diesel version.

In April 2005 the company was officially declared bankrupt and the British government promised £6.5 million in *ad hoc* state aid to keep paying wages and thus try to stave off 6,000 job losses. SAIC said it has ruled out becoming involved with Rover again while it is in administration or buying it as a going concern. A Russian millionaire, who had bought TVR (another British automaker) in 2004, and Iran's Khodro expressed interest in Rover to the company's administrators.

Sources: "More subsidy for a failing car firm," *The Economist*, April 7, 2005; "Who's to blame for MG Rover" and "Last rights," *The Economist*, April 14, 2005; "Rescuing Rover," *Financial Times*, November 29, 2004; "Iranian company in talks to buy Rover cars," *Financial Times*, May 2, 2005; and "Wealthy Russian mulls Rover rescue," *Financial Times*, May 4, 2005.

outdated assets and provided greater job stability than alternative investors. More than two decades ago, the Dutch government "welcomed the entry of [Kuwait Petroleum Company] into Holland despite the privileged position of Shell" and workers "were willing to negotiate concessions, in part because they believed that the new Kuwaiti owners could provide greater job stability than Gulf" (Tétreault 1997: 389).

9.5 A complex issue

From the foregoing discussion, it is clear that most arguments deployed in Western countries to block foreign acquisitions, especially by EMNCs, are specious and more often than not amount to not-so-veiled protectionism. Nevertheless, it is not enough to argue that blocking the doors of the global economy to Chinese and other up-and-coming investors – after opening the doors of their markets and praising the mostly positive consequences – is unfair. The global economy is going through a phase of profound change, and in industrial nations the efforts to gain a better understanding of the underlying trends, the emerging issues, and the necessary adaptations to the policy environment must encompass all stakeholders. This does not obviously translate into protectionism, but helps us understand why "nearly every country wants FDI, but only on its own terms" (Wilkins 1990: 627).

The main consequence for OECD-based companies is obviously the emergence of strong global competitors. What is possibly of more immediate concern is the fact that the presence of new actors changes the context in which bids for assets and properties take place. Different corporate governance rules and behaviors, especially in the case of state-owned and family-controlled companies, respectively, means that EMNCs may have less trouble and more flexibility in accessing capital than listed MNCs that are restricted by the volatile will of shareholders, market regulators, or analysts.[20] Nonetheless, even when EMNCs offer a nominally higher price, the possibility that the associated risk is higher may convince shareholders to prefer rival bids from established companies.

The complexity of the issues is also revealed by the interpenetration of domestic and international, political and economic motivations. Obviously, the behavior of exchange rates influences the decisions of investors, including EMNCs. The world economy is currently characterized by imbalances and misalignments, and in many corners voices are to be heard asking for a revaluation of emerging economies' currencies (*in primis* the Chinese renminbi) as a step in the direction of redressing global imbalances (*in primis* the US trade deficit). By softening tensions in the United States, such a policy would also avert the risk of a resumption of protectionism in the world's largest economy. This is obviously not the place to discuss the underlying causes of the so-called twin deficit in the United States or the viability of using the exchange rate as a policy to address such a problem. What is important to stress is that the purchasing power of Chinese and other investors would obviously be reinforced by a depreciation of the US dollar and that FDI flows from China and other emerging economies to the United States would therefore increase. It is far from certain that such a development would be welcome and that protectionism pressures would correspondingly abate.

10
Conclusions – The Way Ahead

This study has provided a broad overview of a phenomenon that – while certainly not new in absolute terms – has grown in importance and accelerated over the past few years. The long-term trend is for such dynamics to accelerate further: McKinsey's research, for instance, suggests that up to US$250 billion of Gulf investment will be directed to Asia in 2006–11 (Barton and de Boer 2006). An analysis of available data, in addition to pointing to the limitations that are intrinsic to all FDI figures and are even more serious in the case of Southern home investors, has highlighted that some emerging economies have become relevant players in the global economy – and even more so in selected regional and national contexts – and that some EMNCs may by now claim the status of real "global players." The motivations for the corporate decision to internationalize via overseas investment are largely similar to those of OECD-based MNCs – to seek market access, resources, and capabilities – and justify the gamble of operating in foreign territories rather than exporting from the home country. Nonetheless, the international business environment has changed – product cycles are shorter, time-to-market imperatives faster, regionalism and economic liberalization processes more widespread, and network alliances of increasing importance – and firms are pushed to internationalize via direct investment much earlier in their lifecycle.

Future work ought to move toward more explicit generalizations. How, specifically, do the phenomena observed in this book differ from what conventional theory (whatever that is) says about rich-country MNCs? Will EMNCs begin to be much like other MNCs when their home countries become richer? Or, on the contrary, will certain distinguishing features (such as family and state ownership, as well as conglomerate structure) persist, either because they actually contribute to

EMNCs' dynamic advantages or because institutional systems are characterized by a high degree of path dependency?

There can be little doubt that existing theories of international business – and in particular the versatile OLI paradigm – also serve for the analysis of EMNCs. In turn, research into EMNCs contributes to the development of international business studies, especially because firms from developing countries internationalize through FDI at an earlier stage in their life than their counterparts from industrial nations. If they do so, it is because they possess some dexterity in combining non-proprietary skills, even if they remain inherently different from the inimitable capabilities (say, a brand or a patent) traditionally associated with formidable global competitors. Possibly no firm better epitomizes the skills of EMNCs and the ability to use information and communications technologies and organizational dynamics, even in a mature sector such as cement, than Cemex.

An important point that emerges from this study is the heterogeneity of internationalization patterns and the need to explore in great depth the linkages between the political and institutional environment, on the one hand, and corporate trajectories, on the other. Naïve beliefs that globalization heralded the end of distance and geography have now given way to a much richer approach to understanding the inherently embedded and spatial nature of corporate competitiveness.[1] This point has even greater heuristic pertinence in the case of MNCs based in countries where, on account of weaker entrepreneurship, government institutions and policies, as well as ethnic characteristics, have been so crucial in influencing economic successes and failures. In this sense, the study of EMNCs is another building block toward a coherent history of big business in developing countries, in which traditional elements and watershed changes coexist and give rise to a hybrid form of capitalism that is both modern and more open. Insofar as economic and business theories alone are not sufficient for this endeavor, ideas and insights from history, political science, and the other social sciences – in brief, a true "political economy" – must be called upon. Moreover, culture also matters in international business, although the risk of self-reification must be studiously avoided.

The interpenetration of business and political dynamics is obviously germane to the study of MNCs from their very origins. As summarized by Jones (2005), "from the [19th] century, governments were aware that national diplomatic influence and national economic influence were related" (p. 218). The accusations leveled at EMNCs these days of acting as instruments of the foreign policy ambitions of their home governments are therefore naïve, when they do not simply try to conceal deep-rooted protectionist reflexes. At the same time, there is no doubt that many EMNCs have closer ties with their governments than their OECD peers, often because they remain state-owned or state-controlled (this being the case in particular in oil and other natural resources). It would be unfortunate if government support and weak checks and balances on the part of other stakeholders led EMNCs to adopt subpar behavioral and operational standards in low-income developing countries, especially in Africa. As has been argued above, OFDI is a further form of engagement with the global economy and as such brings new forces to bear in the direction of better political and corporate governance.

The other side of the coin is that policymakers in emerging economies should not view the relocation of their firms to labor-abundant countries as a challenge. When the parent company carries out labor-intensive activities abroad, upgrading usually take place in the (by now) relatively capital-abundant home country. In other words, to the extent that EMNCs invest overseas to optimize the use of their resources, corporate relocation of production through multinational activity is an additional instrument that emerging economies have to exploit their comparative advantage to the fullest. For this potential to fully materialize, the business environment at home must be conducive to resource accumulation and eventual internationalization. Once again, the debate taking place in Korea is strongly reminiscent of the controversy regarding restructuring and hollowing out that has been traditionally associated with MNCs at all latitudes.

The research agenda remains at least as vast as the body of information and knowledge accumulated so far. It is well known that the form of entry into a foreign market is an important determinant of the subsequent success of a corporate deal. While some early work has been done, especially in smaller economies such as Chile and Singapore, the topic of the corporate returns of fast-paced internationalization through investment is one where deeper insights are needed to guide public policy no less than corporate decisions.[2] Insofar as the determinants of alternative expansion strategies are closely related to firm-specific characteristics, it is crucial to collect better and broader information. A number of possible conjectures are possible regarding the links between corporate motivation, entry mode, and performance. When exploitation is the purpose of cross-border expansion, entry into other emerging markets is more likely through greenfield investment or acquisition of existing assets, for instance through privatization. For the raw material seekers, for instance, would they be better off simply buying their inputs on open markets rather than investing in resource production? On the other hand, when the EMC is interested in exploring new business possibilities in an industrial country, the difficulties of operating according to more complex schemes and the risk of investing in a business environment that is culturally and managerially remote may make a joint venture more appropriate.[3]

There are hardly any studies that investigate the effect of multinationality on shareholders' wealth – and this is a domain where even in industrial countries the findings are contradictory. Who will survive? If diversification of risk is a driver, for example, are the investors making a mistake, with no real advantage to exploit? Would they be better off simply making portfolio investments abroad? In this case the study of investors from the Gulf countries may provide useful insights, as there are early indications that financial holdings such as Istithmar or the Abu Dhabi Investment Authority are taking a more active interest in the way companies they own are managed.

For an EMNC aspiring to become a profitable international player and recognized brand, the edge of low labor costs – one of emerging economies' advantages in competing with Western rivals – is becoming less and less important. While many Asian companies and a few Latin American and South African ones have gained the scale of multinationals, few are able to manage differences in a multicultural firm; to transfer a business model from a low-cost market to a rich foreign market; to compete via innovation rather than just with cheap manufactured goods. In countless international industries, the big winners are mainly masters of ultra-efficient management of suppliers, assembly, and distribution. Acquisitions may improve the firm's chances, but maximizing the return on deals demands smooth post-merger integration, and this is difficult enough for Western companies that have had decades to build a corporate culture, social values, and well-tested operational routines.

Recent management literature has discussed the existence of learning in a number of contexts. To the extent that EMNCs grow in size and international activity, they have to enlarge the number and enhance the quality of their management processes in order to cope with the added complexity of their overseas operations and the need for control and coordination. Some of the more mundane – and yet crucial – choices have to do with the degree of centralization and hierarchical control (a "national baron," a "product champion," or a "country prince"?) and of product and strategy adaptation to local needs and characteristics.[4] Equally important are the feedback mechanisms into the home economy of the processes of business adaptation and organizational change that characterize multinational expansion. Finding how all this happens in practice, and how cultural differences between home and host nations undermine or enhance multinational acquisitions, is hence another major task for researchers. This can be accomplished through business history research that relies on aggregating case studies. This approach, which also underpins the Harvard management or process approach, is followed by Bonaglia *et al.* (2006) in their study of three EMNCs in white good appliances.

Finally, the recurrent emphasis in policy discourse on the positive influence of South–South cooperation cannot be simply accepted at face value. If, on the one hand, there is an expectation that FDI can play a positive role in facilitating home economies' competitive insertion into the world economy, on the other hand there is a wide consensus that a number of factors must be in place to maximize the developmental impact of FDI. There is no reason to expect EMNCs to be treated differently, unless there is hard evidence to suggest that their *modus operandi* is more conducive to economic growth and sustainable development. Indeed, the risk, if any, is that the poor might be less able to benefit from these developments if most FDI from China and India, and the developing world more broadly, went to resource-intensive industries.

Appendix 1 Selected EMNCs' acquisitions in the OECD market

EMNC	Target OECD company	Description
China		
BOE Technology Group	Hynix (Korea)	Bought the display business in 2003 to become a serious player in the computer screen business. But it still trails industry leaders, with the added burden of hefty debt
Chalkis (subsidiary of Xinjiang)	Le Cabanon (France)	Bought 55% of the production and marketing subsidiary, Conserves de Provence. Under the terms of the merger, Conserves de Provence buys tomato products from China – mainly tomato juice – and resells them in Europe after processing and packing
China National Blue Star	Adisseo (France)	Acquired the animal nutrition supplement producer for €400 m. in January 2006
China National Oil Offshore Corporation	MEG Energy (Canada)	Invested Can$150 m. (US$122 m.) to acquire 16.7%
Huaneng Group	OzGen (Australia)	Paid US$227 m. for a 50% share
Huapeng	Welz (Germany)	Purchase of the insolvent pressurized cylinder manufacturer in Brandenburg gave 30% share of the domestic market

Continued

Appendix 1 Continued

EMNC	Target OECD company	Description
Lenovo	IBM (USA)	Bought the PC business for US$1.75 billion in cash, stock, and debt. IBM will hold an 18.9% stake for three years with an option of extending it. The unit employs some 10,000 people worldwide, of whom 40% already work in China
Qianjiang Group	Benelli (Italy)	Bought the celebrated motorcycle maker from Gruppo Merloni in 2005
Shanghai Automotive Industry Corporation (SAIC)	Ssangyong (Korea)	Bought a 48.9% stake to enhance R&D capabilities in sport utility vehicles and add weight to overseas listing plans
Shanghai Electric	Akiyama and Ikegai (Japan)	Purchased two of Japan's oldest and largest machine tool builders, both bankrupt, in 2002 and 2004
Shougang Group	Mt. Gibson Iron (Australia)	Paid US$120 m. for half of an iron ore mine in June 2005
TCL	Schneider (Germany)	Bought from bankruptcy for US$10.4 m in 2002. A plant in Germany was closed and TTE manufacturing is being shifted to either Poland or Thailand
TCL	Thomson (France)	Signed a deal in November 2003 to combine television and DVD businesses. TCL International owns 67% of TCL-Thomson Electronics (established in July 2004)
TCL	Alcatel (France)	Purchased 55% of the mobile phone activities for €55 m. The goal is to turn it into the world's fifth-largest producer (at the moment, their combined share is equal to 3.7%). R&D, conception, marketing, and sales will be kept in France (Centre de Recherche de Colombes)

Wanxiang (Chinese for universal joint)	Universal Automotive Industries (USA)	Following half-a-dozen acquisitions of smaller auto-parts makers since 1994, in 2001 purchased 21% of the Nasdaq-listed company for US$2.8 m.
Yanzhou Coal Mining Co.	Austar Coal Mine	Paid US$23 m. for a mine in Hunter Valley in 2004
Hong Kong		
AS Watson	Kruidvat (Netherlands)	Acquired the health and beauty group for €1.3 bn. in 2002
AS Watson	Marionnaud (France)	Acquired Europe's largest perfumery for €900 m. in January 2005
AS Watson	Merchant Retail (UK)	Acquired in May 2005 for £222 m.
CLP Holdings	Singapore Power	Bought retail and generation assets in Australia in March 2005 for US$1.68 bn.
Dickson Concepts	ST Dupont (France)	Bought in 1987
Dickson Concepts	Harvey Nichols (UK)	Bought in 1991
Fang Brothers Knitting	Pringle (UK)	Bought the embattled Scottish luxury label for £5 m. in 2000
Li & Fung	Briefly Stated (USA)	Acquired the US$100 m. apparel maker for US$124 m. in August 2005
Sportswear Holdings	Tommy Hilfiger (USA)	Acquired in 1989
Sportswear Holdings	Asprey & Garrard (UK)	Acquired one of Britain's oldest jewelers in 2002
Yangtzekiang Garment Manufacturing	Guy Laroche (FR)	The YGM Trading spin-off paid US$17 m. in 2004 for the French fashion house

Continued

Appendix 1 Continued

EMNC	Target OECD company	Description
Singapore		
Dabicam	InterContinental Hotel	The GIC affiliate bough the Paris property for €315 m. in September 2005
SembCorp Waste Management	Pacific Waste Management (Australia)	Bought 40% in 2000 for US$91 m.
SembCorp Marine	Sabrine Shipyard (USA)	Bought the Texas repair facility in summer 2005 to convert it into its US base
Singapore Airlines	Virgin Atlantic (UK)	Bought 49% of Britain's second-largest international airline in 1999 for US$960 m.
Singapore Airlines	Air New Zealand	Bought 25% in 2000
Singapore Power	SPI PowerNet and TXU Australia	Paid US$5.5 bn. in 2000–04 to become the country's largest private sector utility player
Singapore Telecom	Optus (AU)	Bought the second-largest telecom operator in Australia for US$8 bn. in 2001
South Korea		
Samsung	AST Research (USA)	Bought 40% of the world's sixth-largest PC maker in 1995 for US$378 m.
Samsung Aerospace	Rollei (Germany)	Bought in 1996; massive injection of capital sustained turnaround; management buyout in 1999 following the Asian crisis

Taiwan

Acer	Texas Instruments (USA)	Bought the personal notebook division in 1997
BenQ	Siemens (Germany)	Acquired the US$5.8 bn., 6,000-employee handset unit, with development and manufacturing locations in Brazil and Germany, in exchange for a 2.5% stake
Foxconn's (HonHai)	Eimo (Finland)	Purchased one of Nokia's largest subcontractors in 2003 to get business that had otherwise eluded the firm
TPV	Philips (Netherlands)	Bought the PC monitor and entry-level flat-screen television business for US$358 m. (half in new shares equal to 15% of TPV's capital) and expects sales of Philips-branded products to grow 80% per year on average until 2008

Other ASEAN Countries

Berjaya (Malaysia)	Taiga (Canada)	Bought 60% stake of largest distributor of building materials in 1994
Dusit Thani (Thailand)	Kempinski (Germany)	Bought 83% stake in January 1995 for US$165 m. Sold it in 1997 to Siam Sindhorn, which is controlled by the Crown Property Bureau, an agency that manages assets for the monarchy
Proton (Malaysia)	Lotus (UK)	Bought an 80% stake in the sports automaker in 1996
Proton (Malaysia)	MV Agusta (Italy)	Underwrote €70 m. share issue in 2004 and owns 57.75% of the automaker
Salim (Indonesia)	Futuris (Australia)	Bought a 4.85% interest in the rural services group in 2003; sold to grains group Cooperative Bulk Handling in 2004 to form a 50/50 joint venture, Pacific Agrifoods

Continued

Appendix 1 Continued

EMNC	Target OECD company	Description
San Miguel Corp (Philippines)	National Foods (Australia)	After a five-month contest with Fonterra, acquired the company for US$1.4 m. Owns premium beer J. Boag & Son and Australia's largest fruit juice manufacturer, Berri
Thai Union Frozen Products (Thailand)	Tri-Union Seafoods (USA)	Bought second-largest US tuna cannery, which owns the Chicken of the Sea brand, in 2001. In 2003 it acquired Empress, a leading importer and distributor of frozen shrimp and shellfish. Combined companies' annual revenues of US$550 m.
India		
Bharat Forge	Carl Dan Peddinghaus (Germany)	Now the world's second-largest forgings maker, its ambition is to achieve US$1 billion in global sales by 2008. CDP's operating margin is just 12.5% against Bharat Forge's 30%
Bharat Forge	Federal Forge (USA)	Bought in June 2005 from bankruptcy
Dr. Reddy's Laboratories	Trigenesis Therapeutics (USA)	Acquired the privately owned dermatology company in June 2004 for US$11 m.
Dr. Reddy's Laboratories	Betapharm (Germany)	Acquired the fourth-largest German generics manufacturer in February 2006 for almost €500 m.
Essel Propack	Telcon Packaging (UK)	Latest acquisition by the world's largest manufacturers of tubes used to package toothpaste. The company, with 17 plants in 11 countries, is aiming to double capacity by 2005 in its existing units in China, Egypt, and Latin America

Four Soft	DCS Transportation (UK)	Bought the software logistics developer for US$19 m. in September 2005
I-flex	Equinox (USA)	Acquired a 33% stake in French treasury software specialist Login
Infosys Technologies	Expert Information Services (Australia)	First overseas purchase, in December 2003, aimed at cross-selling call-center services to Infosys's long-standing software services clients in Australia
Jindal Polyester	Rexor (France)	The 2003 purchase created the largest polyester manufacturer of PET film in India and the fifth largest in the world
Ranbaxy	RPG (France)	Bought the fifth-largest generics maker in France (2002 sales of €44 million, 18 out of the 20 best-selling generic drugs) from Aventis in late 2003
Reliance Infocomm	FLAG Telecom (UK)	Acquired the bandwidth supplier with intercontinental undersea cable in 2004 for US$211 m.
Reliance Industries	Trevira (Germany)	The acquisition of the former polyester division of Hoechst for €80 m. in June 2004 made it the world's largest polyester fiber and yarn producer
Satyam	Citisoft (UK)	In 2005, a US$39 m. all-cash purchase signaled its intention to broaden business beyond simple outsourcing into higher-margin, specialist consulting services
Suzlon Energy	EVE Holding (Belgium)	In March 2006, the €465 m. deal gave the world's sixth-largest wind turbine maker indirect ownership of Hansen Transmissions International, the world's second-largest maker of industrial and wind turbine generator gear boxes

Continued

160 *Multinational Companies from Emerging Economies*

Appendix 1 Continued

EMNC	Target OECD company	Description
Tata Consultancy Services	Phoenix Global Solutions (USA)	Bought the global provider of business technology solutions to insurance companies in May 2004
Tata Consultancy Services	Pearl Assurance (UK)	As part of an US$847 m. deal over 12 years to provide business processing services, it will take on close to 1,000 Pearl staff in northern England
Tata Motors	Hispano Carrocera (Spain)	Paid €12 m. for a 21% stake, covering the license for technology and brand rights, and has a call option on the remaining 79%.
Tata Motors	Incat (UK)	Paid £53.4 m. to buy the Aim-listed engineering and design services company
Tata Tea	Tetley Tea (UK)	Acquired in 2001 for £275 m.
Tata Tea	Glaceu (USA)	Acquired a 30% stake in 2006 for US$677 m.
Torrent	Heumann Pharma (Germany)	Bought the €50 m. marketing and distribution arm from Pfizer in June 2005
VSNL	Tyco International (USA)	Paid US$130 m. for 60,000 km of undersea cables
Videocon	Thomson (France)	Bought five cathode-ray tube plants in China, Italy, Poland, and Mexico, employing 14,000 people, in February–June 2005 in exchange for an equity stake
Wipro	NewLogic (Austria)	Paid €47 m. to acquire a leading semiconductor design services company with facilities in Austria, Germany, and France

Latin America

Cemex (Mexico)	RMC (UK)	Completed the US$4.1 bn. acquisition in February 2005
CVRD (Brazil)	Canico (Canada)	Paid US$749 million for a controlling stake in the junior resource company focused on the development of the Onça Puma nickel laterite project in Brazil
Colcerámica (Colombia)	Mansfield Plumbing Products (USA)	In 2004, bought 34% of one of the world's largest producers of plumbing products (more than 750 employees and three plants in Ohio and Texas)
Embraer (Brazil)	OGMA (Portugal)	Partnered with EADS in 2004 to buy 65% stake from government. In the future, the participation of EADS can reach a maximum of 19.5%
Gerdau (Brazil)	Ameristeel (USA)	Currently the fourth-largest overall steel company and the second-largest mini-mill producer in North America
Gruma Corporation (Mexico)	Nuova De Franceschi & Figli (Italy)	The world's largest tortilla producer bought 51% of the US$27 m. maize manufacturer in July 2004, with a view to integrate it with its UK factory
Gruma Corporation (Mexico)	Ovis Boske (Netherlands)	Took over Europe's biggest flour tortilla manufacturer (sales €20 m.) in 2004
IAT Group (Chile)	Fresh Del Monte (USA)	Bought the company in December 1996 from difficult financial challenges and took it public in 1997 on the New York Stock Exchange
KoSa (Mexico)	Hoechst Celanese's polyester fiber plants (Germany)	Bought when the German company decided to move to higher-value synthetics. KoSa, a US–Mexican joint venture managed by Mexicans, is now the world's leading polyester maker

Continued

Appendix 1 Continued

EMNC	Target OECD company	Description
Siderca (Argentina)	Dalmine (Italy)	Bought from government in 1996 and merged with other units to create Tenaris in 2004
Votorantim Cimentos (Brazil)	St. Marys Cement (Canada)	Acquired in 2002 from Lafarge, it has 2 cement plants, 1 cement and grinding plant in Michigan, 9 cement distribution terminals in the Great Lakes region and, 39 concrete and aggregate facilities located in Ontario
South Africa		
Mondi	La Rochette (France)	Bought the €127 m. packaging business in March 2002
Netcare	General Healthcare Group (UK)	Acquisition of a controlling stake in leading private hospital group
Old Mutual	Skandia (Sweden)	Paid US$5.9 bn. in December 2005 to win control of the biggest Nordic insurer
SABMiller	Peroni (Italy)	Bought in May 2003 in a deal valuing the privately held firm at €563 m.
Sappi	Potlatch (USA)	Bought the coated fine paper assets for US$480 m. in March 2002 to supply the US market with locally produced European-style coated paper
Sasol	Condea Vista (USA)	In early 2001, acquired the chemical division of Conoco, which operates facilities in Louisiana, Maryland, and Arizona
South African Breweries	Miller (USA)	Bought for US$5.6 bn. in July 2002 from Philip Morris/Altria and changed name to SABMiller. Altria took a 36% stake (25% of the voting rights)

EMNCs' Acquisitions in the OECD Market 163

New Europe

Agrofert (Czech Republic)	SKW Piesteritz (Germany)	Acquired a controlling stake from Degussa for €50 m. in June 2002
Arçelik (Turkey)	Blomberg (Germany)	Acquisition in 2002 was the largest in a series that also included Leisure and Flavel (UK) and Elektra Bregenz (Austria)
Evraz (Russia)	Palini (Italy)	In August 2005 bought 75.1% plus one share of the US$183 m. rolled steel producer for an undisclosed sum
Lukoil (Russia)	Getty Petroleum (USA)	In 2000 became the first Russian firm to acquire a publicly traded US company
Norilsk (Russia)	Stillwater Mining (USA)	Paid US$257 m. for the palladium and platinum metals producer group
PKN Orlen (Poland)	BP (UK)	Bough 500 petrol stations in eastern Germany in December 2002
Severstal (Russia)	Rouge Industries (USA)	In a competitive bid process, bought the fifth-largest US integrated steel producer in January 2004 for US$285.5 m.
Severstal (Russia)	Lucchini (Italy)	Took a 62% stake in Italy's second-largest steel manufacturing group, producing mainly engineering steel long products, in February 2005
Severstal (Russia)	Stelco (Canada)	Bought the Hamilton steel maker while restructuring under creditor protection
Severstal (Russia)	Carrington Wire (UK)	Subsidiary Metiz bought the wire producer in April 2006 for an undisclosed sum

Continued

Appendix 1 Continued

EMNC	Target OECD company	Description
Sinan Solmaz (Turkey)	Duralex (France)	Bought in December 2005 from receivership. The wholesale retailer accounts for half of the glassmaker's turnover
Sistema (Russia)	Intracom (Greece)	Bought a 51% stake in the ICT equipment vendor for €120 m. in February 2006
Unimil (Poland)	Condomi (Germany)	Bought its German parent and became Europe's biggest condom producer
Other countries		
Ashanti Goldfields (Ghana)	SAMAX Gold (Canada)	In 1998, the acquisition for US$140 m. realized synergies through the development of the adjoining licenses in the Geita district of Tanzania
Dubal (United Arab Emirates)	Global Alumina (Canada)	Paid US$200 m. in August 2005 for a 25% stake
Naser International and other Kuwaiti investors	PGO Automobiles S.A. (France)	Acquired 51% of auto manufacturer listed on Euronext Paris Marché Libre from Germany's Casalva
Orascom (Egypt)	Wind (Italy)	The May 2005 €12.1 bn. deal for the third-largest mobile phone company and second-largest fixed-line provider is Europe's biggest leveraged buyout and the second largest in history
Qatar Petroleum (with ExxonMobil)	Edison (Italy)	Bought 90% of the company in charge of the planned 8 bn. m³ per annum offshore Isola di Porto Levante LNG terminal for €20.75 m. in May 2005

Appendix 2 Representative disputes between EMNCs and host governments in developing countries

Host country	Description of dispute
Ghana[a]	In 1996 a consortium led by Telekom Malaysia bought a 30% stake in Ghana Telecom, in a deal worth US$38 million. Although it was a minority owner, the five-year technical service agreement (TSA) granted the G-Com consortium the power to name four seats on the seven-member board. Among the goals was to roll out 400,000 lines and triple Ghana's telephone capacity. Firms from Malaysia were awarded contracts for network switches (Pernec), towers (Vitraco), and telephone handsets (Sapura). Ghana Telecom arranged for a locally syndicated loan package of US$60 million, together with a Chinese facility of US$150 million arranged by Alcatel Shanghai Bell. In 2001 IFC also extended debt financing for US$100 million, of which US$60 was syndicated to commercial banks, to expand the fixed-line network, develop a nationwide GSM network, and invest in a regional fiberoptic cable. This was the institution's largest investment in Ghana. Currency devaluation in Ghana and a change of government in 2002 complicated the situation. The incoming Kufuor administration granted the Malaysian firm three-month's extra stay and did not renew the TSA. The government claimed that the Malaysian equipment was of inferior quality, that the Ghanaian partners were awarded juicy non-competitive contracts, and that G-Com had not met the contractual targets in respect of improvement in call completion rates, fault clearance, and telecom service installations. On December 16, 2002, the government signed a management services contract with a Norwegian company, Telenor. After very difficult negotiations with Telekom Malaysia, a new board of directors was established to which the government appoints six members and G-Com appoints three members. Telekom Malaysia then sued the Ghanaian government, claiming US$300 million, while its local partners (Dr. Nii Narku Quaynor of NCS, Alhaji Mohammed Said Seidu Sulemana of Sulana Engineering Co., and Michael Attipoe of Giant International Ltd.) issued a writ at the Accra High Court seeking a perpetual injunction restraining Ghana Telecom from accessing local and foreign loans it has contracted to improve on its operations. IFC ultimately cancelled its investment before disbursement

Continued

166 *Multinational Companies from Emerging Economies*

Appendix 2   Continued

Host country	Description of dispute
	because of these prolonged shareholder disputes (also at Westel), as well as the lack of an effective regulator, which put Ghana Telecom in a dominant position with respect to cellular companies.
Indonesia[b]	In the 1970s, Indian motorcycle manufacturer Bajaj had a joint venture to assemble three-wheeled vehicles in Indonesia, then its biggest foreign market. At the height of the Suharto regime in the 1980s, Bajaj was forced out of the country. Djakarta city officials are now committed to replace the old motorized rickshaws with cleaner and quieter, gas-fueled vehicles. The Indian company has formed a joint venture to assemble them locally, but the first contract was awarded to a small, inexperienced company controlled and managed by a retired military intelligence chief with strong links to the military and former Suharto generals. The new Bajaj, on the other hand, were banned by the capital's city transportation agency on the grounds that any replacement for the old model must have a four-stroke engine and four wheels.
Iran	In February 2004 a consortium controlled by Turkcell, one of Turkey's biggest companies, won the license to establish a second GSM network. One year later, citing security reasons, Parliament passed a measure stipulating that managerial and operational control of the Irancell joint venture must lie with the local partner.
Iran	The Turkish-led Tepe-Akfen-Vie consortium signed a US$193 million deal with the Ministry of Road and Transport in September 2003 to handle the new Imam Khomeini International Airport in Tehran. In May the Revolutionary Guards shut down the airport after just one flight had landed, arguing that the operators also had business dealings with Israel, which endangered Iran's security. Later in the year Parliament passed a censure motion against Minister Ahmad Khorram and management is now with a consortium of four Iranian airlines.
Peru[c]	Colombia's Bavaria saw its attempt at securing control over Backus & Johnston severely thwarted by various problems. Already the dominant beer producer in Ecuador, in 2001 Bavaria bought the leading brewer in Panama, while an

Appendix 2 Continued

Host country	Description of dispute
	offer to acquire Panama's other brewery was blocked by competition authorities. In June 2002 Bavaria expanded into a third neighboring country by taking 24.5% of Backus, paying a 127% premium over the prevailing share price. A few days later, Venezuela's Cisneros Group announced it had acquired for US$200 million "irrevocable options" to buy, also off-market, a 16% stake in Backus. Polar, the Venezuela-based brewer that already owned 24% of Backus, alleged that Bavaria and Cisneros were acting in concert to take over the company without individually surpassing the threshold of 25% that would trigger a public tender offer. In December 2002, Peru's stock exchange regulator (CONASEP) cleared the Bavaria offer with no obligation of tendering for all shares. In 2004 an investigation was launched in Peru in response to allegations that Bavaria had paid some members of CONASEP. The allegations were first made in the leading Lima newspaper. This paper is owned by the country's largest media conglomerate, which has a joint venture with the family that owns the Colombian brewery.
Peru	In 1992 Shougang International Trade & Engineering Corp. bought the Hierro Peru iron mine from the state for US$120 million, even though the company was valued at only US$22 million. Shougang has doubled its annual production to 4.5 million tonnes, while shedding half its workforce. The company exports half its production to China, accounting for 1.5% of total Chinese iron ore imports. In 2002 a congressional report cited various failures to meet required investment targets, leading the government to levy fines of US$12 million against the company. Further fines were issued in 2002 after deficient design, non-compliance with prevention and safety rules, and the lack of an emergency plan caused the collapse of a containment area. The mine was attacked in April 2005 after police removed people living on nearby land. Peru's Congress has repeatedly tried to review the privatization contract.
Turkmenistan[d]	During the Soviet era, Turkmenistan was an important gas producer. But in the first decade of independence, dealings with Moscow were marred by price disputes and output plummeted. When Putin took office in 2000, Russia launched an initiative to form a "gas OPEC" with Kazakhstan, Uzbekistan, and Turkmenistan, the only country with developed fields. Gazprom's contract with Turkmenistan provided for

Continued

Appendix 2 Continued

Host country	Description of dispute
	annual imports of 5–6 billion m^3 in 2004 at an estimated US$29 per 1,000 m^3, rising to as much as 80 billion m^3 during 2009–29. These arrangements will allow Gazprom to delay the development of its own expensive reserves in the Yamal and Arctic regions. They will also reduce Gazprom's need to buy gas from independent Russian producers. Furthermore, they will effectively eliminate Central Asian producers as competitors for sales to Europe and other export markets, as most of their production will go to Russia. However, it is uncertain whether these deals will proceed as planned. In January 2005 President Saparmurat Niyazov imposed an embargo on gas deliveries to Gazprom. The government is demanding US$58 per 1,000 m^3 for its gas, about 30% more than its current supply agreement.
Peru	Chilean investors faced negative public reactions based on nationalist feelings. Enersis Lan removed the whole top management echelon after thousands marched in the border city of Iquitos, singing the Peruvian national anthem and destroying the airline's office, to protest against the showing of a video on a Lan international flight.

[a] "Ghana Telecom paralysed," *Business News*, March 17, 2004; personal communications with people involved in the deal.
[b] "New 'bajaj' scorned as city falls for mousy deer on wheels," *The Jakarta Times*, July 30, 2004; "Jakarta rickshaws' demise oils wheels of political controversy," *Financial Times*, September 1, 2004.
[c] "Brewers scramble for Peruvian foothold," *Financial Times*, July 29, 2002; "Trago amaro," *Revista Cambio*, December 3, 2004; "Guerra de Bitácoras," *Caretas*, February 24, 2005.
[d] "Gazprom launches emergency talks with Turkmenistan in bid to end gas embargo," *Financial Times*, April 14, 2005.

Notes

1 Introduction

1. "Mechai's franchise to open in Singapore," *The Nation*, July 28, 2004.
2. See "Churrascarias 'exportam' garcons para os EUA," *O Estado de S. Paulo*, June 14, 2004.
3. In September 2004, a consortium led by Minmetals and including four other state-owned companies – Baoshan Iron & Steel, CITIC, Jiangxi Copper, and Taiyuan Iron & Steel – offered to buy Noranda for approximately US$4.7 billion. The negotiations subsequently became bogged down. The notion that one of Canada's leading corporations, let alone one in the critical resource sector, could come under indirect control of the Chinese government was loudly protested. Negotiations were ended in March 2005, although Minmetals has reaffirmed its interest.
4. According to the 1984 United Nations Centre on Transnational Corporations (UNCTC) definition, an MNC is "an enterprise (a) comprising entities in two or more countries, regardless of the legal form and the fields of activity of those entities, (b) which operates under a system of decision making permitting coherent policies and a common strategy through one or more decision making centres, (c) in which the entities are so linked, by ownership or otherwise, that one or more of them may be able to exercise a significant influence over the activities of others, and, in particular, to share knowledge, resources and responsibilities with others." As the OECD membership has widened to include emerging economies such as Mexico, Korea, the Czech Republic, Hungary, Slovakia, and Poland, the traditional OECD versus non-OECD dichotomy, which held until the early 1990s, has now lost relevance for our purposes. To be true to the truth, Turkey has been an OECD country since 1964 even though its income level was substantially lower than the OECD average. The definition of developed countries used in this study follows the United Nations Department of Economic and Social Affairs (UN/DESA) country classification and includes all members of the OECD Development Assistance Committee. Korea and Singapore are defined as non-developed countries, even if they are by now net contributors to the World Bank Group (in other words, they are no longer eligible for loans). On the other hand, Israel is excluded. The terms "emerging" and "Southern" multinationals are used interchangeably in this book.
5. According to evolutionary economic theory, for each firm, technological change is localized around the very limited range of techniques that it knows and understands. This contrasts with the neoclassical view that firms face a menu of operational technologies, choose among them to reflect factor prices, and can effortlessly switch to a new technique if profit maximization requires them to do so.
6. Li (2003) advances the hypothesis that the superficial knowledge about EMNCs may be due to either neglect or the inability of existing MNC theories to explain what is a different phenomenon.

2 Trends in Southern OFDI

1. Lipsey (2000) observes that balance-of-payments data include all kinds of financial flows and stocks that have little to do with production and are more akin to portfolio investment. This is particularly true for figures that relate to OECD direct investment stock in fiscal havens such as the Netherlands Antilles, which can amount to many billions of dollars even when the whole operation is a tax-induced transformation of portfolio borrowing into nominal direct investment transactions involving little or no production. An additional and fundamental flaw of existing statistics is uncertainty concerning the country of the ultimate beneficial owner.
2. Still different is the case of companies in emerging economies that are controlled and managed by Western entrepreneurs. Any foreign investment made by such entities is classified as flowing from the emerging economy, although strictly speaking the managerial skills are "Western." An example is Rolf Group, Russia's largest car dealer, owned by a Briton who emigrated to Moscow to help relaunch Pepsi in the mid-1990s.
3. As of August 2005, the only non-South African national on the executive committee (and the only woman) was the corporate affairs director, a Briton.
4. I thank Mira Wilkins for drawing my attention to this similarity.
5. The fifth edition of the Balance of Payments Manual (BPM5) and the subsequent instructions provide guidance on the classification of offshore transactions. The OECD has collaborated with the IMF on an extensive meta-analysis exercise to document the sources and definitions used in data collection. This has provided the basis for a number of initiatives aimed at improving the collection methodology and consistency of definitions based on BPM5. These initiatives include intensified training for compilers in various member countries. The Foreign Investment Advisory Service has also provided advisory assistance in Egypt, China, Jamaica, Indonesia, and El Salvador. For example, the Egypt data no longer include workers' remittances and China is now gradually applying a sample survey methodology (although the round-tripping issue has not been resolved).
6. The difficulty of reconciling FDI flow data in the balance of payments with FDI stock data obtained from surveys on international investment positions must be highlighted.
7. The official names for the latter two of these entities are Hong Kong (China) and Taiwan Province of China, shortened here for simplicity's sake.
8. "Poland invests in the EU," *Warsaw Voice*, March 29, 2006.
9. In an important foreign investor such as Malaysia, for instance, no data are available on stocks/flows by country. Only data at the aggregate level are available (Wan Ramlah bt Wan Abd. Raof, Director, Balance of Payments Statistics Division, Department of Statistics, Malaysia, personal communication, September 8, 2005).
10. The breakdown of Chinese FDI stock by sector and industry shows that a full third is in these sectors, although the flows figures suggest a much lower relative share (Giroud and Mirza 2006).
11. At least in the case of Brazil, the relative weight of tax havens is indeed in all likelihood underestimated, since destinations such as Ireland, Luxembourg, and Switzerland receive abnormally high FDI outflows. Owing to government restrictions and tax benefits, Taiwanese investment in China is often routed

through third countries. Because official Chinese FDI statistics report immediate origin instead of original source, the British Virgin Islands currently rank as China's second-largest source of FDI. Bilateral FDI flows between Colombia and Panama are also abnormally high, suggesting that Colombian firms may use the financial center both to invest in third countries and to channel funds back into Colombia (Franco and De Lombaerde 2000).

12. For instance, in spring 2002 Rolly Co. – a company registered in the British Virgin Islands, but in reality a subsidiary of the China National Oil and Gas Exploration and Development Corporation (CNODC) – bought a 50 percent participation in an oil company in Oman. Another example is provided by Essel Propack's acquisition of Telcon Packaging in the United Kingdom in April 2005, which was made through Lamitube Technologies Ltd., Mauritius, a wholly owned subsidiary of the Indian company.
13. In Moldova, Russia contributes one-quarter of the inward FDI stock (Hunya 2006: table 5).
14. This phenomenon, however, is not fully captured in Table 2.4, as a major Brazilian investment, AmBev's takeover of Quilmes, was registered in Luxembourg, where the latter is incorporated. CVRD is also undertaking its first investment in Argentina, in Neuquén.
15. "Fusiones y compras más caras," *La Nación*, December 22, 2005.
16. For providing unpublished data used in this section, I thank Jean-Willem Angel (Insee), René Dell'mour (Oesterreichische Nationalbank), Marco Mutinelli (Politecnico di Milano), Ronnie O'Toole (Forfas), Eric Ramstetter (ICSEAD), Jean Ritzen (Statistics Netherlands), David Sabourin (Statistics Canada), Dietmar Scholz (Bundesbank), and William Zeile (US Bureau of Economic Analysis).
17. This survey is an annual census of employment in all known manufacturing, internationally traded and financial services, and other service companies supported by the development agencies – Enterprise Ireland, IDA Ireland, Shannon Development, and Údarás na Gaeltachta. To put this figure in context, at the end of 2004 employment in agencies' client companies was approximately 300,000, while the total number of those employed was approximately 1.9 million (CSO 2004).
18. Clarke Thompson, Director, International Trade, South Carolina Department of Commerce, and John X. Ling, Managing Director, South Carolina–Asian office, personal communications, June 2005.
19. To put this figure in perspective, according to Hannah (1998), "20 of the top 100 firms in 1912 were still in the top 100 of 1995" (p. 63).
20. See also "A Odebrecht está em Angola para perpetuar a sua actividade," *Jornal de Angola*, November 1, 2005.
21. "Tata sees Bangladesh ventures by 2008," *Financial Express*, October 14, 2004.

3 Toward an Industry Categorization

1. Multinational financial service providers headquartered in emerging and developing economies do obviously also exist, but FDI in banking and insurance presents specificities that demand a different analytical framework. For this reason, this theme is not analyzed here.
2. In April 2002, the British Treasury raised its taxation of North Sea oil producers by 10 percent; in 2005, the state of Alaska added US$88 million to

companies' annual liability by changing tax rules to face declining production in the North Slope field (see "Rush to secure oil supplies shifts the balance of power," *Financial Times*, July 13, 2005).
3. Properly speaking, Gazprom is not a national oil company, although its strategy is similar. It has a strategic alliance with the Gas Authority of India and big investments in Germany, including Wingas, a pipeline and gas marketing joint venture with BASF subsidiary Wintershall. In 2006 the press reported its interest in Centrica of the United Kingdom and Hera of Italy.
4. Non-weighted state ownership for the ten largest OECD oil companies (as listed in *Fortune*'s 2004 Global 500) is 3.031 percent (July 2005) and fully corresponds to the residual stake held by the Italian government (Ministry of the Economy and CDP) in ENI. On the other hand, among the companies included in Table 3.2 only Gazprom, Petrobrás, Petrochina, and Sinopec are listed, although in each case governments still maintain majority control. Possibly the only large-scale oil privatization in developing countries took place in Argentina and eventually led to the takeover of YPF by Spain's Repsol.
5. India had in addition been seeking to secure a fixed-price contract for long-term gas purchase from Iran, but has been obliged to accept a deal that will see the price largely pegged to that of Brent crude, subject to a ceiling of US$31 per barrel.
6. International investment in financial services is also huge, and institutions from emerging, developing, and transition economies are also active, but this sector has specificities that prompt me not to treat the topic in this book.
7. "Empire of the Sun," *International Herald Tribune*, August 19/20, 2006.
8. These include the Dorchester in London, Beverly Hills Hotel in California, Hôtel Meurice Plaza Athénée in Paris, and Hotel Principe di Savoia in Milan. Most recently, Ananda Krishnan, one of the richest men in Malaysia, bought a 50 percent stake in Hotel des Bergues in Geneva.
9. "Jumeirah plans to expand its US presence," *Financial Times*, April 17, 2006.
10. Norwegian Telenor, which owns 27 percent of VimpelCom's shares and controls KyivStar through a joint venture with Altimo, opposed the transaction, claiming that it lacked business sense.
11. Lan was originally LanChile; it dropped the reference to Chile as part of its internationalization strategy.
12. "Up in the air over dithering," *The New Zealand Herald*, October 6, 2001; "Air NZ needs new partner for survival," *The New Zealand Herald*, September 10, 2003; "Sale of SIA's Air NZ stake enlivens market," *The New Zealand Herald*, October 6, 2004.
13. The transition from fragmented, local markets to larger, centralized wholesale markets that took various decades in core OECD countries in the North Atlantic has been largely accomplished in a decade. In Brazil, for instance, supermarkets' share of food sales went from 30 percent in 1990 to 75 percent in 2000. East and Southeast Asia are about five years behind Latin America, but supermarkets in that region are growing at an even faster pace. In China, between 1999 and 2002 the share of the sales value of organized retailing in total retailing sales revenue rose from 1 percent of US$385.5 billion to 9 percent of US$492.2 billion (Digal and Goldstein in progress).

14. See "Avalados por dinamismo económico retailers chilenos trasladan su guerra al exterior," *Estrategia*, December 6, 2004; "La nueva conquista de Falabella," *Qué pasa*, May 27, 2005.
15. "Fortress faces tussle to fend off Chinese assault," *Financial Times*, November 17, 2003.
16. A similar venture is a €9 million software development center set up by Poland's Comarch in Dresden, eastern Germany.

4 The New Asian Multinationals

1. Korea and China established diplomatic relations only in 1992.
2. See "Korea's LG," *Business Week*, January 24, 2005.
3. Chery, one of China's most aggressive new automakers, is also planning to build a new factory in Eastern Europe within five years (see "Chery plans factory in Eastern Europe," *Financial Times*, October 27, 2004).
4. SembCorp Parks Management is majority-owned by SembCorp Industries (SCI), Asia's largest engineering and construction company outside Japan and Korea. Temasek holds 51.46 percent of SCI.
5. Taiwanese and foreign manufacturers have relocated processing and assembly to mainland China. Many intermediate products and raw materials for these operations are imported from Taiwan; final products, in turn, are re-exported from China to final customers in developed markets. The biggest category of Taiwanese exports to China is integrated circuits and microcomponents. Taiwan's strong semiconductor industry remains mainly in Taiwan, while China is still unable to produce advanced semiconductors. In 2003, China's three biggest exporting companies were all subsidiaries of Taiwanese electronics/IT manufacturers. The Shenzhen manufacturing base of the Foxconn Group alone accounted for approximately 1.5 percent of China's total exports in 2003. It is estimated that Taiwanese companies now produce 50–70 percent of China's IT exports.
6. Taiwan has long had its own "Go South" strategy. The policy, first announced in 1994 and reintroduced by President Chen Shui-bian in 2002, aims to lessen Taiwan's economic dependence on China by encouraging business firms to invest in Southeast Asian countries.
7. "Trade week promotes investment in Honduras," *Taiwan Journal*, November 26, 2004.
8. Some 40 percent of total intermediate goods and materials procured by Korean affiliates come from Korea, while these affiliates exported only approximately 20 percent of their sales to Korea.
9. The first joint venture was established in Tokyo in November 1979 by Beijing Friendship Commercial Service.
10. "China eases control on overseas investment," *Financial Times*, October 12, 2004.
11. See "Government to boost China's overseas investment," *Asia Times*, December 7, 2004.
12. "Un géant de l'Empire du milieu s'invite dans l'industrie française de la tomate," *Le Monde*, April 13, 2004.
13. "Des Chinois montent une usine de recyclage dans le Lot," *Le Monde*, April 13, 2004.

14. At the end of 2003, more than 3/4 China's main commodities were characterized by excess supply.
15. "TCL profits switched off," *Financial Times*, April 19, 2005.
16. "Microwave power," *Fortune*, November 24, 2003.

5 Multilatinas

1. A special operative unit (Grupo de Trabalho de Exploração no Exterior – GTEE) was created in 1968 and a separate company (Petrobrás Internacional S.A. – Bráspetro) was set up four years later.
2. In the new-generation factories, the proportion of components that can be manufactured on-site has reached unprecedented levels and, as a result, far fewer suppliers are now required. At Volkswagen's innovative truck plant in Resende, parts are manufactured off-site and then installed into the trucks by the components suppliers themselves, rather than by Volkswagen.
3. Another example of "follow-the-customer" investment is provided by India's Sundram Fasteners, which decided to acquire a plant in Jiaxin, in the Haiyan economic zone, to supply Ford.
4. Similarly, Estonian banks and other financial institutions have leveraged their earlier exposure to market reforms to expand to other transition economies (Stare 2002).

6 Existing Theories and Their Relevance to EMNCs

1. In Africa, Chinese companies reportedly pay their own workers salaries that are lower than those paid to local managers ("La Chine destabilize l'Europe," *J.A./L'intelligent*, November 28, 2004). See also Pheng and Hongbin (2003).
2. "The Chinese either have the skills to a large extent and [for] skills they don't have ... they are very clever at acquiring them in joint ventures," says Carlos Möller, international director at Germany's Bilfinger Berger. "But they are reluctant to give out a large share." See "Firms cautious despite uptick," *Engineering News Record*, August 23, 2004.
3. Implicit in the model is the strong emphasis on individuals as the holders of market-specific knowledge.
4. Buckley and Casson (1976) criticize the monopoly advantage approach, claiming that considering the MNC as a monopolistic rent seeker obscures its Coasian efficiency-seeking properties.
5. See, e.g., Álvarez (2001) on Spain; Barry *et al.* (2003) on Ireland; Bellak (2000) on Austria; Castro (2004) on Portugal.
6. Since the United States is the most important source of FDI flows into Ireland and also the most important destination for Irish outflows, Barry *et al.* (2003) utilize US data on the bilateral Irish–US FDI relationship to test the IDP hypothesis.
7. See also Papandreou's (1952) intuition that the firm should be treated as a specific case of the general phenomenon of social organization and a system of communication and coordination.
8. Their definition of "emerging" is broader than the one used in this book as they include Australia, considering it a "prosperous yet still peripheral nation."

9. March (1991) defined exploitation as "such things as refinement, choice, production, efficiency, selection, implementation, execution" and exploration as "terms such as search, variation, risk taking, experimentation, play, flexibility, discovery, innovation" (p. 71).
10. Although most models in financial economics predict that minority shareholders are adversely affected by family ownership (e.g., Burkart *et al.* 2003), according to Anderson and Reeb (2003) family firms perform better than non-family firms. Additional analysis reveals that the relationship between family holdings and firm performance is non-linear and that when family members serve as CEO, performance is better than with outside CEOs.
11. Note also the recent experience of Iceland, where three diversified family-controlled conglomerates have accumulated a sizeable portfolio of foreign assets following financial deregulation in the early 1990s.
12. Ratan Tata, in "Tata takes its wares to the world," *Financial Times*, September 26, 2003.
13. "A giant so big it's a proxy for India's economy," *The New York Times*, June 4, 2004.
14. "A retail invasion from Turkey," *Business Week*, December 15, 2003; "Strong growth in the pipeline for Koc [sic]," *Financial Times*, December 3, 2004.
15. A second Portuguese plant was opened in 2003, with a strong emphasis on research and development functions ("COFICAB: quand le Groupe Elloumi se distingue à l'international," *l'Economiste Maghrébin*, 309).

7 The Role of Governments

1. This applies to Indian rupee investments.
2. A liberalized mechanism for acquisition of software companies in the overseas market permits stock swap options up to US$100 million on an automatic basis. For acquisition in other sectors, the ceiling under the automatic route has been increased from US$15 million to US$50 million, and beyond this approval is through the Committee on Overseas Investment.
3. The Board of Investment takes a facilitating role, while the Exim Bank provides financing facilities for overseas investment in construction projects and in Thai restaurants.
4. The Brazilian company agreed to remit dividends equal to 1.5 times the US$80 million credit. In its press statement to announce the deal, BNDES stated that by supporting the acquisition, it prevented a non-Brazilian competitor from buying the Argentine company and exploiting its so-called Hilton quota to export to the EU ("En Brasil hay 30 transnacionales," *La Nación*, September 11, 2005).
5. "New horizons," *Financial Mail*, May 5, 2006.
6. "AmBev says merger is in national interest," *Financial Times*, July 5, 1999.
7. See "Le géant de la bière InBev veut mondialiser ses marques pour grossir encore," *Le Monde*, March 23, 2005.
8. See "A bet on a Brazilian brewery pays off for 3 investors," *The New York Times*, March 4, 2004. In July 2005, SABMiller took over Grupo Empresarial Bavaria, the Colombian brewery with large operations in other Andean countries, for US$8 billion. To the extent that the raider is a UK-based MNC, the deal amounts to the disappearance of an EMNC and may signal a trend that

large viable (Latin American) EMNCs will be absorbed into still larger OECD entities. I thank Mira Wilkins for drawing my attention to this possibility.
9. See "Belgian brewer acquires a taste for Brazilian frugality," *The New York Times*, September 27, 2005.
10. In 1999 Spain's competition authorities cleared the sale of state-owned intercity transport company Enatcar to Alsa on the condition that the bidder did not buy any other domestic company before 2005. Over the next few years, Alsa expanded abroad in Morocco, Chile, and Germany ("Alsa rudea por Europa del Este," *El País*, April 17, 2005).
11. Telmex controls 94 percent of all fixed phone lines in Mexico, and América Móvil controls an estimated 80 percent of the country's mobile phone market ("Mexico competition chief pushes for reform," *Financial Times*, March 15, 2006). Qatar Telecom (Qtel), the sole provider of fixed, mobile, Internet, and Datacomm services in Qatar, is also astonishingly profitable – its net profit margin reached 65 percent in 2004.
12. The economies are Hong Kong, India, Kazakhstan, Malaysia, Pakistan, Singapore, South Africa, Thailand, and Tunisia.
13. Austria's OMV and Sweden's Lundin made a highly publicized departure from Sudan in 2002 in response to insecurity and embarrassment over association with the government. In Angola, Sinopec was recently awarded two concessions (blocks 3/80 and 8) that were previously exploited by France's Total. This decision is widely thought to reflect the worsening of Franco-Angolan relations caused by prohibited arms sales during the 1990s ("Bonne gouvernance: fort de son pétrole, l'Angola se tourne vers la Chine pour échapper aux exigences du FMI," *Le Monde*, July 6, 2005).
14. Ibid.
15. The governments of the two countries are proposing jointly to construct a 7,000 megawatt hydropower plant on the Salween river, more than three times Thailand's current total power generation capacity. Several companies, including Thailand's partly state-owned and listed upstream PTT Exploration and Production, are exploring in the Gulf of Martaban. Gas exports to Thailand are worth US$1 billion a year and represent 40 percent of legal exports ("Thailand scouts for energy," *Asia Times*, February 23, 2005).
16. To "counteract the media dictatorship of the big international news networks," president Chávez is also promoting a region-wide television station, Televisión del Sur (Telesur). A venture that involves Argentina, Cuba, Brazil, and Uruguay but is 70 percent financed by Venezuela, the station begun broadcasting in July 2005 ("And now, the news in Latin America's view," *The New York Times*, May 17, 2005).
17. "ONGC chairman threatens to resign," *Financial Times*, August 31, 2005; "India slams Goldman Sachs for 'moving goalposts' on Kazakhstan oil auction," *Financial Times*, October 17, 2005.
18. "DP World strives to contain dispute in India," *Financial Times*, April 6, 2006.
19. Because of alleged Chinese connections, in 2004 the central government security agencies removed the company from a shortlist of candidates bidding to operate a terminal at Jawaharlal Nehru Port in Mumbai; in 2005 it failed to win security clearance to build and operate the Mumbai Port Trust container terminal. In January 2006 India announced that it will consider more sympathetically

Chinese bids to take part in developing the country's infrastructure. Fears of a "Chinese domination" over the Panama Canal, the world's busiest shipping corridor, emerged in August 1997. In a letter to Defense Secretary William Cohen, Senate Majority Leader Trent Lott stated that "US naval ships will be at the mercy of Chinese-controlled pilots, and could even be denied passage through the Panama Canal by Hutchinson Whampoa, an arm of the People's Liberation Army." In 2003, a negative review by the Committee of Foreign Investment in the United States caused Hutchinson Whampoa to withdraw a bid for Global Crossing, the telecommunications carrier.

20. See "Mongolia weaves new relationship with 'enemy' China," *Financial Times*, September 17, 2004.
21. In April–June 2005, Transneft cut overall crude supplies to Mazeikiu to 1.8 million tonnes, compared with the 2.25 million tonnes forecast. Instead, the monopoly has allocated the reduced volumes among several Russian state-owned or state-friendly companies, including Lukoil and Rosneft. Following the control shift to Poland's PKN Orlen in May 2006, the new owner said that it has contingency plans to ship oil from a Baltic Sea terminal if Russian supplies are ever cut off, but declined to provide more details as "they have to remain confidential" ("Battle is on to reclaim refinery," *Petroleum Economist*, May 2005; "Mazeikiu sale aims to alleviate pressure from Russia," *Financial Times*, May 30, 2006).
22. "A Slav's best friend," *The Economist*, April 28, 2005; "Sale of slumbering, poisonous giant is key to awakening growth," *Financial Times*, July 12, 2005.
23. Thai Petrochemical Industry (TPI) suffered the biggest and most fiercely disputed of the many bankruptcies brought on by the Asian crisis. In June 2005, the government signed a memorandum of understanding to sell a 61.5 percent stake to domestic state-owned strategic partners. Later in the month CITIC Resources Holdings and Prachai Leophairatana, the firm's founder, presented a rival proposal to buy the loan back from creditors. The Finance Ministry opposed the CITIC move in the courts and Prime Minister Thaksin Shinawatra raised the issue during a visit to China in July.
24. "Tata sees Bangladesh ventures by 2008," *Financial Express*, October 14, 2004; "Natural gas a mixed blessing," *Financial Times*, May 4, 2005.
25. I thank Timothy J. Power for drawing my attention to this dimension.
26. According to a survey conducted by Vinaye Dey Ancharaz, University of Mauritius (personal communication, December 1, 2004).

8 Some Key Questions

1. As Khanna and Palepu (2004a) note in their discussion of the software industry in India, when the necessary institutions for sorting and pricing skills are lacking, foreign companies are unable to exploit an existing abundance of cheap talent. What characterize Indian software companies is hence the ability to develop "business models and organizational capabilities that allow them to match the talent in India with demand in developed markets" (p. 9).
2. They use US data and find that the brain drain and FDI inflows are negatively correlated contemporaneously but that skilled migration is associated

with future increases in FDI inflows. They also find suggestive evidence of substitutability between current migration and FDI for migrants with secondary education, and of complementarities between past migration and FDI for unskilled migrants.
3. No employer can determine whether an employee is deploying his skill in managing low-wage labor or exploiting his local connections to the fullest. Such contracts cannot be monitored, verified, or enforced.
4. "Filipino-Chinese spread their wings," *Financial Times*, October 17, 1995. Overseas Chinese Anthony Salim and Mochtar Riady from Indonesia and Robert Kuok from Malaysia teamed up with Li Ka-shing of Hutchison Whampoa and mainland Chinese investors to invest heavily in China after 1992.
5. The total FDI stock would be lowered by about 45 percent if China's economic center were located in New Delhi and would be lowered by about 70 percent if China's economic center were located in New Delhi and there were no cultural ties.
6. The brothers have been involved in a kickbacks scandal in India. In 1986, the government signed a US$1.3 billion contract with Bofors, a Swedish arms manufacturer, for the supply of 155 mm howitzers to the Indian army. The brothers are alleged to have received kickbacks amounting to SKr80 million (US$11 million) from Bofors for securing the contract. The scandal brought down Rajiv Gandhi's government.
7. "Gas pipeline bounces between agendas," *Washington Post*, October 5, 1998.
8. "Kocharian meets with Eduardo Eurnekian," *Asbarez*, March 10, 2005.
9. "Seeking the most hardy investors," *Financial Times*, September 30, 2004.
10. "Venir a un hotel así con tu propia pareja le añade emoción y morbo," *EPS*, August 7, 2005.
11. Indeed, while we follow UNCTAD and consider this an EMNC, Wells (1983) does not, arguing that "not only must the ownership be in the hands of developing country nationals but management must be from the local culture" (p. 7).
12. Although the Keswicks hold less than 10 percent of the group, the family dominates voting rights through a complex ownership structure that in theory is supposed to render Jardine raider-proof.
13. See, e.g., "China's people problem," *The Economist*, April 14, 2005.
14. In September 2004 Acer appointed as president an Italian executive who had joined the Taiwanese firm at the time of its acquisition of a division of Texas Instruments.
15. Anglo-American Corporation appointed a British chairman in 2002, Royal Dutch/Shell's former chairman Sir Mark Moody-Stuart. In September 2001 Goran Lindahl, the Swedish former chief executive of ABB, had been designated but had subsequently to resign as details emerged of his pension package at ABB.
16. In 2005 foreign non-executive directors at CNOOC hired independent advisors to review the management's plans for a possible bid for Unocal. The move was unusual and indicated uneasiness with the level of information provided by the management.
17. "Chinese companies acquire a taste for Western targets," *Financial Times*, October 19, 2004.
18. "India's mini-multinationals make waves in Western markets," *International Herald Tribune*, September 1, 2005.

19. See "Winning Unocal only the start of the challenge," *Financial Times*, June 30, 2005; "Antagonists argue over Chinese group's financing," *Financial Times*, July 6, 2005.
20. "Russia sees its shares emigrate," *International Herald Tribune*, February 16, 2006.
21. A similar initiative by Wal-Mart in Argentina allowed SMEs to export goods for US$14 million in 2004. See "Exportar mediante los supermercados," *La Nación*, April 15, 2005.
22. I thank Kenneth Davies for drawing my attention to this link.

9 Consequences for OECD Governments, Firms, and Workers

1. Expansionary R&D investment takes place when an EMNC opens a facility in another developing country with the objective of supporting second-generation technology transfer or other business activities.
2. "Haier reaches higher," *Fortune*, September 12, 2002.
3. A 1998 Wanxiang deal to buy Guidion, an engine-parts manufacturer in Muskegon, Michigan, fell apart when the union balked at the Chinese suitor's insistence on slimmer benefits. The company went bankrupt, dealing a blow to the Muskegon economy. See "China investing in Rust-Belt companies," *The Wall Street Journal*, November 26, 2004.
4. "Il padronato 'giallo'? Riga dritto o ti licenzia," *Corriere della Sera*, October 18, 2004.
5. See "Sweet smell of success," *Far Eastern Economic Review*, March 18, 2004.
6. Bluestar beat out General Motors, DaimlerChrysler, and Shanghai Automotive Industry Corp (SAIC) to take control of the SUV maker despite the fact that its only connection to car manufacturing is a chain of auto repair shops from which it derives approximately 16 percent of sales. The rest of its business comes from detergents, petrochemicals, and a chain of noodle shops. An interesting twist was added to the affair by an SAIC announcement that the government had anointed it as the sole Chinese bidder for the deal and Bluestar did not have permission to take over Ssangyong.
7. "Finnish ministers face pressure as Indian group targets Valtra," *Financial Times*, August 29, 2003. AGCO, a US manufacturer and distributor of agricultural equipment, eventually purchased Valtra in January 2004.
8. "Lenovo chief dismisses US security fears," *Financial Times*, February 3, 2005.
9. "Sale of I.B.M. unit to China passes US security muster," *The New York Times*, March 10, 2005.
10. After the State Department purchased 16,000 desktop computers from Lenovo, Representative Frank R. Wolf wrote in a letter to Secretary of State Condoleezza Rice that because of the Chinese government's "coordinated espionage program" intended to steal American secrets, they "should not be used in the classified network." Wolf, a Virginia Republican, is the chairman of the House subcommittee that oversees the budget appropriations for the State Department, Commerce Department, and Justice Department. In May 2006 the State Department agreed to keep the PCs off its networks that handle classified government messages and documents.

11. In the late 1990s Unocal had been instrumental in blocking the attempts by Argentina's Bridas to develop a gas production and transmission business in Turkmenistan (Rashid 2000).
12. That politics plays a crucial role in the energy business is obviously nothing new, nor is this restricted to non-OECD countries. The Australian government in 2001 rejected a takeover bid from Shell for Woodside because it would have given a foreign company control over the extraction and marketing of a major Australian energy resource. In the meanwhile China has become Australia's biggest trading partner and is soon expected to overtake Japan, which might make officials in Canberra more flexible if CNOOC pursued Woodside ("Aggressive search by CNOOC for new oil and gas seen," *The New York Times*, August 5, 2005).
13. "Bush would veto any bill halting Dubai port deal," *The New York Times*, February 22, 2006.
14. "China buys into oilsands," *Edmonton Sun*, June 1, 2005.
15. "Integrity surfaces as key concern in Arcelor battle," *Financial Times*, February 1, 2006; "Présent dans l'Ain depuis 1999, Mittal est plutôt un bon employeur," *Le Monde*, February 3, 2006.
16. "Dichiarazione alla stampa del Presidente della Repubblica Carlo Azeglio Ciampi, in visita di Stato nella Repubblica Popolare Cinese, al termine del colloquio con ,il Presidente Hu Jintao," December 6, 2004; "Address by Prime Minister Paul Martin to the Canada-China Business Council," January 21, 2005.
17. "Blair to back Indian plans for UK jobs," *Financial Times*, September 7, 2005.
18. "West is still best for some Poles," *Financial Times*, April 11, 2006.
19. "Ingegneri italiani blocaccti al confine," *Il Sole 24 Ore*, May 21, 2005.
20. This may apply, in particular, to the oil business, although the past few years have also seen the emergence of so-called juniors (small companies involved in exploration, and primarily financed by risk capital out of Canada).

10 Conclusions – The Way Ahead

1. For a different view that "national, regional and First World-Third World differences between transnational corporations will diminish over time," see Sklair and Robbins (2002: 97).
2. Zhang (2003) presents sketchy evidence on the strategic behavior of Greater China FDI flows into the United States from 1974 to 1994.
3. Aybar and Thirunavukkarasu (2004) use monthly share price returns collected over the 1996–2003 period and annual accounting data to explore the risk and performance characteristics of 79 EMNCs from 15 countries. They find that EMNCs on average perform better than their respective country market indices, although their returns remain volatile and highly sensitive to local market shocks. Their analysis indicates that performance is not affected by the degree of internationalization, that investments in developed markets have a positive impact on the value, and that EMNCs in less risky emerging markets enjoy higher firm value.
4. Some examples of firms running according to a transnational model, which place their top executives and core corporate functions in different countries to gain a competitive edge through the availability of talent or capital, low costs, or proximity to their most important customers, are provided in "Borders are so 20th century," *Business Week*, September 22, 2003.

References

Acha, Virginia and John Finch (2005), "Paths to Deepwater in the International Petroleum Industry," in K. Green, M. Miozzo, and P. Dewick (eds.), *Technology, Knowledge and the Firm: Implications for Strategy and Industrial Change*, Cheltenham and Northampton, MA: Edward Elgar Publishing, 73–91.

Álvarez, Montserrat (2001), "España y la senda de desarrollo de la inversión directa: una aproximación," Institut d'Economia de Barcelona, Document de treball No. 2001/11.

Amsden, Alice (2001), *The Rise of 'the Rest': Challenges to the West from Late-Industrializing Countries*, Oxford: Oxford University Press.

Amsden, Alice and Takashi Hikino (1994), "Project Execution Capability, Organizational Know-How and Conglomerate Growth in Late Industrialization," *Industrial and Corporate Change*, Vol. 3, No. 1: 111–47.

Anderson, Ronald C. and David M. Reeb (2003), "Founding-Family Ownership and Firm Performance: Evidence from the S&P 500," *Journal of Finance*, Vol. 58, No. 3: 1301–27.

Andreff, Wladimir (2003), "The New Transnational Corporations: Outward Foreign Direct Investment from Post-Communist Economies in Transition," *Transnational Corporations*, Vol. 12, No. 2: 73–118.

Andrews-Speed, Philip, Xuanli Liao, and Roland Dannreuther (2004), "Searching for Energy Security: The Political Ramifications of China's International Energy Policy," Smithsonian Institution, China Environment Series No. 5.

Ashton, David N. and Johnny Sung (2002), *Supporting Workplace Learning for High-Performance Working*, International Labour Office.

Athukorala, Premachandra and S. K. Jayasuriya (1988), "Parentage and Factor Proportions: A Comparative Study of Third-World Multinationals in Sri Lankan Manufacturing," *Oxford Bulletin of Economics and Statistics*, Vol. 50, No. 4: 409–23.

Aybar, Bülent and Arul Thirunavukkarasu (2004), "Emerging Market Multinationals: An Analysis of Performance and Risk Characteristics," paper presented at the 11th Annual Conference of the Multinational Finance Society, Istanbul, July 3–8.

Aykut, Dick and Dilip Ratha (2004), "South–South FDI Flows: How Big Are They?" *Transnational Corporations*, Vol. 13, No. 1: 149–77.

Baah, Anthony (2003), "Woolworths – Your Quality Store?" *South African Labour Bulletin*, Vol. 27, No. 1: 17–19.

Baena, Cesar (2002), "Growth beyond National Borders: A Policy-Making Analysis of PDVSA's Internationalization Strategy," *Latin American Business Review*, Vol. 3, No. 1: 31–55.

Bain & Company (2004), *China Goes West – An Opportunity for the German Economy*, Bain & Company.

Balsevich, Fernando, Julio Berdegué, Luis Flores, Denise Mainville, and Thomas Reardon (2003), "Supermarkets and Produce Quality and Safety Standards in Latin America," *American Journal of Agricultural Economics*, Vol. 85, No. 5: 1147–54.

Barragán, Juan Ignacio and Mario Cerruti (2003), "CEMEX: del mercado interno a la empresa global," in M. Cerruti (ed.), *Del mercado protegido al mercado global. Monterrey, 1925–2000*, Mexico City: Trillas/Universidad Autónoma de Nuevo León.

Barry, Frank, Holger Görg, and Andrew McDowell (2003), "Outward FDI and the Investment Development Path of a Late-Industrialising Economy: Evidence from Ireland," *Regional Studies*, Vol. 37, No. 4: 341–49.

Bartlett, Christopher A. and Sumantra Ghoshal (1989), *Managing across Borders*, Harvard Business School Press.

—— and —— (2000), "Going Global: Lessons from Late Movers," *Harvard Business Review*, No. 78: 133–42.

Barton, Dominic and Kito de Boer (2006), "The Need for Reform along the New Silk Road," *Financial Times*, July 4.

Bellak, Christian (2000), "The Investment Development Path of Austria," Vienna University of Economics, Working Paper Series No. 75.

Black, J. Stewart (1990), "The Relationship of Personal Characteristics with the Adjustment of Japanese Expatriate Managers," *Management International Review*, Vol. 30: 119–34.

Blomqvist, Hans C. (2002), "Extending the Second Wing: The Outward Direct Investment of Singapore," University of Vaasa, Department of Economics, Working Paper No. 3.

Blythman, Joanna (2004), *Shopped. The Shocking Power of British Supermarkets*, London and Glasgow: HarperCollins UK.

Bonaglia, Federico and Andrea Goldstein (2006), "Egypt and the Investment Development Path: Insights from Two Case Studies," *International Journal of Emerging Markets*, Vol. 1, No. 2: 107–27.

——, —— and John Matthews (2007), "Accelerated Internationalization by Emerging Multinationals in the Home Appliances Sector," *Journal of World Business*, forthcoming.

Boué, Juan Carlos (2002), "El programa de internacionalización de PDVSA: ¿triunfo estratégico o desastre fiscal?," *Revista Venezuelana de Economía y Ciencias Sociales*, Vol. 8, No. 2: 237–82.

—— (2004), "The Internationalisation Programme of Petróleos de Venezuela S.A. (PDVSA)," study commissioned from Oxford Institute for Energy Studies by PDV (UK) S.A.

Bräutigam, D. (2005), "Strategic Engagement: Markets, Transnational Networks, and Globalization in Mauritius," *Yale Journal of International Affairs*, Vol. 1, No. 1: 447–67.

Buckley, Peter J. (1991), "Kojima's Theory of Japanese Foreign Direct Investment Revisited," *Hitotsubashi Journal of Economics*, Vol. 32, No. 2: 103–09.

—— and Mark Casson (1976), *The Future of Multinationals*, London: Macmillan.

Burkart, Mike, Fausto Panunzi, and Andrei Shleifer (2003), "Family Firms," *Journal of Finance*, Vol. 58, No. 5: 2167–202.

Busjeet, Vinod (1980), "Foreign Investors from Less-Developed Countries: A Strategic Profile," Doctoral thesis, Graduate School of Business Administration, Harvard University.

Cantwell, John and Grazia D. Santangelo (2002), "M&As and the Global Strategies of TNCs," *The Developing Economies*, Vol. 40, No. 4: 400–34.

Cantwell, John and Paz Estella Tolentino (1990), "Technological Accumulation and Third World Multinationals," University of Reading, Discussion Papers in International Investment and Business Studies No. 139.

Casanova, Lourdes (2004), "East Asian, European, and North American Multinational Firm Strategies in Latin America," *Business and Politics*, Vol. 6, No. 1: 1074.

Castro, Francisco Barros (2004), "FDI in a Late Industrializing Country: The Portuguese IDP Revisited," Faculdade de Economia do Porto, Working Papers No. 147.

Chabane, Neo, Andrea Goldstein, and Simon Roberts (2006), "The Changing Face and Strategies of Big Business in South Africa: More Than a Decade of Political Democracy," *Industrial and Corporate Change*, Vol. 15, No. 3: 549–77.

Chen, Tain-Jy and Ying-Hua Ku (2002), "Creating Competitive Advantages out of Market Imperfections: Taiwanese Firms in China," *Asian Business & Management*, Vol. 1, No. 1: 79–99.

Chen, Tain-Jy and Ying-Hua Ku (2003), "The Effects of Overseas Investment on Domestic Employment," *NBER Working Paper*, No. 10156.

Chew, Irene and Frank Horwitz (2004), "Human Resource Management Strategies in Practice: Case-Study Findings in Multinational Firms," *Asia Pacific Journal of Human Resources*, Vol. 42, No. 1: 32–56.

Choi, Youngrak (2003), "Sources of Corporate Growth: Experiences of Korean Enterprises," Science and Technology Policy Institute (STEPI), Working Papers No. 155.

Chua, Amy (2003), *World on Fire: How Exporting Free Market Democracy Breeds Ethnic Hatred and Global Instability*, Doubleday.

Chudnovsky, Daniel, Bernardo Kosacoff, and Andrés López, with Celso Garrido (1999), *Las multinacionales latinoamericanas: sus estrategias en un mundo globalizado*, Buenos Aires: Fundo de Cultura Económica.

Cross, Adam, Liu Xin, and Hui Tan (2004), "China and the 'Round-Tripping' Phenomenon: A Re-evaluation and Future Trends," mimeo, Leeds University Business School, Centre for Chinese Business and Development.

CSO (2004), *Foreign Direct Investment 2003*, Central Statistics Office Ireland.

Cuervo, Javier C. and Low Sui Pheng (2003a), "Ownership Advantages/Disadvantages of Singapore Transnational Construction Companies," *Construction Management and Economics*, Vol. 21, No. 1: 81–94.

—— and —— (2003b), "Significance of Location Factors for Singapore Transnational Construction Corporations," *Engineering, Construction and Architectural Management*, Vol. 10, No. 5: 342–53.

Cuervo-Cazurra, Alvaro (2004), "Explaining the Non-Sequential Internationalization across Countries," mimeo, University of Minnesota, Carlson School of Management.

Debaere, Peter and Hongshik Lee (forthcoming), "A New Giant Sucking Sound? The Impact of Outward Multinational Activity in South Korea," *mimeo*, University of Texas at Austin.

del Sol, Patricio (2005), "Why Join a Chilean Firm to Invest Elsewhere in Latin America?," Pontificia Universidad Católica de Chile, Departamento de Ingeniería Industrial y de Sistemas, Documento de Trabajo No. 182.

—— and Pablo Duran (2002), "Responses to Globalization in Asia and Latin America: Chilean Investment Alliances across Latin America," LAEBA Working Papers No. 5.

—— and Joe Kogan (2004), "Global Competitive Advantage Based on Pioneering Economic Reforms: The Case of Chilean FDI," mimeo, Pontificia Universidad Católica de Chile.

Diaz-Alejandro, Carlos F. (1977), "Foreign Direct Investment by Latin Americans," in T. Agmon and Charles Kindleberger (eds.), *Multinationals from Small Countries*, Cambridge, MA: MIT Press.

Digal, Larry and Andrea Goldstein (in progress), "Supermarkets in the Philippines," *mimeo*, OECD Development Centre.

Dosi, Giovanni, Richard R. Nelson, and Sidney G. Winter (eds.) (2000), *The Nature and Dynamics of Organizational Capabilities*, Oxford: Oxford University Press.

DPE (2006), *Continental Investments Project: A Report on SOE Investments in the Continent*. South Africa: Department for Public Enterprises.

Dunning, John H. (1979), "Explaining Changing Patterns of International Production: In Defence of an Eclectic Theory," *Oxford Bulletin of Economics and Statistics*, Vol. 41, No. 4: 269–95.

—— (1980), "Toward an Eclectic Theory of International Production: Some Empirical Tests," *Journal of International Business Studies*, Vol. 11, No. 2: 317–35.

—— (1981), "Explaining the International Direct Investment Position of Countries: Towards a Dynamic or Developmental Approach," *Weltwirtschaftliches Archiv*, Vol. 117, No. 1: 30–64.

—— (1986), "The Investment Development Cycle Revisited," *Weltwirtschaftliches Archiv*, Vol. 122, No. 4: 667–77.

—— (1993), *Multinational Enterprises and the Global Economy*, Wokingham, UK: Addison-Wesley.

—— (1995), "Reappraising the Eclectic Paradigm in an Age of Alliance Capitalism," *Journal of International Business Studies*, Vol. 26, No. 3: 461–91.

—— (2006), "Comment on *Dragon Multinationals: New Players in 21st Century Globalization*," *Asia Pacific Journal of Management*, Vol. 23, No. 2: 139–41.

Dunning, John H. and Rajneesh Narula (1996), "The Investment Path Revisited: Some Emerging Issues," in *idem* (eds.), *Foreign Direct Investment and Governments: Catalysts for Economic Restructuring*, London and New York, NY: Routledge, 1–41.

Edwards, Christine and Miao Zhang (2003), "Human Resource Management Strategy in Chinese MNCs in the UK: A Case Study with Six Companies," *Research and Practice in Human Resource Management*, Vol. 11, No. 1: 1–14.

Erdilek, Asim (2003), "A Comparative Analysis of Inward and Outward FDI in Turkey," *Transnational Corporations*, Vol. 12, No. 3: 79–105.

Feenstra, Robert and Gordon H. Hanson (2004), "Intermediaries in Entrepôt Trade: Hong Kong Re-Exports of Chinese Goods," *Journal of Economics & Management Strategy*, Vol. 13, No. 1: 3–35.

Findlay, Christopher and Andrea Goldstein (2004), "Liberalization and Foreign Direct Investment in Asian Transport Systems: The Case of Aviation," *Asian Development Review*, Vol. 21, No. 1: 37–65.

Foxley, Alejandro (1983), *Latin American Experiments in Neoconservative Economics*, Berkeley, CA: University of California Press.

Franco, Andrés and Philippe De Lombaerde (2000), *Las empresas multinacionales latinoaméricanas: el caso de la inversión colombiana directa en Ecuador, México, Perú y Venezuela*, Tercer Mundo.

Frynas, Jedrzej George, Kamel Mellahi, and Geoffrey Allen Pigman (2006), "First Mover Advantages in International Business and Firm-Specific Political Resources," *Strategic Management Journal*, Vol. 27, No. 4: 321–45.

Gao, Ting (2005a), "Foreign Direct Investment in China: How Big Are the Roles of Culture and Geography?" *Pacific Economic Review*, Vol. 10, No. 2: 153–66.

—— (2005b), "Foreign Direct Investment from Developing Asia: Some Distinctive Features," *Economics Letters*, Vol. 86, No. 1: 29–35.

Ghoshal, Sumantra, Gita Piramal, and Sudeep Budhiraja (2001), *World Class in India: A Case of Companies in Transformation*, New Delhi: Penguin India.

Giroud, Axèle and Hafiz Mirza (2006), "Chinese Outward Foreign Direct Investment," mimeo, United Nations Conference on Trade and Development.

Goldstein, Andrea (2004a), *Regional Integration, FDI and Competitiveness in Southern Africa*, OECD.

—— (2004b), "The Dynamics of Foreign Direct Investment and A-B-C Competitiveness," in *Trade and Competitiveness in Argentina, Brazil and Chile: Not as Easy as A-B-C*, OECD.

—— (2005), "Un jugador global latinoamericano se dirige a Asia: embraer en China," *Boletín Informativo Techint*, No. 316.

—— (2006a), "Multinazionali emergenti – una nuova geografia degli investimenti internazionali?," in Istituto per il Commercio Estero, *Rapporto sul commercio estero*.

—— (2006b), "Who's Afraid of Emerging Multinationals? Or, Are Developing Countries Missing Something in the Globalization Debate?," paper prepared for the International Conference "The Rise of TNCs from Emerging Markets: Threat or Opportunity?" Columbia University, New York, October 24–25.

—— and Serge Perrin (2006), "La Stratégie internationale d'un groupe nord-africain de télécommunications: le cas d'Orascom," in M. Mezouaghi (ed.), *Les Trajectoires d'insertion dans l'économie numérique: le cas du Maghreb*, Editions Maisonneuve & Larose.

—— and Omár Toulan (2006), " 'Multilatinas' Go to China: Two Case Studies," in R. Grosse (ed.), *How Can Latin American Firms Compete?*, Oxford: Oxford University Press.

Guedes, Ana Lucia and Alexandre Faria (2003), "Internacionalização de empresas: explorando interfaces governo-empresa e governança-gerência," paper presented at the 3rd International Conference of the Iberoamerican Academy of Management, São Paulo.

Guha, Ashok and Amit S. Ray (2000), "Multinational versus Expatriate FDI: A Comparative Analysis of the Chinese and Indian Experience," Indian Council for Research on International Economic Relations, Working Papers No. 56.

Guimaraes, Eduardo Augusto (1986), "The Activities of Brazilian Firms Abroad," in Charles Oman (ed.), *New Forms of Overseas Investment by Developing Countries: The Case of India, Korea and Brazil*, Paris: OECD Development Centre.

Guislain, Pierre and Christine Zhen-Wei Qiang (2006), "Foreign Direct Investment in Telecommunications in Developing Countries," in *Information and Communications for Development 2006: Global Trends and Policies*, The World Bank.

Gunduz, Lokman and Ekrem Tatoglu (2003), "A Comparison of the Financial Characteristics of Group Affiliated and Independent Firms in Turkey," *European Business Review*, Vol. 15, No. 1: 48–54.

Guriev, Sergei and Andrei Rachinsky (2005), "The Role of Oligarchs in Russian Capitalism," *Journal of Economic Perspectives*, Vol. 19, No. 1: 131–50.

Gurushina, Natalia (1998), "British Free-Standing Companies in Tsarist Russia," in Mira Wilkins and Harm Schröter (eds.), *The Free-Standing Company in the World Economy, 1830–1996*, Oxford: Oxford University Press.

Hakkala, Katariina and David Zimmermann (2005), "Foreign Operations of Swedish Manufacturing Firms: Evidence from the IUI Survey on Multinationals 2003," The Research Institute of Industrial Economics, Working Paper No. 650.

Hannah, Leslie (1998), "Survival and Size Mobility among the World's Largest 100 Industrial Corporations, 1912–1995," *American Economic Review*, Vol. 88, No. 2: 62–65.

Hashai, Niron and Tamar Almor (2004), "Gradually Internationalizing 'Born Global' Firms: An Oxymoron?," *International Business Review*, Vol. 13: 465–83.

Heenan, David A. and Warren J. Keegan (1979), "The Rise of Third World Multinationals," *Harvard Business Review*, January–February: 101–109.

Heinrich, Andreas (2004), "EU Enlargement and the Challenges for the Internationalization of Companies from Central and Eastern Europe: Insiders and Outsiders in the Energy Sector," paper presented at the Conference "New Europe 2020 – Visions and Strategies for Wider Europe," Turku, August 27–28.

Hoskisson, Robert, Lorraine Eden, Lau Chung Ming, and Mike Wright (2000), "Strategy in Emerging Economies," *Academy of Management Journal*, Vol. 43, No. 3: 249–67.

Hunya, Gábor (2006), "FDI in the New EU Borderland," mimeo, The Vienna Institute for International Economic Studies.

IEA (2004), *World Energy Outlook*. International Energy Agency.

ITPS (2005), *Utlandsägda företag 2004*. Institutet för Tillväxtpolitiska Studier.

Jacob, Raúl (2004), *Cruzando la frontera*, Montevideo: Editorial Arpoador.

Jauch, Herbert (2005), "Namibia," in Herbert Jauch and Rudolf Traub-Merz (eds.), *The Future of the Textile and Clothing Industry in Sub-Saharan Africa*, Friedrich-Ebert-Stiftung.

Johanson, J. and J.-E. Vahlne (1977), "The Internationalization Process of the Firm—A Model of Knowledge Development and Increasing Foreign Market Commitments," *Journal of International Business Studies*, Vol. 8, No. 1: 23–32.

Jomo, K. S. (2002), *Ugly Malaysians? South–South Investments Abused*, Select Books.

Jones, Geoffrey (2005), *Multinationals and Global Capitalism from the Nineteenth to the Twenty-First Century*, Oxford: Oxford University Press.

—— and Tarun Khanna (2006), "Bringing History (Back) into International Business," *Journal of International Business Studies*, Vol. 37, No. 4: 453–68.

Kabelwa, George (2004), "Technology Transfer and South African Investment in Tanzania," Economic and Social Research Foundation, Globalisation and East Africa Working Paper Series No. 10.

Kalotay, Kálmán (2003), "Outward Foreign Direct Investment from Economies in Transition in a Global Context," *Journal for East European Management Studies*, Vol. 8, No. 1: 6–24.

Kang, Sung Jin and Hongshik Lee (2004), "Location Choice of Korean Companies in China," mimeo, Korea University and KIEP.

Khanna, Tarun and Jan Rivkin (2001), "Estimating the Performance Effects of Business Groups in Emerging Markets," *Strategic Management Journal*, Vol. 22, No.1: 45–74.

—— and Krishna G. Palepu (1999), "The Right Way to Restructure Conglomerates in Emerging Markets," *Harvard Business Review*, July–August.

—— and —— (2004a), "Globalization and Convergence in Corporate Governance: Evidence from Infosys and the Indian Software Industry," *Journal of International Business Studies*, Vol. 35, No. 6: 484–507.

—— and —— (2004b), "Emerging Giants: Building World-Class Companies From Emerging Markets," *mimeo*, Harvard Business School.

Kobrin, Stephen J. (2001), "Sovereignty@bay: Globalization, Multinational Enterprise, and the International Political System," in Alan Rugman and Thomas Brewer (eds.), *The Oxford Handbook of International Business*, Oxford: Oxford University Press.

Kock, Carl J. and Mauro F. Guillén (2001), "Strategy and Structure in Developing Countries: Business Groups as an Evolutionary Response to Opportunities for Unrelated Diversification," *Industrial and Corporate Change*, Vol. 10, No. 1: 77–113.

Kogut, Bruce and Ugo Zander (1993), "Knowledge of the Firm and the Evolutionary Theory of the Multinational Corporation," *Journal of International Business Studies*, Vol. 34, No. 6: 516–29.

Kojima, Kiyoshi (1960), "Capital Accumulation and the Course of Industrialisation, with Special Reference to Japan," *The Economic Journal*, Vol. 70: 757–68.

Kosacoff, Bernardo, Jorge Forteza, María Inés Berbero, and E. Alejandro Stengel (2001), *Globalizar desde Latinoamérica: el caso Arcor*, McGraw-Hill Interamericana.

Krugman, P. (2000), "Fire-Sale FDI," in S. Edwards (ed.), *Capital Flows and the Emerging Economies: Theory, Evidence and Controversies*, University of Chicago Press.

Kugler, Maurice and Hillel Rapoport (2005), "Skilled Emigration, Business Networks and Foreign Direct Investment," paper presented at the Royal Economic Society Annual Conference.

Kumar, Sree, Sharon Siddique, and Yuwa Hedrick-Wong (2005), *Mind the Gaps: Singapore Business in China*, Institute of Southeast Asian Studies.

Lall, Sanjaya (ed.) (1983), *The New Multinationals: The Spread of Third World Enterprises*, Chichester, UK: Wiley.

Lecraw, Donald J. (1977), "Direct Investment by Firms from Less Developed Countries," *Oxford Economics Papers*, Vol. 29, No. 3: 442–57.

Lecraw, Donald J. (1993), "Outward Direct Investment by Indonesian Firms: Motivation and Effects," *Journal of International Business Studies*, Vol. 24, No. 3: 589–600.

Lee, Hongshik (2003), "The Decision to Invest Abroad: The Case of South Korean Multinationals," Korea Institute for International Economic Policy, Working Paper No. 03–12.

—— (2004), "Expansion Strategies of South Korean Multinationals," Korea Institute for International Economic Policy, Working Paper No. 04–05.

Lee, Keun, Justin Y. Lin, and Ha-Joon Chang (2005), "Late Marketisation versus Late Industrialisation in East Asia," *Asian-Pacific Economic Literature*, Vol. 19, No. 1: 42–59.

Leff, Nathaniel (1978), "Industrial Organization and Entrepreneurship in the Developing Countries: The Economic Groups," *Economic Development and Cultural Change*, Vol. 26, No. 3: 661–75.

Leproux, Vittorio and Douglas H. Brooks (2004), "Viet Nam: Foreign Direct Investment and Postcrisis Regional Integration," Asian Development Bank, ERD Working Paper No. 56.

Li, Peter Ping (2003), "Toward a Geocentric Theory of Multinational Evolution: The Implications from the Asian MNEs as Latecomers," *Asia Pacific Journal of Management*, Vol. 20, No. 2: 217–42.

Lim, Hyunjoon (2004), "Is Korea Being Deindustrialized?" *The Bank of Korea Economic Papers*, Vol. 7, No. 1: 115–40.

Lin, Huilin and Ryh-Song Yeh (2004), "To Invest or Not to Invest in China," *Small Business Economics*, Vol. 22, No. 1: 19–31.

Lipsey, Robert E. (2000), "Interpreting Developed Countries' Foreign Direct Investment," National Bureau of Economic Research, Working Paper No. 7810.

London, Ted and Stuart L. Hart (2004), "Reinventing Strategies for Emerging Markets: Beyond the Transnational Model," *Journal of International Business Studies*, Vol. 35: 370–91.

Mägi, Rasmus (2003), "Estonian Foreign Direct Investment to Latvia," Bachelor thesis in Economics and Business Administration, Stockholm School of Economics in Riga.

Makino, Shige, Chung-ming Lau, and Rhy Song Yeh (2002), "Asset Exploitation versus Asset Seeking: Implications for Location Choice of Foreign Direct Investment," *Journal of International Business Studies*, Vol. 33, No. 3: 403–21.

March, James G. (1991), "Exploration and Exploitation in Organizational Learning," *Organization Science*, Vol. 1, No. 1: 71–87.

Mariotti, Sergio and Marco Mutinelli (2005), *Italia Multinazionale: Le partecipazioni italiane all'estero ed estere in Italia*, Istituto Nazionale per il Commercio Estero.

Martínez, Jon I., José Paulo Esperança, and José de la Torre (2003), "From 'Multilatinas' to Multinationals: Evolving Management Processes in Latin American Operations," mimeo, ESE, Graduate School of Business, Universidad de los Andes.

Matheson Connell, Carol (2003), "Jardine Matheson & Company: The Role of External Organization in a Nineteenth-Century Trading Firm," *Enterprise & Society*, Vol. 4, No. 1: 99–138.

Mathews, John A. (2002a), *Dragon Multinational: Towards a New Model of Global Growth*, Oxford: Oxford University Press.

—— (2002b), "Competitive Advantages of the Latecomer Firm: A Resource-Based Account of Industrial Catch-Up Strategies," *Asia Pacific Journal of Management*, Vol. 19, No. 4: 467–88.

—— (2006), "Dragon Multinationals: New Players in 21st Century Globalization," *Asia Pacific Journal of Management*, Vol. 23, No. 1: 5–27.

Matsuno, Hiroshi and Elly Lin (2003), "The Globalization of Chinese Companies and Advances into Japan," Nomura Research Institute, *NRI Papers*, No. 68.

Mattlin, Mikael (2004), "Trade Effects of Taiwanese Investment in Mainland China," Bank of Finland, BOFIT China Review No. 4.

Meyer, Marshall W. and Xiaohui Lu (2005), "Managing Indefinite Boundaries: The Strategy and Structure of a Chinese Business Firm," *Management and Organization Review*, Vol. 1, No. 1: 57–86.

Mistry, Percy S. and Niels E. Olesen (2003), "Mitigating Risks for Foreign Investments in Least Developed Countries: Executive Summary," prepared for Sweden's Ministry of Foreign Affairs.

Nachin, Dashnyam (2004), "Foreign Direct Investment in Mongolia," ERINA Report No. 58.

Nam, Young-sook (2004), "China's Industrial Rise and the Challenges Facing Korea," *East Asian Review*, Vol. 16, No. 2: 43–64.

Narula, Rajneesh (1997), "The Role of Developing Country Multinationals in the Acquisition of Industrial Technology in Nigeria: A Pilot Study," *Science, Technology and Development*, Vol. 15, No. 1: 140–61.

Nicholas, Stephen and E. Maitland (2002), "International Business Research: Steady-States, Dynamics and Globalisation," in Bijit Bora (ed.), *Foreign Direct Investment: Research Issues*, London: Routledge.

Nicholson, Nigel and Ayako Imaizumi (1993), "The Adjustment of Japanese Expatriates to Living and Working in Britain," *British Journal of Management*, Vol. 4, No. 2: 119–35.

Ocampo, José Antonio (2004), "Latin America's Growth and Equity Frustrations During Structural Reforms," *Journal of Economic Perspectives*, Vol. 18, No. 2: 67–88.

Olivier, Daniel, Francesco Parola, Brian Slack, and James J. Wang (2005), "The Time Scale of Internationalisation: The Case of the Container Port Industry," presented at the International Workshop on New Generation Port-Cities and Their Role in Global Supply Chains, Hong Kong, December.

Oman, Charles (ed.) (1986), *New Forms of Overseas Investment by Developing Countries: The Case of India, Korea and Brazil*, Paris: OECD Development Centre.

Ottaway, Marina (2005), "Tyranny's Full Tank," *The New York Times*, 31 March.

Oxelheim, Lars and Trond Randöy (2003), "The Impact of Foreign Board Membership on Firm Value," *Journal of Banking and Finance*, Vol. 27, No. 12: 2369–92.

—— and —— (2004), "The Effect of Internationalization on CEO Compensation," The Research Institute of Industrial Economics (IUI), Working Paper No. 611.

Pangarkar, Nitin (2004), "The Asian Multinational Corporation: Evolution, Strategy, Typology and Challenges," in Kwok Leung and Stephen White (eds.), *Handbook of Asian Management*, Kluwer Academic.

—— and Junius R. Lie (2004), "The Impact of Market Cycle on the Performance of the Singapore Acquirers," *Strategic Management Journal*, Vol. 25, No. 12: 1209–16.

—— and Hendry Lin (2003), "Performance of Foreign Direct Investment from Singapore," *International Business Review*, Vol. 12, No. 5: 601–24.

Papandreou, Andreas (1952), "Some Basic Problems in the Theory of the Firm," in B. F. Haley (ed.), *A Survey of Contemporary Economics*, Homewood, IL: Richard D. Irwin.

Park, Beom and Keun Lee (2003), "Comparative Analysis of Foreign Direct Investment in China," *Journal of the Asia-Pacific Economy*, Vol. 13, No. 1: 57–84.

Park, Jongsoo (2004), "Korean Perspective on FDI in India," *Economic and Political Weekly*, July 31: 3551–55.

Patey, A. Luke (2006), "A Complex Reality: The Strategic Behaviour of Multinational Oil Corporations and the New Wars in Sudan," The Danish Institute for International Studies, DIIS Report No. 2006/2.

Pavida, Pananond (2001), "The Making of Thai Multinationals: A Comparative Study of the Growth and Internationalization Process of Thailand's Charoen Pokphand and Siam Cement Groups," *Journal of Asian Business*, Vol. 17, No. 3: 41–70.

—— (2004), "Thai Multinationals After the Crisis: Trends and Prospects," *ASEAN Economic Bulletin*, Vol. 21, No. 1: 106–26.

Pegg, Scott (2003), "Globalization and Natural-Resource Conflicts," *Naval War College Review*, Vol. 56, No. 4: 82–96.

Penrose, Edith (1955), "Limits to the Growth and Size of Firms," *American Economic Review*, Vol. 45, No. 2: 531–43.

Pereira, Alexius A. (2004), "State Entrepreneurship and Regional Development: Singapore's Industrial Parks in Batam and Suzhou," *Entrepreneurship & Regional Development*, Vol. 16, March: 129–44.

Pheng, Low Sui and Jiang Hongbin (2004), "Internationalization of Chinese Construction Enterprises," *Journal of Construction Engineering and Management*, Vol. 129: 589–98.

Pitelis, Christos (2002), "Stephen Hymer: Life and the Political Economy of Multinational Corporate Capital," *Contributions to Political Economy*, Vol. 21, No. 1: 9–26.

PPIAF (2005), *Developing Country Investors and Operators in Infrastructure*, Phase 1 Report, Public Private Infrastructure Advisory Facility, The World Bank.

Pradhan, Jaya Prakash (2003), "Outward Foreign Direct Investment from India: Recent Trends and Patterns," mimeo, Centre for the Study of Regional Development, Jawaharlal Nehru University, New Delhi.

—— and Manoj Kumar Sahoo (2005), "Case Study on Outward Foreign Direct Investment by Indian Small and Medium-Sized Enterprises," mimeo, United Nations Conference on Trade and Development.

Prahalad, C. K. (2005), *The Fortune at the Bottom of the Pyramid: Eradicating Poverty through Profits*, Upper Saddle River, NJ: Wharton School Publishing.

Rajan, K. Sreenivas and Nitin Pangarkar (2000), "Mode of Entry Choice: An Empirical Study of Singaporean Multinationals," *Asia Pacific Journal of Management*, Vol. 17, No. 1: 49–66.

Rashid, Ahmed (2000), *Taliban: Islam, Oil and the New Great Game in Central Asia*, I.B. Tauris.

Rialp-Criado, Alex, Josep Rialp-Criado, and Gary A. Knight (2005), "The Phenomenon of Early Internationalizing Firms: What Do We Know After a Decade (1993–2003) of Scientific Inquiry?" *International Business Review*, Vol. 14, No. 2: 147–66.

Rodrik, Dani (2004), "Industrial Policy for The Twenty-First Century," *mimeo*, Harvard University, John F. Kennedy School of Government.

Rugman, Alan M. and Alain Verbeke (2004), "A Perspective on Regional and Global Strategies of Multinational Enterprises," *Journal of International Business Studies*, Vol. 35, No. 1: 3–18.

Sachwald, Frédérique (ed.) (2001), *Going Multinational: The Korean Experience of Direct Investment*, London: Routledge.

SA Foundation (2004), "South Africa in Africa: Development Partner or Investment Predator?" SA Foundation, Occasional Paper No. 3/2004.

Sakong, Il (1993), *Korea in the World Economy*, Washington, DC: Institute for International Economics.

Sandvold, Tore (2004), "NOC to IOC? National Oil Companies and International Oil Companies," *Oxford Energy Forum*, May: 12–13.

Save the Children (2005), *Beyond the Rhetoric: Measuring Revenue Transparency in the Oil and Gas Industries*, Save the Children.

Shen, Jie (2004), "Compensation in Chinese Multinationals," *Compensation & Benefits Review*, Vol. 36, No. 1: 15–25.

Shimizu, Katsuhiko, Michael A. Hitt, Deepa Vaidyanath, and Vincenzo Pisano (2004), "Theoretical Foundations of Cross-Border Mergers and Acquisitions: A Review of Current Research and Recommendations for the Future," *Journal of International Management*, Vol. 10, No. 3: 307–53.

Sindipeças (2005), *Desempenho do Setor de Autopeças*, Sindipeças.

Sinha, Yashwant (2000), "Union Budget 2000–2001 Speech," 29 February.

Sklair, Leslie and Peter Robbins (2002), "Global Capitalism and Major Corporations from the Third World," *Third World Quarterly*, Vol. 23, No. 1: 81–100.

Spányik, Péter (2003), "The Role of ITD Hungary in Promoting FDI by Hungarian Enterprises Abroad," presentation prepared by the Hungarian Investment and Trade Development Agency (ITDH).

Stare, Metka (2002), "The Pattern of Internationalisation of Services in Central European Countries," *The Service Industries Journal*, Vol. 22, No. 1: 77–91.

Strange, Susan (1992), "States, Firms and Diplomacy," *International Affairs*, Vol. 68, No. 1: 1–15.

Suarez, Fernando F. and Rogelio Oliva (2002), "Learning to Compete: Transforming Firms in the Face of Radical Environment Change," *Business Strategy Review*, Vol. 13, No. 3: 62–71.

Sull, Donald N. and Martin Escobari (2004), "Creating Value in an Unpredictable World," *Business Strategy Review*, Vol. 15, No. 3: 14–20.

Sullivan, Daniel (1994), "Measuring the Degree of Internationalization of a Firm," *Journal of International Business Studies*, Vol. 25, No. 2: 325–42.

Sung, Yun-Wing (1996), "Chinese Outward Investment in Hong Kong: Trends, Prospects and Policy Implications," OECD Development Centre, Technical Papers No. 113.

Sutton, John (1991), *Sunk Costs and Market Structure*, Cambridge, MA: MIT Press.

Svetličič, Marjan and Matija Rojec (eds.) (2003), *Facilitating Transition by Internationalization: Outward Direct Investment from Central European Economies in Transition*, London: Ashgate.

Tan, Chia-Zhi and Hanry Wai-chung Yeung (2000), "The Regionalization of Chinese Business Networks," *Professional Geographer*, Vol. 52, No. 3: 437–54.

Tavares, Márcia (2006), "Las multilatinas: tendencias y política pública," *Boletín Informativo Techint*, No. 320: 13–31.

Taylor, Robert (2002), "Globalization Strategies of Chinese Companies: Current Developments and Future Prospects," *Asian Business & Management*, Vol. 1, No. 2: 209–25.

Tétrault, Mary Ann (1997), "Political Consequences of Restructuring Economic Regimes: The Kuwait Petroleum Corporation," *Millennium*, Vol. 26, No. 2: 379–401.

Te Velde, Dirk Willem and Dirk Bezemer (2004), "Regional Integration and Foreign Direct Investment in Developing Countries," mimeo, ODI.

Tolentino, Paz Estrella (1993), *Technological Innovation and Third World Multinationals*, London: Routledge.

—— (2002), "Hierarchical Pyramids and Heterarchical Networks: Organisational Strategies and Structures of Multinational Corporations and Its Impact on World Development," *Contributions to Political Economy*, Vol. 21, No. 1: 69–89.

UNCTAD (various years), *World Investment Report*, Geneva, United Nations Conference on Trade and Development.

—— (1997), *Sharing Asia's Dynamism: Asian Direct Investment in the European Union*, Geneva, United Nations Conference on Trade and Development.

—— (2004a), "India's Outward FDI: A Giant Awakening?," UNCTAD/DITE/IIAB/2004/1, United Nations Conference on Trade and Development; available at www.unctad.org/sections/dite_dir/docs/diteiiab20041_en.pdf.

UNCTAD (2004b), "South–South Investment Agreements Proliferating," UNCTAD/PRESS/PR/2004/036, Geneva, United Nations Conference on Trade and Development; available at www.unctad.org/Templates/webflyer.asp?docid=5637&intItemID=2807&lang=1.

—— (2005a), *World Investment Report*. United Nations Conference on Trade and Development.

—— (2005b), "Case Study on Outward Foreign Direct Investment by Russian Enterprises," Geneva, United Nations Conference on Trade and Development; available at http://www.unctad.org/en/docs/c3em26d2a4_en.pdf.

—— (2006), "Report of the Expert Meeting on Capacity Building in the Area of FDI: Data Compilation and Policy Formulation in Developing Countries," TD/B/COM.2/EM.18/3, Geneva, United Nations Conference on Trade and Development; available at www.unctad.org/en/docs/c2em18d3_en.pdf.

UNCTC (1984), *Code of Conduct on Transnational Corporations*. United Nations Center on Transnational Corporations.

Vahtra, Peeter (2006), "Expansion or Exodus? Trends and Developments in Foreign Investments of Russia's Largest Industrial Enterprises," Turku School of Economics and Business Administration, Pan-European Institute, Electronic Publications No. 1.

—— and Kari Liuhto (2004), "Expansion or Exodus? Foreign Operations of the Russia's Largest Corporations," Turku School of Economics and Business Administration, Pan-European Institute, Electronic Publications No. 8.

van Ark, Bart and Erik Monnikhof (2000), "Productivity and Unit Labour Cost Comparisons: A Data Base," International Labour Office, Employment Paper No. 2000/5.

Vasquez-Parraga, Arturo Z. and Reto Felix (2004), "Investment and Marketing Strategies of Mexican Companies in the United States: Preliminary Evidence," *Thunderbird International Business Review*, Vol. 46, No. 2: 149–64.

Vernon, Raymond (1966), "International Investment and International Trade in the Product Cycle," *Quarterly Journal of Economics*, Vol. 80, No. 2: 190–207.

—— (1970), "Foreign Enterprises and Developing Nations in the Raw Materials Industries," *American Economic Review*, Vol. 60, No. 2: 122–26.

von Zedtwitz, Maximilian (2006), "Globalization of R&D and Developing Countries," UNCTAD, Geneva, 117–40.

Wagner, Don, Keith Head, and John C. Ries (2002), "Immigration and the Trade of Provinces," *Scottish Journal of Political Economy*, Vol. 49, No. 5: 507–25.

Wall, David (1997), "Outflows of Capital from China," OECD Development Centre, Technical Papers No. 123.

Walters, S. S. and J. W. Prinsloo (2002), "The Impact of Offshore Listings on the South African Economy," *SA Reserve Bank Quarterly Bulletin*, September: 60–71.

Warhurst, Alyson (1994), "South–South Cooperation: Opportunities in Minerals Development," in L. Mytelka (ed.), *South–South Cooperation in a Global Perspective*, Paris: OECD Development Centre.

Wells, Louis T., Jr. (1983), *Third World Multinationals: The Rise of Foreign Investment from Developing Countries*, Cambridge, MA: MIT Press.

—— (1998), "Multinationals and Developing Countries," *Journal of International Business Studies*, Vol. 29, No. 1: 101–14.

Wilkins, Mira (1974), *The Maturing of Multinational Enterprise. American Business Abroad from 1914 to 1970*, Cambridge, MA: Harvard University Press.

—— (1981), "Venezuelan Investment in Florida: 1979," *Latin American Research Review*, Vol. 16, No. 1: 156–65.

—— (1990), "Japanese Multinationals in the United States: Continuity and Change, 1879–1990," *Business History Review*, Vol. 64, No. 4: 585–629.

—— (2004), *The History of Foreign Investment in the United States, 1914–1945*, Cambridge, MA: Harvard University Press.

—— (2005), "Dutch Multinational Enterprises in the United States: A Historical Summary," *Business History Review*, Vol. 79, No. 2: 193–273.

World Bank (2004), *Patterns of Africa–Asia Trade and Investment: Potential for Ownership and Partnership*, prepared for TICAD Asia–Africa Trade and Investment Conference (AATIC), Tokyo, November 1–2.

Wright, Mike, Igor Filatotchev, Robert E. Hoskisson, and Mike W. Peng (2005), "Strategy Research in Emerging Economies: Challenging the Conventional Wisdom," *Journal of Management Studies*, Vol. 42, No. 1: 1–33.

Xiao, Geng (2004), "Round-Tripping Foreign Direct Investment in the People's Republic of China: Scale, Causes and Implications," ADB Institute, Discussion Paper No. 7.

Yang, Y.-H. and Y.-Y. Tu (2004), "Analysis of Factors Influencing Taiwan's Unregistered Overseas Investment Behavior," *Asian Economic Journal*, Vol. 18, No. 2: 213–31.

Yeung, Henry Wai-chung (ed.) (1999), *The Globalisation of Business Firms from Emerging Economies*, 2 Vols., Cheltenham, UK: Edward Elgar.

Yeung, Henry Wai-chung (2002), *Entrepreneurship and the Internationalisation of Asian Firms: An Institutional Perspective*, Cheltenham, UK: Edward Elgar.

―― (2004), "Strategic Governance and Economic Diplomacy in China: The Political Economy of Government-Linked Companies from Singapore," *EAST ASIA*, Vol. 21, No. 1: 39–63.

Yi, Ren (2004), "Motivations for Chinese Investment in Vietnam," mimeo, The University of Melbourne.

Zhang, Ruimin (2005), "Haier, Already a Success, Aims Higher," interview with Wharton management professors Michael Useem and Marshall W. Meyer; available at http://www.knowledgeatwharton.com.cn/index.cfm?fa=viewfeature&languageid=1&articleid=1111.

Company Names Index

3NOD, 139
Aeropuertos Argentinos, 120
Africof, 121, 122
AGIP, 36
Air New Zealand, 56
Al Furat, 128
Alfa, 90
Algosa, 121
Alpargatas, 67
Altria, 8
AmBev (American Beverages), 100, 101
America Mòvil, 102
AmorePacific, 142
Amtel-Vredestein, 131
Andrade Gutierrez, 68
Anglo-America, 15
Anheuser-Busch, 125
Antartica, 100
Antofagasta, 9
Aral, 36
Arçelik, 89
Arcelor, 8, 143
Arcor, 124
AutoVAZ, 90

Banco do Brasil, 98
Bangkok Bank, 118
Banque Islamique de Guinée, 122
Barako, 35
Barlow Tractors International Limited, 104
BenQ, 138
Birla, 89
Bitech Petroleum, 36
Bluestar, 142
BMW, 145
BNDES, 98
Bosch-Siemens, 64
BP, 36, 114
Brahma, 100, 101
Bràspetro, 68
Bridas, 120

Brightstar, 8
British Gas (BG), 35, 114
Bunge y Born, 67
Business Connexion (BCX), 90
Business Development Bank, 91

Cabbages and Condoms, 1
Caledonia, 128
Camargo Corrêa, 68
Carl Dan Peddinghaus, 138
Castel, 125
CCT Holdings, 66
Celtel, 128
Cementos Mexicanos (Cemex), 1, 33, 85, 86, 111, 138, 149
Cerveceria Hondureña, 124
CEZ, 16
Chakira-Cable, 89
Chalkis, 63
Charoen Pokphand (CP) Group, 64, 89, 91
Chesapeake Energy, 128
Chevron, 35, 110, 128, 143
China Bicycles Corp., 63
China Export and Credit Insurance Corporation (Sinosure), 99
China International Marine Containers (Group) (CIMC), 140, 141
China International Trust and Investment Corp. (CITIC), 31
China Merchants Holdings, 140
China Minmetals, 2
China Mobile, 129
China National Chemical Import and Export Co-operation (SinoCement), 31
CNPC (China National Petroleum Corp.), 35, 106
China Ocean Shipping (Group) Company (COSCO), 140
China Resources Enterprises, 124

Company Names Index

China State Construction & Engineering Corp. (CSCEC), 76
Citgo, 107, 108
CNOOC (China National Offshore Oil Corp.), 35, 110, 128, 129, 143
Coca-Cola, 121
Cofap, 68, 70
COFAT, 89
COFICAB, 89, 90
Columbia, 128
Comarch, 144
Comcraft Group, 120
Comstar, 131
Condumex, 70
Confab, 121
ConocoPhillips, 36
Conserves de Provence, 63
Construmix, 86
Continental Baking, 71
Copersucar, 68
COSCO [China Ocean Shipping (Group) Company], 140
CP Trading Group, 91
CP, 119
Cubapetroleo, 37
CVRD, 2
CxNetworks, 86

D'Long Strategic Investment, 92
Daastan, 142, 145
Daewoo, 90
DaimlerChrysler, 126
Dalmine, 121
DBS, 55
De Beers, 15
Delphi, 70
Dexcel Electronics Designs, 120
DP World, 112, 143
Dragòn, 73

E.ON, 128
East Asiatic Company Ltd., 140
Eaton, 92
Efes Breweries, 131
Eimo, 138
Electrolux, 64, 65
Elloumi Group, 89
Embraco, 9
Enarsa, 35

EnCana, 35, 128
EnCana, 128
Endesa, 72
Engen, 100
Eskom Enterprise, 109
Etilsalat, 128
Eurofind, 121
Evraz, 130, 131
Eximbank, 110
Export-Import Bank of Thailand, 98
Exxon Mobil, 35

Fairchild Dornier, 92
Federal Forge, 138
Fiat Engineering, 120
Fillony, 66
FLAG Telecom, 89
Four Soft, 138
Foxconn, 138
Friboi, 98

Galanz, 66
GAZ, 90
Gazprom, 37
GE (General Electric), 64, 65, 66, 70
GE Capital, 86, 92
General Motors, 71
Gerdau, 68
Getty Petroleum Marketing, 36
Glencore, 101
Gradiente, 68
Grundig, 92
Grupo Bimbo, 71
Grupo Industrial Saltillo, 70
Guangdong International Trust and Investment Corporation, 93
Guihou Tianan Pharmaceutical, 91
Gulzar International, 120

Haier, 63, 64, 65, 66, 138, 139, 140
Hankook, 54
Harvard, 66
Heidelberg, 111
Himart, 66
Holcim, 86
HPA Monon, 141
Huaneng Power Group, 63
Huawei, 139
Humax Electronics, 54

Hutchinson Port Holdings, 112
Hyundai Motors, 132
Hyundai, 53, 54

IBM, 138, 142, 143
ICIIE (Islamic Corporation for the Insurance of Investment and Export), 103
Ikegai, 1
INA, 16
InBev, 101
Indian Oil Corporation (IOC), 35
INN CableNet, 120
Inpex, 128
Interbrew, 101
Investcom, 128, 129
Investec, 139
IOC-OIL, 106
Islamic Corporation for the Insurance of Investment and Export (ICIIE), 103
Islamic Development Bank, 103

Jardine Matheson, 122
Jet Airways, 120

Kaco, 71
KAP, 113
Kazakhgold, 131
Kazakhmys, 131
Kazkommertsbank, 131
KazMunaiGaz, 131
Kerr-McGee, 128
KFC, 91
Khodro, 145
Kia, 53, 54
KNI, 56
Koç, 89
Konka, 139
KPC, 34
Krung Thai Bank, 91
Kuwait Petroleum Company, 145
Kuwait Petroleum Corp., 36
Kuwait Petroleum International (KPI), 36

Lafarge, 86, 111
Latinexus, 86
Leciva, 9

Lenovo, 1, 138, 142, 143
LG Electronics, 53, 66
Lieberhaier, 64
Lolita, 73
Lucchini, 138, 144
Lukoil, 36, 37, 90, 106, 128
Lundim Petroleum, 9

Mabe, 70
Maersk, 128
Mahindra & Mahindra, 142
MAN, 92
Marcopolo, 73
MASSCORP (Malaysian South-South Corp. Berhad), 98
Maurel & Prom, 35
Mazeikiu Nafta, 15, 113
McDonald's, 71
Medco, 55
Media-Clinic, 100
MEGEnergy, 35
Meneghetti Equipment, 65
Metcombank, 90
MG Rover, 90, 144, 145
MIDROC (Mohammed International Development Research & Organization Companies), 120
MIGA (Multinational Investment Guarantee Agency), 104
Miller Brewing, 125
Millicom, 129
Minsheng Banking, 55
Mittal, 8, 9, 143
Mobil, 36
MOL, 16
Moltech, 138
Morton Custom Plastics, 65
MTC, 128
MTN, 128, 130
Murray, 92

NamPower, 134
NamWater, 134
National Iranian Oil Co., 37
NatSteel, 90
Nelson Resources, 36, 128
Neoris, 86
Neptune Orient, 55

Netcare, 100
NKK, 121
Noranda, 2
Norilsk Nickel, 90
Norsk Hydro, 37, 128
Northwest, 128
Novatek (INI), 131
Novopolipetsk (INI), 131
Nuritech, 54
Nynäs Petroleum, 107

Occidental, 128
Odebrecht, 68
Oil India, 35
Old Mutual, 139
OML, 128
OMV, 16
OMZ, 131
ONGC (Oil and Natural Gas Corp.) Videsh, 36, 106, 110, 128
Optus, 56
Orascom, 139, 144
Orascom Construction Industries, 115
Ozgen, 63

P&O, 143
Paladin, 128
Park Lane Confectionery, 71
PAZ, 90
PDVSA (Petròleos de Venezuela), 34, 37, 107
Pemex, 37
Perez Companc, 37
Pertamina, 37
PetroAméerica, 108
Petrobrás, 34, 37, 68, 113, 114, 115
PetroCaribe, 108
Petrochina, 37
PetroKazakhstan, 110, 128
Petrominera, 73
Petronas, 100
Petronas, 106
Petronas, 34
PETROPARS, 35
Philippine Airlines (PAL), 118
Philips, 138
Phillips Electronics, 64

Pick'n'Pay, 133
Pilkington, 121
PKN Orlen, 15
Pogo, 128
Posco, 110
Proton, 55, 145
Provida, 72
PSA, 55, 112
PTCL, 128
PTTEP-Mitsui, 128
Pyaterochka, 130, 131

Qingdao Air Conditioner, 64
Qingdao Electroplating, 64
Qingdao Haier Refrigerator, 66
Qingdao Red Star, 64
Quanta, 33
Quinenco, 9

Raiffeisenbank, 104
Rajawali, 111
Ramatex, 133, 134, 138
Repsol YPF, 37, 114, 121
Reliance Industries, 89
Reliance Infocomm, 89
Rhino Garments, 135
Rouge Industries, 138
RMC, 86, 138
Rosneft, 131
Royal Dutch/Shell, 36, 37
RusAl, 14, 101, 113
Russian Tobacco Company, 14

Sabancı, 89
SABMiller, 8, 9, 33, 87, 124, 138
Sabó, 70, 71
SAIC (Shanghai Automotive Industry Corporation), 145
Salim Group, 127
Sampo, 66
Samsung Electronics, 65, 66
Samsung Semiconductors, 54
Samsung, 4, 33, 54, 138
San Luís, 70
Sanson, 85
Santa Fe, 36
Sanyo, 65, 66

Sappi, 126
Sasol, 100, 126
Saudi Oger Group, 121, 128
Schneider, 63
SembCorp Park Management (SPM), 56
SembLog, 55
Semen Gresik, 111
Severstal, 14, 90, 144
Shanghai Electric, 1
Shanghai Tyre & Rubber Company, 138
Shangri-La Asia, 126
Sheksna Insurance Company, 90
Shell, 35, 145
Shin Corp., 112
Shinawatra Group, 91
Shoprite, 133
Shougans (Capital Steel), 31
Siam Cement, 119
Siderca, 121
Siemens, 138
Singapore International Airlines (SIA), 55
Singapore Technologies (ST), 55, 112
SingTel (Singapore Telecomunications), 55, 112
Sinopec, 35, 106
SinoCement (China National Chemical Import and Export Co-operation), 31
Sistema (INI), 131
Sistema/MTS, 90
Skandia, 139
Skoda Auto, 9
Slovakofarma, 9
Slovenske Elektrarne
Slovnaft, 16
SNO Telecom, 90
Sonagol, 35
Spinnaker, 128
SsangYong Motor Company, 90, 142
State Power Corp., 63
Statoil, 128
Steeco Gujarat, 120
Sual, 101
SungWoo, 54
Suzuki, 92
Swift, 98
Sy Group, 119

Talisman, 128
Tamsa, 121
Tangguh, 128
Tata, 89, 90, 113
Tata Consultancy Services, 90, 144
Tata Motors, 90
Tata Steel, 90
Tata Tea, 90, 138
Tavsa, 121
TCI, 66
TCL, 63, 138
Teboil, 36
Techint, 120, 121
Teikoku Oil, 128
Telecom Namibia, 134
Telekom Malaysia, 112
Telmex, 101, 102
Telsim, 128
Temasek Holdings, 55, 112
Tenaris, 121
Tesco, 91
Tethyan Copper, 9
Tetley, 90
Tex-Ray Industrial, 60
Thai Beverage, 130
Thomson, 63, 138, 142
Tomkins, 92
Torno, 120
Total, 106
TPV, 138
Transneft, 113
TRW, 71
TTE, 139
Turk Telekom, 128

Uhambo Oil, 100
Ulyanovsk Automobile Factory (UAZ), 90
Unimil, 15
Unipetrol, 15
Unocal, 110, 128, 129, 143
Uralmash-Izhora (INI), 131
Utd Heavy Machinery, 131

Valenciana, 85
Valtra, 142
Vanguard National Trailer Corporation, 141

Veba Oel, 107
Vintage, 128
Vodafone, 128
Volkswagen, 9, 71
VSNI, 90

Wal-Mart, 133
Wanxiang, 123
Wanxiang, 93
Warburg Pincus, 9
Whirpool, 9, 64, 65
Wind, 139, 144
Wipro, 138
Wuhan Freezer Factory, 64

Xiang Torch Investment, 92
Xinjiang Tunhe Investments, 92

YPF, 114, 121
YPFB, 114
Yukos, 113
Yukos, 16

Zavolzhskii Automobile Factory, 90
ZE, 92
Zee Television, 120
Zentiva, 9
ZMA, 90
Zouk, 122
ZTE, 139

Subject Index

Air transport industry, 44–45
Argentinean multinationals, 120–121
Asian multinationals, xv, 11, 29, 52–66, 133–135

Behavioural models, 77–79
Brazilian multinationals, 19, 30, 71
Business services, 49

Central and Eastern Europe multinationals, 14, 16–17
Chinese multinationals, xiv, 61–66, 106, 123, 138–141, 143
Conglomerates, 31, 42, 87–93
Corporate nationality, 5

Data, quality, xv, 10, 12, 21–22, 31
Data, trends, 11, 17–19, 30
Diaspora, 117–122
Dynamic capabilities, 4, 63, 84–87

Eclectic paradigm, 79–84, 149
Egyptian multinationals, 42–43
Ethnic ties, xv, 78, 89, 91, 117–122, 126

Fast-food chains, 48
Financial market issues, 127–130, 151
Foreign directors, 126–127

Government policies, 94–116
Government policies, in Brazil, 98, 100–101
Government policies, in China, 61–62
Government policies, in India, 95–98
Government policies, in Malaysia, 98
Government policies, in OECD countries, 136–139, 142–144
Government policies, in Russia, 101
Government policies, in South Africa, 96, 99–100, 109
Government policies, in Thailand, 98
Government policies, in Venezuela, 107–109

Hospitality industry, 40–41

Indian multinationals, 14, 30, 90–91, 106, 120
Impact on home country, 61, 150
Impact on host country, 60, 130–135
Industrial-township projects, 56–58
International treaties, 102–103

Korean multinationals, 52–54, 142

Latin American multinationals, xv, 3, 14, 67–73

Management issues, 122–127, 151
Market reforms, as a driver of FDI, xv, 68–73
Mexican multinationals, 71–72, 85–86

Oil and gas industry, xv, 33–40, 105–109, 113–115

Performance, 59–60, 139–142
Product cycle model, 2, 74–77
Protectionism, 110–116, 142–144

Regionalization, 15, 78, 103
Retail distribution, 45–46, 119, 132–133
Russian, multinationals, xv, 14

Singaporean multinationals, 55–59
South African multinationals, xv, 15, 19, 109, 124–125, 133

Taiwanese multinationals, 58
Tax havens, 18
Technology, 2
Telecommunications industry, 19, 41–44, 101–102
Thai multinationals, 119
Third world multinationals, 2, 105